SMOKING

SMOKING
PSYCHOLOGY
AND PHARMACOLOGY

HEATHER ASHTON AND ROB STEPNEY

TAVISTOCK PUBLICATIONS
LONDON AND NEW YORK

First published in 1982 by
Tavistock Publications Ltd
11 New Fetter Lane, London EC4P 4EE

Published in the USA by
Tavistock Publications Ltd
in association with Methuen, Inc.
733 Third Avenue, New York, NY 10017

First published in paperback in 1983

© 1982 Heather Ashton and Rob Stepney

Printed in Great Britain at the
University Press, Cambridge

Set in Linoterm Baskerville by
Keyset Composition, Colchester

British Library Cataloguing in Publication Data

Ashton, Heather
Smoking: psychology and pharmacology.
1. Smoking
I. Title   II. Stepney, Rob
613.85   HN5726

ISBN 0-422-77700-5
ISBN 0-422-77710-2 Pbk

Library of Congress Cataloguing in Publication Data

Ashton, Heather.
Smoking, psychology and pharmacology.
Bibliography: p.
Includes indexes.
1. Smoking – Psychological aspects.
2. Tobacco – Physiological effect.
3. Smoking – Social aspects.
I. Stepney, Rob.   II. Title
BF789.S6A83   616.86′5   81-18829
ISBN 0-422-77700-5   AACR2
ISBN 0-422-77710-2 (pbk.)

CONTENTS

ACKNOWLEDGEMENTS

We thank the many people with whom we have worked, with whom we have discussed our ideas and whose ideas in return have contributed to this book.

In particular, we thank John Thompson, Professor of Pharmacology at Newcastle University, who initiated and has guided our interest in smoking. We are grateful also to Dr Ray Thornton, of British-American Tobacco, for his friendly interest over several years, and to Professor I.H. Mills, of Cambridge University, for his encouragement in the writing of this book. Dr Noel Olsen read and provided helpful comments on Chapter 7, and Dr Tony Dickinson and Paul Creighton on Chapter 8.

During two years of work on this book, many people have been involved in the typing of drafts and preparation of illustrations. For their work in Cambridge we thank Christine Bunn, Carol Cassidy, Anne Barcroft, Linda Medlicott, and Lucy Wade, and, in Newcastle, Valerie Wright.

Any publication on smoking is inevitably controversial. We have both worked at times on research projects funded collectively or individually by tobacco companies. We are grateful for their support and co-operation. However, the views presented here are our own.

Cambridge, February 1981

INTRODUCTION

Cigarette smoking is surely one of the strangest of human behaviours. How *is* it that nearly half the adult population regularly performs a bizarre act which is necessary neither for the maintenance of life nor for the satisfaction of social, sexual, cultural, or spiritual needs; an act which is acknowledged, even by its adherents, to be harmful to health and even distasteful?

The ubiquity of cigarette smoking and its persistence in the face of vigorous proscription, and, in our own time, despite the generally agreed health risk, is a remarkable phenomenon. Nearly 500 years after those accompanying Columbus first observed the strange behaviour of American Indians who appeared to 'drink' the smoke from rolls of burning leaves, we still do not really know why people smoke, nor why they cannot easily stop.

The many different forms which smoking takes and the complexity of the smoking act itself make any unitary account of the behaviour difficult. It is likely that different forms of smoking involve rewards derived in differing degrees from social, sensory, and pharmacological sources. The rituals of smoking, taste, and aroma would seem to be particularly important in pipe smoking, for example, where the rubbing of the tobacco, the filling and cleaning of the pipe, and the homely and academic associations, may be as vital a part of the procedure as the act of drawing smoke. In non-inhaling cigar smokers, social and sensory rewards and the image of affluence and success are again likely to be relevant.

The smoking of cigarettes, however, is by far the most important means of tobacco consumption, in terms of both prevalence and health consequences. In Britain 50,000 excess deaths per year are laid at its door and in the United States 325,000. The association between smoking and disease has now been widely accepted for many years – even by smokers themselves. A survey conducted by the US Public

Health Service over ten years ago showed that more than 70 per cent of current smokers agreed that smoking was harmful to health. Yet despite the generally accepted view that smoking is a form of 'slow-motion suicide', the proportion of the population smoking cigarettes today is not radically different from what it was twenty years ago.

In contrast to the pipe and cigar smoker, the cigarette smoker does not present a clearly defined face to the world. Indeed the habit has recently acquired negative rather than positive associations, even for the smoker. Neither do the taste, aroma, and appearance of smoke seem to play much part in the rewards of cigarette smoking. It is

Figure 1 Factors influencing smoking behaviour

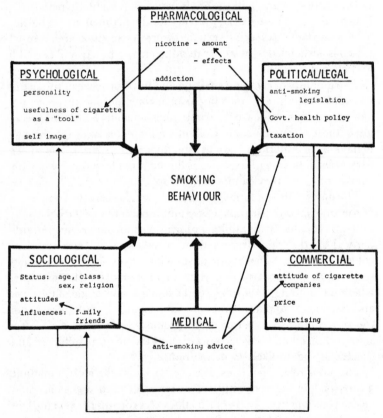

This 'spider's web' of influences can be expected to affect all aspects of smoking – from whether a particular individual will smoke at all to how long an unsmoked butt he leaves.

therefore our thesis that the use of cigarettes can best be understood when viewed as a means of nicotine self-administration. In this way, the unique role of tobacco and the prevalence of inhalation can be explained, together with the fact that smokers habitually take into their bodies quantities of the drug sufficient to have important effects on brain and behaviour.

The apparent primacy of nicotine has implications for our views of smoking motivation and for strategies by which the impact of smoking on health may yet be reduced. However, as with many human activities, the causes of smoking are complex. It is influenced by many factors − sociological, economic, medical, and political (*Figure 1*) − and these will be mentioned. Our main emphasis, nevertheless, lies on the pharmacology of nicotine and its psychological effects.

Having placed cigarette smoking in its historical and current context, Chapters 2 and 3 discuss the role of nicotine and the development of smoking behaviour in the individual. This is followed by an account of how smokers regulate their intake of nicotine; the implications for the view of smoking as addiction to nicotine are discussed. The effect of smoking and nicotine on performance and response to stress is considered in Chapter 5, which presents evidence that smoking is used as a 'psychological tool'. Chapter 6 is concerned with factors which distinguish smokers from non-smokers, and with the interaction between personality and the effects of smoking. In Chapter 7 individual and social attitudes to smoking are examined, and in Chapter 8 smoking is considered as a learned behaviour. Certain effects of smoking on body systems are mentioned in Chapter 9, prefacing a consideration of whether smoking can be made less hazardous to health.

1 THE INDIAN'S REVENGE
A BRIEF HISTORY OF
THE TOBACCO HABIT
AND ITS CURRENT STATUS

The tobacco plant, *nicotiana tabacum*, is surely the most loved and hated member of the vegetable kingdom. Denied the uncontroversial nutritional role of the tomato and potato, or the decorative attractions of the winter cherry and petunia – to all of whom it is related in the family of Solanaceae – an adaptation of plant chemistry, which dictated that it should carry in its leaves quantities of the alkaloid nicotine, gave it instead power over men's minds. The tobacco habit has had a remarkable history, having undergone astonishing trans-formations – from smoking to snuffing to chewing and back again. Yet however great the changes in the method by which tobacco is consumed, the desire for some form of tobacco use, once known, seems never to have weakened.

A legend amongst the Huron Indians of North America tells how the Great Spirit sent a naked girl to restore a land ravaged by famine. Potatoes grew where she touched the ground with her right hand, corn where she placed her left hand, and from where she sat down sprang tobacco. Whatever the origins of the tobacco plant itself, we may speculate that the peculiarly pleasurable consequences of inhaling its smoke were discovered more or less by chance during the use of various plant materials in sacred rituals involving fire and incense. The history of Western man's acquaintance with tobacco has a more clearly defined beginning. We derive our knowledge of tobacco from Columbus. The finding of the enchanted weed must rank somewhere between the introduction of syphilis and the dis-covery of America in terms of the ultimate benefit to mankind of the consequences of his stubborn voyaging.

Inhaling smoke was not totally unknown in the Old World (Koskowski 1955). Europeans had inhaled the fumes of such un-appetizing substances as coltsfoot and dried cow dung for medicinal purposes, and Herodotus reported the use of hemp as an intoxicant by

Scythian tribes (Corti 1931). The use of tobacco, however, was a curious novelty – despite claims once made that a pipe still smelling of nicotine had been unearthed in the ruins of a Greek temple at Constantinople. In spite of their acquaintance with similar habits, the earliest observers of the Indians' behaviour seemed not to have known how to describe what they saw, reporting either that the Indians drank smoke or that they used it to perfume themselves.

One of the first coherent accounts of tobacco smoking was provided by Bartolomé de las Casas in 1527, who wrote:

> 'some dry herbs (are) put in a certain leaf, also dry, in the manner of a musket made of paper . . . and having lighted one part of it, by the other they suck, absorb or receive that smoke inside with the breath, by which they become benumbed, almost drunk, and so it is that they do not feel fatigue. These muskets, as we will call them, they call tobacco.'
>
> (Brooks 1953: 13–14)

Interesting in the light of our present experiences with tobacco are the assertions, firstly, that tobacco use produces an intoxication comparable to that resulting from alcohol (which does not seem an appropriate description of the effect of 'modern' smoking), and, secondly, that tobacco may be used to counter the effects of fatigue – something with which we might be more in agreement. The precise psychological effects of smoking have long been in dispute. One of the most intriguing properties of tobacco is that it seems capable of having contradictory effects – being used both as a sedative and as a stimulant. King James I, who wrote a violent and, many would say, unreasoning (if eloquent) treatise against the use of tobacco, was nevertheless perceptive enough to draw attention to this fact:

> 'Being taken when they goe to bed, it makes one sleepe soundly, and yet being taken when a man is sleepie and drowsie, it will, as they say, awake his braine, and quicken his understanding.'
>
> (James I 1604: C3)

PROPONENTS OF TOBACCO

> There are those who would say that money is more precious than virtue, but that tobacco is more precious still

King James fought a losing battle against the use of tobacco. By the end of Elizabeth's reign tobacco had gained a strong hold over England – and not even the 'Counterblaste' could loosen its grip. James might inveigh against a custom 'lothesome to the eye, hatefull to the Nose, harmfull to the braine, dangerous to the Lungs, and in the blacke stinking fume thereof, neerest resembling the horrible Stigian smoke of the pit that is bottomelesse', but it was clear that few of his loyal subjects were inclined to agree.

In view of the current nearly-unanimous condemnation by the medical profession, it is surprising to learn that tobacco was once much-valued for its supposed medicinal properties (Brooks 1953). It was thought by many to be a prophylactic against the plague, and to have power to cure a variety of diseases including headaches, asthma, gout, ulcers, scabies, labour pains (when leaves were applied to the navel) and, ironically, cancer. Smoke was regarded as valuable in driving moisture from the brain (Inglis 1975), so ridding it of a cold phlegmatic humour, and was used by monks to dull the sexual appetite, although Kant, in contrast, characterized tobacco as 'one of the basest methods of exciting the sensual appetite' (Corti 1931).

Molière, in 'Don Juan' has the character Sganarelle eulogize tobacco (Corti 1931: 179): 'it is the passion of all proper people, and he who lives without tobacco has nothing to live for. Not only does it refresh and cleanse men's brains, but it guides their souls in the ways of virtue, and by it one learns to be a man of honour.' The non-medical use of tobacco had many stout defenders. A contemporary of the Thirty Years War (1618–48) pointed out its varied usefulness (Corti 1931: 101): 'If time hang heavy and he has nothing else to do, a man will drink tobacco. Is he moody, angry or perplexed; he sticks his pipe between his teeth and takes a long pull at it. Should his wife begin to nag, the man will fill his mouth with smoke and puff it in her face.'

J. M. Barrie, who wrote 'My Lady Nicotine' as the panegyric of a man about to forsake for ever his beloved 'Arcadia' mixture, explained how tobacco had turned the tide of history:

'When Raleigh, in honour of whom England should have changed its name, introduced tobacco, the glorious Elizabethan age began . . . men who had hitherto only concerned themselves with the narrow things of home put a pipe in their mouths and became philosophers. Poets and dramatists smoked until all ignoble ideas were driven from them, and into their place rushed such high thoughts as the world had not known before. . . . The whole country was stirred by the ambition to live up to tobacco.'

(Barrie 1890: 106–07)

Many have seen the usefulness of tobacco in the control of emotion; whilst pleasant sensations are accentuated, unpleasant ones seem to become muted, and strong ones like rage or fear are toned down.

Churchill is reported as saying that if he had not smoked so much he would have lost his temper more often. Bismarck would have agreed entirely. During the peace negotiations with a defeated France in 1871 he commented that 'a cigar held in the hand and nursed with care serves, in a measure, to keep our gestures under control . . . as the blue smoke curls upward the eye involuntarily follows it; the effect is soothing, one feels better tempered, and more inclined to make concessions' (Corti 1931: 257). The non-smoker, he argued, is more apt to be guided by the impulse of the moment.

OPPONENTS OF THE HABIT

Love is a brief madness, but smoking a permanent one

Jacob Balde, a Jesuit priest, asked in an anti-tobacco tract published in Nuremberg in 1658, 'What difference is there between a smoker and a suicide; except that the one takes longer to kill himself than the other?' (Corti 1931: 119). Featured on the frontispiece to his book was a skull smoking – an image later to be made powerful use of in health-education campaigns. The view that tobacco was in some way the Indian's revenge on the European was expressed more than once. Louis XIV's physician, Fagon, addressed his fears to the Paris School of Medicine: 'America triumphed over the arrogance of her con-querors by infecting them with her own vices; she hastened on the death of her new masters by giving them venereal disease – and tobacco' (Corti 1931: 185).

Another, more dramatic, spirit imagined meeting the 'tobacco fiend' at the court of Lucifer. The fiend spoke:

'Thus do I take revenge in full upon the Spaniards for all their cruelty to the Indians; since by acquainting their conquerors with the use of tobacco I have done them greater injury than even the King of Spain through his agents ever did his victims; for it is both more honourable and more natural to die by a pike thrust or a cannon ball than from the ignoble effects of poisonous tobacco.'

(Corti 1931: 111)

Practical opposition to the habit took a variety of forms. The aptly named Murad the Cruel of Turkey (1623–40) had smokers beheaded, hung, and quartered. In the Russia of the first Czar, Michael Feodorovitch Romanov, smokers were flogged and exiled to Siberia. In Japan in 1616 the penalties for smoking included imprisonment and the confiscation of property. Surprisingly, severe and immediate punishment proved no more effective in halting smoking than current

Figure 2 Early cigarette smoking

This illustration, redrawn by David Carruthers, is based on that appearing in *A History of Smoking* by Count Corti (1931). Adapted and reproduced by permission of George G. Harrap & Company Ltd.

fears of long-term health consequences. Rulers came and went, but smoking stayed. Later, governments underwent a conversion of sorts, prompted primarily by the realization that tobacco was an excellent source of revenue – derived either from customs dues (such as those introduced by Richelieu in France in 1629) or from the sale of monopolies to deal in tobacco goods. Bohemia was fortified in 1668 with money derived from the tobacco trade, and the Emperor Leopold of Austria used tobacco revenue to finance elaborate hunting expeditions (Corti 1931). The scale of tobacco revenue is regarded by many as underlying present governments' less than whole-hearted espousal of the anti-tobacco cause.

Pockets of resistance to tobacco remained, however. The Berlin police force constituted one notable outpost of anti-smoking senti- ment. The Chief of Police proclaimed in 1810 that smoking in streets and on promenades was as indecent as it was dangerous, and contrary to the character of an orderly and civilized city. In consequence smoking was strictly forbidden and anyone transgressing might expect to be arrested and punished with a fine of five thalers, imprisonment, or corporal punishment. The prohibition was lifted briefly during a cholera outbreak in the 1830s, but was restored and remained in force – 'because non-smokers have a clear right not to be annoyed' – until 1848.

The reference to the rights of non-smokers finds recent echo in the Californian campaign to have greater restrictions placed on the public areas in which smoking may take place. With the aid of £3 million spent on advertising by United States tobacco interests, propositions which would have effected these changes were defeated in referenda held in November 1978 and 1980 (ASH 1980a). The historical precedent for such legislation, anyway, is not encouraging. We might expect that the average nineteenth-century Prussian was more amenable to regimentation than his twentieth-century Californian counterpart – yet 4000 prosecutions for illegal smoking in the year 1846 alone failed to deter Berlin smokers from indulging their habit on the city's streets and promenades.

THE CURRENT CONTEXT

Today, for obvious reasons, little is said in praise of smoking. As is clear from the historical sources already quoted, this was not always so. Yet the cigarette, in contrast to the pipe and cigar, never really had its 'literature of enthusiasm'. The pipe was at worst comforting and homely, and at its best positively inspiring; the cigar affluent, sophisticated, aristocratic, and a feast for the senses. The democratic cigarette, on the other hand, has been rather looked down upon. It is characterized as a convenient way of consuming tobacco, cheap, and, above all, ideally suited to modern techniques of mass production.

Each age, it would seem, gets the form of tobacco it deserves, and the true tobaccophile is clearly not at home in this one. The particular attractions of the cigarette have therefore gone largely unsung – with perhaps one notable exception. Oscar Wilde, in *The Picture of Dorian Gray*, has his character Lord Henry Wotton advise, 'I can't allow you to smoke cigars. You must have a cigarette. A cigarette is the perfect type of a perfect pleasure. It is exquisite, and leaves one unsatisfied. What more can one want?'

Health and economics

In the current context, smoking is clearly on the defensive and likely to remain so. Yet, historically, the strength of opposition to the tobacco habit waxed and waned. For example, between 1895 and 1909 twelve American States banned cigarettes totally, but every ban had been repealed by 1927 (Brooks 1953). The arguments against tobacco traditionally involved appeals to a combination of religious, moral and aesthetic principles, with little emphasis (and what there was, often misplaced) on the health consequences of the habit. A feature of the present situation, however, is that anti-smoking sentiment is firmly anchored in widely accepted medical evidence. In 1931 it was possible for Count Corti to conclude in his *History of Smoking* (Corti 1931: 265) that although the fight between smokers and non-smokers still dragged on, the latter were 'but a feeble and ever-dwindling minority'. This is of course far from true today.

In 1938, Raymond Pearl, Professor of Biology at Johns Hopkins University, indicated the link between non-smoking and longevity. Whereas only 46 per cent of heavy smokers lived to beyond 60 years of age, this was true of 67 per cent of non-smokers. Case reports linking smoking with a specific disease – cancer – had appeared in the nineteenth century and a retrospective study of the relationship between cancer of the lung and smoking habits was carried out in Cologne in 1939. However, it was not until the careful epidemiological studies of Doll and Hill in the UK (e.g. Doll and Hill 1952) and Wynder and others in the USA (e.g. Wynder *et al.* 1956) that the statistical association was clearly established. At more or less the same time known carcinogens were identified in tobacco smoke (Van Proosdij 1960; Wynder and Hoffman 1967). Since then, tobacco smoking has been implicated in a range of diseases including cancer of the oral cavity, larynx, pharynx, oesophagus, and bladder, coronary heart disease,

bronchitis, and emphysema. The current debate on smoking therefore takes place in a context radically different from that influencing
any preceding tobacco controversy.

The tobacco industry itself has not been slow to respond to the
change in climate, and, whilst stoutly resisting legislative measures
which might seriously have imperilled its profitability, has expended
considerable effort on attempts to design cigarettes which carry a
lower associated health risk.

The introduction of filter cigarettes was originally largely unrelated
to questions of 'safer' smoking, being initially a response to the rising
importance of the female smoker, who was suspected of disliking
conventional soggy cigarette ends. A further reason for the introduction of the tipped cigarette was that the filter economized on
expensively taxed tobacco leaf, preserving cigarette length whilst
avoiding wastage of tobacco in the unsmoked butt (Corina 1975).
Many early filter brands in fact yielded more nicotine and tar in their
smoke than some non-filter brands, and there was a suspicion that
manufacturers were taking the opportunity presented by filters to use
higher-yielding but poorer-quality grades of tobacco. The manufacturers of one brand of cigarette (Kent) actually introduced a
genuinely effective filter in 1952, but later reduced the efficiency of the
filter as sales dropped (Van Proosdij 1960). Wynder and Hoffman
summarized the position in the United States in 1967:

> 'As a result of the stress on "taste" and "satisfaction" in cigarette
> advertisements, some of the new filter cigarettes have the same "tar"
> yield as leading non-filter cigarettes. . . . If a manufacturer chooses an
> inefficient filter and at the same time uses tobaccos yielding high
> amounts of "tar", the basic purpose of a cigarette filter is negated.'
>   (Wynder and Hoffman 1967: 506)

This points to a major difficulty, practical and commercial, inherent
in the search for a 'safer' cigarette. A brand yielding smoke which is
effectively filtered may be notionally less harmful, but it will also be
less 'satisfying', less liked, and therefore smoked by fewer people.

Nevertheless, the impression that filter cigarettes are likely to be
less damaging to health has become widespread. Over the longer
term the tar and nicotine yield of filter cigarettes did undoubtedly
become considerably less than that of non-filter brands, and there is
evidence that smokers are being slowly weaned onto a lower diet of tar
and nicotine than they had been accustomed to. The introduction of
specifically low-tar brands has also met with some success (*Figure 3*),
and again there are likely to be measurable – if small – effects on the

Figure 3 The sale of cigarettes 1900–1980

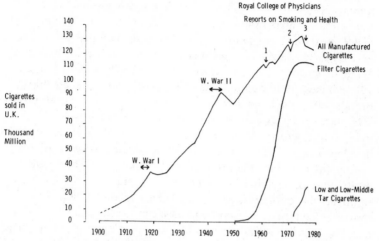

1, 2, and 3 refer to the first, second, and third Royal College of Physicians reports.
Sources: Lee 1976; Capell 1978; Research Services Ltd (private communication) 1980.

level of smoking-related disease. Interestingly, with respect to the introduction of lower-tar brands, cigarette manufacturers seem again to have been motivated by a mixture of commercial factors and genuine concern. One of the ways in which the tar yield of a brand can be reduced is by incorporating into the cigarette a proportion of reconstituted tobacco sheet, formed from stem and tobacco dust. Moshy (1967: 49) argues that 'the development of reconstituted sheet technology throughout the world gave the cigarette manufacturer the opportunity to upgrade his waste tobacco from a product of virtually no value to one usable in the manufacture of cigarettes'.

There is now evidence that the effect of lower-tar cigarettes in reducing the health risks of smoking is beginning to become apparent. Auerbach, Hammond and Garfinkel (1979), compared the histological appearance of the bronchial lining in tissues taken at autopsy from two groups of cigarette smokers who died from causes other than lung cancer. Lung tissues taken from smokers who died in the period 1970–77, who would have smoked cigarettes of relatively low tar and nicotine delivery, showed a significantly *lower* frequency of precancerous histological abnormalities than tissues taken from smokers who died in the period 1955–60, who smoked roughly the same number of cigarettes, but cigarettes of a comparatively high nicotine and tar yield.

It should be emphasized that the frequency of histological abnormality in the 1970–77 sample of smokers was still much greater than in *non-smokers* from either period. Nevertheless, the finding of histological differences in the bronchial epithelia of smokers of high and lower-yielding cigarettes, taken together with epidemiological evidence showing that lung cancer occurred less frequently in people who smoked filter cigarettes than in those who smoked untipped brands, offers the hope that smoking, whilst never likely to be made safe, may yet be made safer (Wynder 1980).

However, whilst the governments and health agencies of the developed world have met with some limited success in their campaigns to reduce the prevalence of smoking and encourage the production of less harmful cigarettes, in many underdeveloped countries the position is reversed (Taha and Ball 1980). Rates of consumption are rising steeply and the cigarettes being smoked (often with the same brand names as in the UK) are of high tar and nicotine yield.

Since the sixteenth century, commerce in tobacco has been of great economic and political importance (Corina 1975). The culture and export of tobacco enabled fledgling English colonies in North America to survive, and the need for a large merchant marine to transport the leaf and then for naval protection of the trade, contributed to England's supremacy at sea. In the late nineteenth century, the tobacco industry, along with those in oil and steel, was a pillar of American monopoly capitalism. Now, seven extremely successful multinational tobacco conglomerates – with diversified interests in food and drink manufacture, retailing, mining, cosmetics, pulp and paper, and many other areas – control the cigarette market in the non-communist world (Clairmonte 1980).

The expanding market for cigarettes in the Third World is supplied primarily by imports or by affiliates and licencees of the major tobacco companies (Wickström 1980). Nevertheless, growing the tobacco itself is becoming a major part of the economy of many countries (such as Malawi and India) and developing nations accounted for 60 per cent of the 1977 world production of 5.6 million tons (Marongiu 1980; Aberg 1980). The number and variety of individuals, companies, and governments vitally interested in the continued growing, trading, and manufacture of tobacco makes it unlikely that the 'smoking epidemic' will be short-lived. If it is improbable that severe restrictions will be *imposed* on the manufacture and sale of cigarettes, it is equally unlikely in present circumstances that consumers will voluntarily abandon the tobacco habit. In this context a better understanding of why it is that people smoke, and of ways in which smoking might be made less harmful, is of considerable importance.

Who smokes what?

Cigarette smoking is overwhelmingly the most important form in which tobacco is consumed, both in terms of the amount smoked and in terms of the consequences for health. The total weight of all tobacco goods sold in the United Kingdom in 1979 was 247 million pounds. Of this, 0.2 per cent was in the form of snuff, 3 per cent cigars and cigarillos, 4 per cent pipe tobacco and 93 per cent cigarettes – hand rolled, plain and filter (Research Services Limited (private communication) 1980). Over 124 thousand million cigarettes were smoked by the country's 18 million cigarette smokers, at an average rate of 19 per day (*Figure 3*). Roughly 42 per cent of the adult male population smoked manufactured cigarettes and 39 per cent of the female population – though there were in fact slightly more female smokers than male smokers. Over the past thirty years the proportion of male smokers has declined steadily from around 65 per cent in 1948, whilst the proportion of women smoking has remained relatively stable. The difference in smoking prevalence between the sexes has therefore narrowed considerably and is now virtually non-existent.

However, whilst the sex difference has become less pronounced, a difference according to social class has emerged (*Figure 4*), social class I having the smallest proportion of smokers and social class V the largest (Capell 1978: Table 3). In certain working-class areas smoking is apparently still nearly ubiquitous. A report in the *Observer Magazine* described life on the Creggan Estate in Londonderry, where stress factors may also be presumed to play a part in the prevalence of smoking:

'In the poorer houses just about everybody smokes, ashtrays are full of butts. It is a place where it is still an act of hospitality to offer a pack or actually toss cigarettes round the room on the assumption that everyone smokes. Finger tips are yellow-brown with nicotine, and clouds of smoke eddy round the television screen.'

(*Observer Magazine* 31 December 1978: 24)

Amongst specific occupational categories, construction workers, labourers, and those employed in the transport and communications

Figure 4 Smoking and social class in men and women, 1976

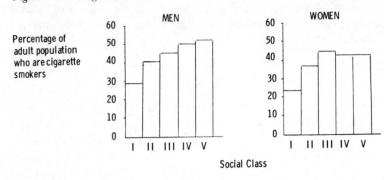

Source: Capell 1978.

Social class   I – higher professional, managerial, and administrative
            II – intermediate professional, managerial, and administrative
            III – supervisory, clerical, and junior
            IV – skilled manual
            V – semi- and unskilled manual

industries were estimated in 1975 to have the highest per capita consumption of cigarettes, whilst professional, technical, and clerical workers had the lowest consumption (Lee 1976: Table 28M). Perhaps surprisingly, members of the armed forces seemed to smoke no more heavily than average. Within England and Wales, the prevalence of cigarette smokers was greater in the non-metropolitan conurbations than in London, and greater in London than in rural areas. When all categories of (male) smokers were considered, the greatest prevalence of smokers by a clear majority, but for no obvious reason, was found in North London (Lee 1976: Table 29).

There is also a quite marked effect of age on smoking. Although admittedly based on a small survey sample, Lee (1976: Table 14) found that cigarette consumption is at its peak amongst men who in 1975 were 50 to 54 years of age. This age group would have been in their late teens when war broke out in 1939, and there seems little doubt that the greater per capita consumption of cigarettes represents the persistent effect of the increase in smoking which accompanied the Second World War. Perhaps surprisingly, the graph relating cigarette consumption to age in women shows no corresponding peak at this point. Another interesting feature of the relationship between age and smoking is the marked decrease in per capita cigarette consumption amongst the oldest age groups. People in this age range will probably have smoked fewer cigarettes all through their lives, though the reduction in consumption may also reflect a genuine lessening of interest in smoking with age. The percentage of ex-smokers increases markedly in the male over-60 age group, and anecdotal evidence suggests that older people are often able to give up smoking without too great difficulty. This would suggest the kind of 'maturing' out of drug use which has been found to occur with alcohol at a similar age (Jessor 1978), and with opiate abuse at a much earlier stage. Increased mortality amongst the heaviest smokers may also have played a part in reducing per capita consumption.

Over the period that the total number of smokers has fallen, sales of cigarettes have continued to rise (Lee 1976: Table 2). This apparent paradox is explained by the fact that consumption of cigarettes per smoker has markedly increased; there are now slightly fewer smokers than 20 years ago, but those who do smoke, smoke more heavily. Between 1949 and 1978 the average consumption by male smokers rose from approximately 100 to 154 cigarettes per week. In women smokers, per capita consumption more than doubled, rising from 50 to 118 cigarettes per week (Lee 1976: Table 17; Research Services Limited (private communication) 1980).

The increase in the number of cigarettes consumed by each smoker has occurred over a period during which the average tar and nicotine yield of cigarettes has decreased considerably (Todd 1975: Table 9; Lee 1976: Table 6). The declining yield of the cigarettes smoked has been due primarily to the by now almost complete switch from high-yielding untipped cigarettes to lower-yielding filter brands (*Figure 3*), although the delivery of both plain and filter cigarettes is also being progressively reduced, and the introduction of specifically low-tar brands over the past six years has made some contribution (Capell 1978). In 1978, over 90 per cent of the cigarettes sold in the UK were filter brands, and over 11 per cent fell in the government's low-tar category (Maxwell International 1979).

An interesting and as yet unanswered question concerns whether those who have followed the government's advice and successfully made the switch to low-tar brands are representative of smokers in general or whether they constitute a particular atypical sub-group. It is certain that many smokers have tried low-tar brands, found them unpleasant or 'unsatisfying' and returned to a higher delivery cigarette. This would suggest that the strategy of reducing cigarette yields and persuading smokers to switch to lower delivery brands might be self-limiting.

With reference to specific brands, Park Drive and Woodbine were the best-selling plain cigarettes in 1978 – but plain cigarettes altogether accounted for under 10 per cent of total sales. King-size cigarettes took 54 per cent of the market – in contrast to only 28 per cent in 1977 – because of the change in January 1978 to an end-product taxation system (*Tobacco* 1979). Benson and Hedges King Size was Britain's best-selling cigarette, with almost 12 per cent of the market share. Player's No. 6 Filter and Embassy Regal followed with 8 per cent and 6 per cent respectively. Silk Cut King Size was the most successful low-tar product – coming eleventh in the rankings with 3.5 per cent of sales.

By way of comparison with the UK, the 54 million smokers in the United States together consumed nearly five times as many cigarettes (615 thousand million), and at a higher rate of consumption per smoker than in Britain (Krasnegor 1980). The proportion of the market taken by filter cigarettes was roughly the same as in Britain, but the emphasis on low-tar low-nicotine products was greater, cigarettes equivalent to our low and low-middle tar categories accounting for 40 per cent of sales (McElheny 1980). Non-filter cigarettes, delivering high yields of tar and nicotine, were still very popular in many Third World countries (notably India, where over three-quarters of the cigarettes sold were plain), but many Dutch, Danish and Norwegians also seem to prefer their tobacco untipped.

APPENDIX: THE DEVELOPMENT OF THE TOBACCO HABIT

Important dates	*Major trends*
1492: 12 October: Columbus first encounters tobacco and later records the incident in his journal.	*Pre-history to 15th century:* the use of tobacco smoke, probably initially for religious and ritual purposes, but later also for pleasure, plays an important role in Mayan civilization and ultimately spreads throughout central and north America.
1519: tobacco leaves brought to Europe. 1543: tobacco recommended for its healing properties. 1556: tobacco seeds arrive in France.	*16th century:* tobacco cultivation and the medicinal use of the leaf becomes widespread in Europe, although the recreational use of tobacco is at first largely confined to American colonists, sailors, and inhabitants of the maritime ports.

1570: tobacco plant named Nicotiana after Jean Nicot, French ambassador to Portugal, who enthused about tobacco's medicinal uses and introduced the leaves to France.

1585–86: English colonists in Virginia take to smoking tobacco and bring the habit to England. Sir Walter Raleigh, a devotee, does much to popularize smoking for pleasure.

1604: the tobaccophobe James I's 'Counterblaste to Tobacco' inveighs against the habit.

17th century: the ascendancy of the pipe
1. Pipe smoking spreads from England to Holland and thence throughout Europe, helped by the marauding armies of the Thirty Years War.
2. Smoking reaches Russia via the Baltic ports and the Near East through the Venetians; the habit proliferates in the Far East where it was introduced by Spanish and Portuguese sailors and merchants.
3. Harsh persecution in Turkey, Persia, Russia and Japan fails to check the habit.

1660: snuff introduced to England from France by courtiers of Charles II.

4. The tobacco trade plays a major part in developing the English North-American colonies; the need for ships to carry leaf to Europe aids the development of England's maritime power and revenue from tobacco subsidizes . military adventure on land.
5. Tobacco is used as a currency, to buy wives in Virginia, slaves and land in Africa.

18th century: during which a good part of the world fell to 'snuffing' and the pipe circumnavigated the globe.

1820s: introduction of flue-curing of tobacco.

19th century: the age of the cigar and the tobacco quid.

1828: Posselt and Reiman isolate the 'active ingredient' in tobacco and call it 'nicotine'.

1840–70: the development of new strains of plant and new methods of curing result in a milder and mellower tobacco.

1848: fall of one of the last bastions against tobacco – smoking is allowed on the streets of Berlin.

1854–56: Europeans introduced to the cigarette by the Crimean War.

1881: the cigarette-making machine patented in the US; with a speed of 200 cigarettes per minute (now over 5000) each machine produces as much in a day as 500 workers, and heralds the era of mass production.

1914–18: The Great War spreads cigarette smoking.

Post-1918: the rise of the female smoker.

1929: the introduction of du Maurier – Britain's first filter cigarette.

1937: for the first time, cancer is produced in laboratory animals by cigarette tar.

1938: Raymond Pearl of Johns Hopkins University produces statistics showing non-smokers live longer than smokers.

1950–56: Doll and Hill and others assemble evidence linking cigarette smoking with cancer of the lung; known carcinogens identified in cigarette smoke.

20th century: the cigarette conquers the world.
1. The low cost and convenience of the cigarette, combined with increasing prosperity, the growth of leisure and the democratization of society, provide unprecedentedly favourable conditions for a massive growth in consumption.
2. The use of mellower tobacco encourages the inhalation of smoke.
3. Detailed epidemiological studies in the 1950s and 1960s confirm the increased health risks associated with cigarette smoking.
4. Governments introduce health-education campaigns and legislation designed to reduce the prevalence of smoking, whilst cigarette manufacturers become interested in the concept of developing a 'safer' cigarette.
5. Great growth in the proportion of the total market taken by filter cigarettes, accompanied by a general downward trend in tar

1962: first report on smoking and health by the Royal College of Physicians.

1964: United States Surgeon General's report on smoking and health.

1965: UK ban on cigarette advertising on television. A health warning appears on cigarette packets sold in the United States.

1970: radio and TV advertising of cigarettes banned in US.

1971: the health warning appears in the UK.

1973: publication by the UK government of tar and nicotine 'league tables'; low-tar 'milder' brands of cigarette introduced.

1977: the introduction and rapid commercial failure of cigarettes containing tobacco substitutes.

deliveries. This trend is especially pronounced in the US and West Germany.

6. In the developed world, the proportion of the population smoking tends to fall and the total consumption of cigarettes plateaus. Perhaps because of this, tobacco companies engage in 'aggressive' marketing in the Third World where consumption rises, governments are slow to take action, and cigarettes remain high in tar and nicotine.

2 THE IMPORTANCE OF NICOTINE

From the incandescent tip of a lighted cigarette, burning at a temperature of 800°C, the smoker with each puff draws along the tobacco rod and into his mouth a hot potpourri of gases and many-sized particles. Hundreds of different chemicals have been identified in cigarette smoke, but there is little doubt that nicotine is the pharmacological agent of prime importance. Smoking doses of nicotine are known to exert profound effects throughout the body, many of which are described in following sections. Nevertheless, non-pharmacological factors are also involved in the act of smoking and before considering the role of nicotine in detail it is worth taking account of the variety of non-nicotine explanations of smoking.

VIEWS OF SMOKING WHICH DO NOT INVOLVE NICOTINE

One of the earliest scientific papers to consider the role of nicotine in smoking listed factors which were thought to be of possible importance in initiating or maintaining the habit:

> 'optical perception of the smoke; fire worship; agreeable smell and taste; mechanical manipulation somewhat resembling the influence of the nipple on the infant; pleasurable irritation of the laryngeal and tracheal sensory branches of the pneumogastric nerve; relief of tension; stimulation; sociability; gives people something to do; permits one to do nothing, gracefully; produces a rise in blood sugar; satisfies a desire or craving; . . . combating hunger and thirst, joy and pain, heat and cold, irritation and languidness.'
>
> (Finnegan, Larson, and Haag 1945: 94)

Certain of these effects are probably related to the pharmacological properties of nicotine; others clearly are not. Explanations which do not regard nicotine as of central importance in smoking motivation include the views that smoking is simply an activity, that it is rewarding because it produces pleasant sensations of smell, taste or irritation, and that it provides some form of 'oral erotic gratification'.

Smoking as a displacement activity

The view that smoking is important simply as an activity has two aspects. First, smoking can be useful in excusing and legitimizing relaxation. This aspect is exemplified in a smoker's self-report about how he started the habit. As a student, with a holiday job on a building site, he noticed that his fellow workers took a few minutes' break every half-hour or so. He followed suit, only to be reprimanded by the foreman for idling. On pointing out that everyone else had regular breaks he was told, 'They're not having a break, they're having a smoke.'

Secondly, smoking can be seen as a valuable 'displacement activity' analogous to behaviours such as scratching and pawing the ground which ethologists have observed in animals in situations of conflict and uncertainty. Desmond Morris (1977: 180) has produced the example of an air traveller, superficially calm, but revealing his anxiety through compulsive tapping of the cigarette to remove ash, crushing out half-smoked cigarettes and dismembering matches. He writes: 'the smoker has an enormous advantage over the non-smoker in moments of stress and can actually create the impression that all his fiddling and fidgeting is really part of a nicotine pleasure and therefore a sign of enjoyment rather than an inner conflict reaction'. The cigarette habit:

> 'Is so much more than a question of inhaling smoke. There is the finding of the packet and the matches or lighter; the extraction of the cigarette from the pack; the lighting up; putting out the flame and getting rid of the lighter, match-box and cigarette packet; shifting the ashtray into a more convenient position; flicking a little imaginary ash from the front of the clothes, and blowing smoke thoughtfully up into the air.'
>
> (Morris 1977: 180)

Like Morris, Chein sees the activity involved in smoking as being valuable to the 'organismic economy' (Chein 1969: 19–20). The suggestion is that smoking provides a routine means both of channelling wandering attention and of providing an outlet for the 'uncoordinated psychomotor irradiation' which might otherwise disrupt both complex behaviour and reverie.

There is evidence suggesting that the frequency and style of smoking does indeed relate to the situation in which the smoker finds himself. In an experiment using electric shocks (ostensibly to measure tactile sensitivity), Schachter *et al.* (1977b) found that smokers exposed to high levels of stress smoked more cigarettes and took 50 per cent more puffs than when the stress level was low. Comer and Creighton (1978) report similar findings; subjects in a (presumably quite demanding) EEG experiment took more frequent puffs of greater volume, and smoked to a shorter butt length, than when they were observed under standard laboratory conditions. However, evidence derived from carefully controlled studies of smokers in non-laboratory environments is relatively sparse, though an unpublished report to the Tobacco Research Council by National Opinion Polls showed that smoking was more intensive under conditions of excitement. Nevertheless, there is prolific anecdotal evidence to reinforce the view that there is a greater incidence of smoking when people are uncertain, anxious, angry and excited. It is likely that having something to do with one's hands and mouth helps under such circumstances, and that non-smokers adopt behaviours such as nail-biting, pen-chewing, and face-scratching which may serve a similar function. However (as we shall see in subsequent chapters) there is also evidence that the pharmacological effects of nicotine may be valuable in assisting in the control of arousal, that the usefulness of nicotine (and therefore the smoker's 'need' for it) varies according to context, and that smokers take different doses of nicotine from a cigarette, depending on their circumstances.

Taste, smell and irritation

The importance of smoking as the source of pleasant sensations of taste and smell is difficult to judge. Anecdotal evidence suggests that these factors are likely to play a role in the enjoyment of a cigar and pipe; Stanley Baldwin is reported to have said, 'my thoughts grow in the aroma of this particular tobacco' (Hamilton 1978: 583). With cigarette smoking, however, the position is probably somewhat different. In a questionnaire study of 1600 people, Zagona and Zurcher (1965) found that only 20 per cent of smokers gave flavour as a reason for enjoying cigarettes. (This compares, for example, with 28 per cent mentioning social comfort, and 45 per cent relaxation.) Indeed it is unclear whether cigarette smokers are capable of judging differences between brands on the basis of taste rather than strength. However, advertisements for cigarettes lay great emphasis on the taste and flavour of particular brands and manufacturers employ panels of trained tasters similar to those used in assessing the acceptability of different blends of tea. Tobaccos, varying widely in strain and geographical origin, presumably differ considerably in taste and aroma and it would be unreasonable to dismiss the possible importance of these influences. Moreover, nicotine itself has a tobacco-like odour.

The psychoanalyst A.A. Brill considered the relevance of taste in a perceptive paper entitled *Tobacco and the Individual* (Brill 1922) which suggests that the great variety of sensory experience available is one of the fundamental distinctions between civilization and savagery. Brill was thinking not only of how music and the arts have extended the range of possible auditory and visual experience far beyond anything provided by the natural world, but also of the wealth of gustatory and olfactory sensations offered to the civilized man. When one considers our elaborate structure of learned taste preferences it is perhaps no more surprising that we should develop a taste for tobacco than that we should have learned to like the many foods and drinks which sophisticated man consumes more for taste than for nutritional value. Nor is the taste for tobacco unique in terms of the strength with which it is desired. Several other substances (salt, refined sugar, chocolate) are not merely enjoyed when they happen to be available, but are actively sought for, sometimes at considerable inconvenience. Brill cites as an example the case of certain South American tribes who could be induced to remain in missionary compounds because the desire they had developed for salt could not be satisfied if they returned to the jungle.

Brill further suggests that the sense of taste, like other senses, craves not only variety but also 'continuous gratification'. Hence, for example, the Roman vomitoria, used so that eating could be emancipated not only from its natural cause – the feeling of hunger – but also from its natural consequence – the filling of the belly. Smoking is a means of taking into the body a substance which excites sensory organs in the lips, mouth, and throat, and which provides sensations of touch, taste, heat, and irritation. Unlike food and drink, however, smoke does not accumulate uncomfortably in the body and is therefore an ideal medium of continuous sensory 'gratification'.

The concept of a sense 'craving gratification' suggests self-indulgence and may seem inappropriate. There is evidence, however, that organisms do seek stimulation – monkeys and children will play with 'interesting' objects, not from any expectation of reward, but from what seems to be a desire for novel experience. One of the most disturbing things that can happen to a human being is to be put in conditions of sensory deprivation, and it is not unreasonable to suppose that smoking could be of value to the organism simply as a source of additional stimulation. The effect of variation in stimuli impinging on the sense organ is to produce an increase in arousal and it is conceivable that part at least of the effect of smoking on arousal is mediated by this mechanism.

An experiment conducted in 1933 investigated smokers' ability to discriminate their own from four other cigarette brands, and found that correct identifications were made at a level greater than chance. Similar results were obtained by Ramond, Rachal and Marks (1950) using three popular American brands. Regular smokers of Camel, Chesterfield and Lucky Strike correctly identified their own cigarettes 73 per cent of the time. However, in this experiment subjects were able to see the cigarettes being smoked (although the brand name was obscured) so that their discriminations may have been based partly on visual cues. It required a later experiment (Prothro 1953) conducted in Beirut, to show that blindfolded smokers could reliably distinguish between and amongst American, British, and Lebanese cigarettes. Prothro's finding is in interesting contrast to that of Hull (1924). In his classic experiment on the psychological effects of smoking, Hull had pipe smokers draw into their mouths either tobacco smoke or warm moist air. Provided the experimenter stood by with a genuinely lit pipe of tobacco, the blindfolded subjects were apparently unable to distinguish puffing smoke from puffing air. This would suggest that the sensations accompanying the presence of smoke in the mouth are not of any real importance in determining the satisfaction of smoking. The sensations accompanying inhalation, however, may assume a somewhat greater role.

Cain (1980) draws the distinction clearly. He argues that the fundamental taste qualities (sweet, sour, salty, bitter) play little part in the sensory impact of smoking, and suggests that the use of sweet additives – traditional in American cigarettes – serves more to disguise bitterness than to enhance flavour. The sense of smell, which very rapidly habituates, is probably equally unimportant, except at the time the cigarette is lit. The effect of inhaled smoke, on the other hand, may be longer lasting, stimulating the 'common chemical sense' (mediated by the glossopharyngeal and vagus nerves) responsible for the perception of pungency, warmth and pain:

'Upon inhalation of cigarette smoke, the smoker stimulates this entire perceptual system, but seems to focus on the feel produced in the soft palate at the back of the mouth and in the sublaryngeal region. For uncertain reasons, the magnitude of this feel, a composite of chemical attributes, seems strongly dependent on the amount of nicotine in mainstream smoke.'

(Cain 1980: 243)

It is not known whether nicotine causes, or is merely correlated with, this immediate sensory impact. Neither is it clear whether the sensations accompanying inhalation are themselves part of the pleasure of smoking. Since the extent of the irritation caused by the smoke relates closely to the amount of nicotine present, the sensations may act merely as a measure of the pharmacological effects to come. Their value to the smoker would therefore be secondary, and might disappear, if the association with nicotine were broken. Furthermore, a tremendous variety of other vegetable substances exist which produce a pleasant smell when burned, and possibly a not unpleasant taste. The smoke from these substances, if drawn into the mouth and inhaled, would probably provide most of the sensations which normally accompany tobacco smoking. The fact that tobacco smoke has been so generally preferred to other equally available, equally flavoursome, and probably equally irritant substances suggests that it has uniquely valuable properties. These properties are probably not unrelated to the fact that the smoke contains a drug with powerful physiological and psychological effects. (The only other vegetable materials widely smoked – opium and marijuana – also, of course, contain psychologically active drugs.)

The Freudian and psychoanalytic view

There can be few aspects of human behaviour so utterly lacking in real or imagined significance as to have avoided Freud's attention. Not surprisingly, the act of smoking – at once apparently trivial and yet rich in many levels of potential meaning – did not escape his scrutiny. The phallic shape of the cigar or cigarette, the oral nature of the behaviour and its affinity with taking milk from the breast, the symbolism of fire, might all have attracted the analytic eye. Yet Freud's involvement with tobacco is interesting as much for the stubborn strength of his personal relationship with the habit as for any theoretical contribution he may have made to our understanding of smoking behaviour (Brecher 1972).

Freud was in many ways a classic casualty of tobacco. Through forty years of suffering from an intermittent but severe 'affection of the heart', and through thirty-three operations for a cancer of the oral cavity which eventually was to prove fatal, Freud persisted in smoking. His doctors implicated nicotine in the etiology of both conditions and strongly recommended abstinence, but without result. Freud's biographer wrote, 'He was always a heavy smoker – twenty cigars a day were his usual allowance – and he tolerated abstinence from it with the greatest difficulty' (Jones 1953, I: 339). During one brief but miserable attempt to give up, Freud himself commented, 'renouncing the sweet habit of smoking has resulted in a great diminution of my intellectual interests' (Jones 1953, II: 128). Earlier, when Freud had been confronted by one of his doctors with the clear choice of continuing to smoke at great risk to his heart, or of forsaking the habit, Freud had replied, 'I am not following your interdict from smoking; do you think then it is so very lucky to have a long miserable life?' (Jones 1953, I: 339). When Freud's pathologist accused nicotine of causing the 'leucoplastic growth' (in fact clearly cancerous) which had recently been removed from his mouth, Freud is said merely to have shrugged his shoulders. Freud's great desire to smoke not only placed his own health in continuing danger but also, on one occasion, put the well-being of others at risk. In 1931, when the export of goods from Germany to Austria was forbidden, and when Freud felt he simply could not smoke anything obtainable in Austria, he persuaded friends to smuggle cigars across the border.

Yet Freud apparently did not possess a character which was peculiarly susceptible to addiction. He had after all been one of cocaine's earliest enthusiasts – advocating its use in a variety of clinical contexts (including anaesthesia), distributing it liberally amongst family and friends, and himself taking regular doses of the 'magical' substance (Jones 1953, I: 89) against depression and indigestion. Though the dangers inherent in his cavalier use of the drug became apparent to others in the tragic addiction of several colleagues, Freud himself suffered no ill-effects and judged the danger in the employment of cocaine to arise not from the drug itself but from its administration by the newly-developed hypodermic needle.

Although there is no evidence that Freud considered in detail the origins of his own 'tobaccomania', the motivation to smoke was incorporated in his general theory of sexuality (Freud 1905). Freud argued that thumb-sucking was both a re-experiencing of the pleasures of suckling and a source in its own right of desirable sensations. In this latter capacity, the behaviour could be regarded as an 'auto-erotic' manifestation of primitive sexuality. Amongst children in whom there was a 'constitutional intensification of the erotogenic significance of the labial region' (Freud 1905: 98), thumb-sucking would be a natural childhood behaviour. As adults, such people would be 'epicures in kissing' and, if males, would have a powerful motive for smoking and drinking. Further exploring the supposedly sexual nature of smoking, Green suggested that a pipe had significance as a symbol of the male sexual organ:

'one may note that English women still dislike, in many cases, a man to smoke in the street. But many of these profess to like a pipe in the house. I have heard women say that a man does not seem at home unless he smokes a pipe and again that a man does not seem a man without a pipe. All this seems in line with an unconscious identification of the pipe with the phallus.'

(Green 1923: 324)

Bergler (1946: 302) wrote of the childhood antecedents of smoking 'getting something orally is the first great libidinous experience of life: breast, milk bottle, pacifier, food. The smoker reassures himself by getting something into his mouth too'. In general, there was nothing untoward in this behaviour; smoking was an 'excellent outlet'. Brill (1922: 444) commented: 'I have never seen a single neurosis or psychosis which could definitely be attributed in any way to tobacco. On the other hand one is more justified in looking with suspicion at the abstainer . . . most of the fanatic opponents of tobacco I have known were all bad neurotics'. Freud would no doubt have approved these sentiments. Nevertheless, psychoanalysts claimed that smoking sometimes had its origins in a disorder of personality. In this respect smoking by certain individuals has been regarded as anything from a substitute for masturbation (Brill 1922) and an expression of the death wish against the father (Green 1923) to a manifestation of masochism (the latter idea arising from the belief that continued smoking in the face of the risk to health may be part of an unconscious wish for self-injury). Bergler demonstrates the kind of convoluted logic peculiar to certain religious and psychoanalytic interpretations in his account of 'pathological smoking'. Having suggested that moderate use of tobacco (along with kissing and gourmanderie) are aspects of oral eroticism, he subsequently argues (Bergler 1953: 214) that compulsive smoking is used 'for expression NOT of the wish to get (the simple continuation of smoking pleasure) but as the unconscious defence against the inner reproach of wanting to be refused'!

Whilst the psychoanalytic interpretations of compulsive smoking approach the wilder flights of fancy, the explanation of moderate smoking in terms of orality is at least intuitively plausible. W.H. Auden, for example, is said to have explained his heavy smoking as 'insufficient weaning – I must have something to suck'. In the psychoanalytic literature, interpretation of the singular circumstances of a particular case history is usually paramount. It is therefore rare to find hypotheses which are general and unambiguous enough to be tested. Freudian ideas on the childhood origins of smoking, however, can – and have been – measured against conventional yardsticks of scientific validity. Is there then any evidence that smoking is a feature of an 'oral personality'? More particularly, do smokers differ from non-smokers in the degree to which they experienced 'oral-frustration' as children?

Perhaps surprisingly there is some slight indication that age at weaning, although unrelated to whether or not people are smokers, and unrelated to amount smoked, may be associated with the ability to give up the habit (McArthur, Waldron, and Dickinson 1958). Thus light smokers able to stop were found to have spent an average of 8 months at their mother's breast and heavy smokers able to stop 6.8 months, whilst smokers who had never tried to give up were weaned at an average age of 5 months, and those who had tried and failed at 4.7 months. A further association with childhood experience was found in a survey which related smoking and drinking in late-adolescent males to birth order and birth interval (Zucker and van Horn 1972). An interaction was found between the two variables such that first-borns who had been closely followed by a second child showed a significantly greater frequency of smoking and problem drinking. This phenomenon could be related to the fact that such children would have received less maternal attention specifically during feeding (a narrow interpretation of oral frustration). Or, on a broader view of the Freudian concept, the greater degree of maternal deprivation can be seen as having occurred simply during the oral phase of development (Jacobs et al. 1965). However, oral frustration, although correlated with subsequent smoking, is not thereby proven to be causally related to it. It is quite conceivable that weaning practices and adult smoking are both reflections of much wider differences in child-rearing, and indeed in family circumstances as a whole. Evidence that smoking is a part of a wider 'oral personality' is slight. Howe and Summerfield (1979) reported the findings of a study which had considered whether smokers and non-smokers differed in orality – as measured by such behaviours as sucking pencils, sweets, or one's thumb, food-chewing and nail-biting. The smokers and non-smokers in their group of 97 student subjects did not differ in any of these respects. There was some evidence of greater orality amongst smokers who had never succeeded in giving up for any length of time, compared with subjects whose pattern of smoking was more inter-mittent; but even here, although pencil-sucking and nail-biting discriminated between the two groups, thumb-sucking and sweet-eating still did not.

An association between smoking and alcohol – and coffee-drinking – (both basically non-nutritive oral behaviours) has been consistently demonstrated in a variety of studies. Coffee consumption by smokers is twice that of non-smokers (Matarazzo and Saslow 1960), and cigarette consumption correlates very highly with both alcohol intake (Borgatta and Evans 1968) and the existence of problem drinking (Prendergast and Preble 1973). However, the fact that use of tobacco, coffee and alcohol tend to occur together in the same people can readily be explained without reference to such a concept as orality. To a large extent all three substances are consumed in the kind of social context which might be more attractive to a particular kind of person. There is also the possibility that nicotine, caffeine and alcohol – all mood-altering substances – may be of greater usefulness to those with difficulties in the self-regulation of affect, irrespective of any early childhood experience or of any constitutionally intensified 'erotogenic significance of the labial region'.

The argument that people smoke as a symbol, or as substitute suckling, suffers also from the same general objection that was brought against the view that the factors of taste and smell or activity are important. This approach to the habit fails to account for the primacy of tobacco over similar vegetable substances not containing nicotine. In addition, the psychoanalytic view is not able to explain why it is that 80 to 90 per cent of cigarette smokers inhale (Lee 1976: Table 34). All the supposed satisfactions of smoking related to oral and manual manipulation and taste and aroma can be obtained without drawing tobacco smoke into the lungs. Why then do smokers inhale? The inhalation of smoke is not a natural behaviour – it has to be learned, often at the cost of some initial discomfort. It is, however, an exceptionally fast and efficient way of getting a drug into the body, and in this respect is rivalled only by intravenous injection. It is therefore our view that both the unique role of tobacco, and the prevalence of inhalation, can best be accounted for by the assumption that smoking is essentially a means of nicotine self-administration.

THE INTAKE OF NICOTINE

Smokers rarely smoke substances (such as those available in the wide variety of herbal cigarettes) which do not contain nicotine. They also tend not to smoke cigarettes which (although made of tobacco) yield only small amounts of the drug.

A 'league table' entitled *Tar and Nicotine Yields of Cigarettes* is issued at six-monthly intervals by the Health Departments of the UK Government. It reports the tar and nicotine produced by cigarettes of every commercially available brand, each smoked on a machine to standard specifications of puff number, frequency, duration, and volume. The standardized puff parameters are based on what is taken to be an average 'real' smoking style. Of course human smokers do not all smoke in the same 'average' way and individual smokers may change the way they smoke according to circumstances. In par-

Figure 5 Distribution of brands according to nicotine delivery

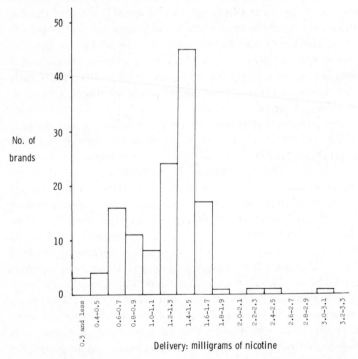

Source: May 1980 league table of tar and nicotine yields, Health Departments of the United Kingdom.

ticular, there is good evidence (which will be reviewed) that smokers take more frequent and larger puffs when smoking a relatively weaker (i.e. lower tar and nicotine yield) cigarette. The league table figures therefore do not represent the amount of tar and nicotine that a particular smoker obtains from a particular cigarette on a particular occasion. They do, however, give a reliable and objective indication of the relative yields of the different brands.

The tar yields of the brands listed in the May 1980 table ranged from under 4 to 28 milligrams and the nicotine yields from under 0.3 to 3.1 milligrams, with a broad spread of standard deliveries in between. (As the nicotine yield of a cigarette increases, its tar yield increases also; the high degree of correlation being due to the close association of nicotine and tar in the smoke produced by the combustion of tobacco.) Amongst the 130 or more kinds of cigarette listed in the league tables, the smoker has a wide range of delivery, taste and brand image from which to choose. Yet in 1977, even though the proportion of the market accounted for by the lower delivery cigarettes had doubled since 1972, at least 79 per cent of all cigarettes sold had a nicotine yield of 1.2 mg or above. Despite being urged over a period of years to switch to lower delivery brands, and then to switch still lower, the majority of smokers are clearly unable or unwilling to do so. The most likely explanation for this is that the nicotine delivery (or tar) of the lower yielding brands is inadequate. The fact that the distribution of brands peaks in the 1.3–1.6 mg nicotine range, presumably reflects commercial awareness of this fact (*Figure 5*).

Absorption of nicotine into the body

Nicotine is an alkaloid containing carbon, hydrogen and nitrogen in the proportion $C_{10}H_{14}N_2$, combined together to form a double ring-like structure. In its pure state it is a colourless, volatile, strongly alkaline liquid which turns brown on exposure to air and gives off a characteristic tobacco smell. It is so powerfully toxic that one drop of the free substance placed on the tongue or skin will kill a dog (or a man) within minutes (Larson, Haag, and Silvette 1961). In an unlit cigarette the nicotine is dissolved in the moisture of the tobacco leaf as water soluble salts, but in a burning cigarette the nicotine volatilizes and is present in the smoke as free nicotine suspended on minute droplets of tar. Those droplets, less than one thousandth of a millimetre across, are small enough, if inhaled, to reach the smallest passages and air sacs (alveoli) in the depths of the lungs.

The nicotine in cigarette smoke has to be inhaled to be absorbed to any great extent. Non-inhaling cigarette smokers, who merely take the smoke into their mouths, do not absorb much nicotine (Armitage *et al.* 1975). This is partly because most cigarette smoke is acid and, for physicochemical reasons, dissolved nicotine is not well absorbed in acid conditions. In addition, the surface area available for absorption in the mouth and nose is limited.

It is interesting to note that the position with cigar and pipe smoking is probably somewhat different, though the current evidence on this point is a little confused. In 'primary' pipe and cigar smokers (that is those people who have not previously also smoked cigarettes) it is usual for the smoke to be retained in the mouth, but not inhaled. If the smoke from pipe and cigar tobacco were identical to that from cigarettes, this would suggest that nicotine was not an important factor in pipe and cigar smoking. However, pipe and cigar tobacco, which has been differently cured, furnishes an alkaline rather than an acidic smoke (in an experiment reported by Armitage and Turner (1970) the pH of cigarette smoke was found to be 5.4 and that of cigar smoke 8.5). The balance of evidence suggests that nicotine under these conditions can be absorbed from the mouth – considerably more slowly than following inhalation, but in sufficient quantities to have a pharmacological effect (Armitage 1973). When snuff is taken, nicotine is also absorbed (Russell, Jarvis, and Feyerabend 1980a), and this is likely to be the case also when tobacco is chewed. It can therefore be argued that the behaviours which tobacco users have adopted are all, in their different ways, effective means of self-administering nicotine.

The lungs have a vast surface area for absorption in the regions where thousands of small blood vessels course under the linings of the air sacs into which the smoke is drawn, and the surface fluids into which the nicotine dissolves are slightly alkaline. When cigarette smoke is inhaled, absorption of nicotine is therefore both efficient and rapid. It has been estimated that around 90 per cent of the nicotine present as inhaled smoke is absorbed (Creighton 1973). As for the speed with which nicotine enters the blood, the increase in plasma nicotine concentration following repeated puffs from a cigarette closely parallels that found with bolus intravenous injection of a similar dose (Russell and Feyerabend 1980). Nicotine absorption, following various methods of administration, might be expected to follow the idealized patterns shown in *Figure 6*, in which an attempt has been made to summarize the findings of a number of experiments.

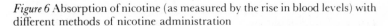

Figure 6 Absorption of nicotine (as measured by the rise in blood levels) with different methods of nicotine administration

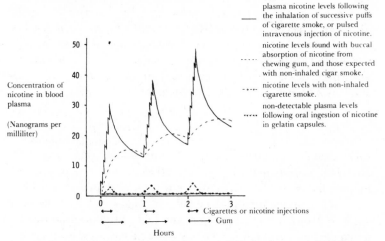

plasma nicotine levels following
the inhalation of successive puffs
of cigarette smoke, or pulsed
intravenous injection of nicotine.

nicotine levels found with buccal
absorption of nicotine from
chewing gum, and those expected
with non-inhaled cigar smoke.

nicotine levels with non-inhaled
cigarette smoke.

non-detectable plasma levels
following oral ingestion of nicotine
in gelatin capsules.

Sources: Isaac and Rand 1969, 1972; Haines *et al*. 1974; Armitage *et al*. 1975; Russell, Feyerabend, and Cole 1976b; Armitage *et al*. 1978; Russell and Feyerabend 1980.

When a cigarette is smoked and the smoke inhaled, blood nicotine levels rise very rapidly and probably peak at roughly the time the cigarette is extinguished. There is then a steep decline in nicotine concentration until the next cigarette is smoked. If cigarettes are smoked at frequent and regular intervals (for example, once an hour), the effect is cumulative so that even in the 'trough' periods, nicotine levels are higher than the baseline. In addition to the peak levels corresponding to each cigarette, there is evidence that each inhalation produces a peak of its own. Though the precise pattern shown in the figure is conjectural, peaking of nicotine levels in arterial blood following each of a number of successive forced inhalations of cigarette smoke has been demonstrated in the dog (Isaac and Rand 1969). Repeated inhalations also had a cumulative effect.

In contrast, non-inhaled cigarette smoke seems to have very little effect on blood nicotine levels (Haines *et al*. 1974; Armitage *et al*. 1975) although *alkaline* smoke held in the mouth is likely to have an intermediate effect (Armitage *et al*. 1978), similar to that found when gum containing nicotine is slowly chewed (Russell, Feyerabend, and Cole, 1976b). Such absorption would be sufficient to attain the trough nicotine levels experienced by the average cigarette smoker, but would not approach the peak levels obtained with inhalation. It should be mentioned, however, that Turner, Sillett and McNicol (1977) found little absorption of nicotine in a small group of non-inhaling primary cigar smokers. This unexpected result, although subject to criticism (Roe and Lee 1978), is sufficient to cast some doubt on the accepted view that significant amounts of nicotine are absorbed from cigar smoke. A similar absence of nicotine absorption has recently been reported in the case of non-inhaling pipe smokers (Turner, Sillett, and McNicol 1981).

Distribution of nicotine within the body

Once taken up into the blood flowing through the lungs, some of the absorbed nicotine immediately enters the lung tissues, while the rest follows the course of the circulation into the left side of the heart. From there it is pumped rapidly to all parts of the body. The vanguard of nicotine molecules obtained from the first puff of a cigarette may reach the brain in about 7 seconds and the big toe in 15–20 seconds.

Over 30 per cent of the nicotine in blood exists in the free form, the remainder being present as dissociated salts (ions). In its free form nicotine is exceedingly lipid (fat) soluble and, since the membranes surrounding the cells of the body are largely composed of lipids, it can easily penetrate through these membranes into tissue cells. As free nicotine leaves the blood, more is continually formed from the salts left behind, and this in turn can pass into the tissues. Thus the major part of absorbed nicotine has ready access to the vital cellular structure of most organs – including those of the foetus, if the smoker happens to be pregnant.

However, a feature of the distribution of nicotine (and of many other drugs) among body tissues is that it is unequal and the relative concentration of nicotine in different tissues varies over time. Studies with many species of animals (rats, mice, cats, dogs, guinea pigs, and monkeys) have shown that nicotine is taken up with great rapidity by the brain and other nervous tissues (e.g. Mazière et al. 1976; Schmiterlow et al. 1967; Larson, Haag, and Silvette, 1961; Larson and Silvette 1975). For example, in the mouse, maximum brain concentrations of nicotine are reached within one minute of the injection or direct application of nicotine to the respiratory tract, and at this time the concentration of nicotine in the brain is more than five times greater than that in the blood. This avid sequestration of nicotine by the brain is no doubt important in determining its swift psychological effects. Other structures in the nervous system which quickly take up nicotine from the blood are the medulla of the adrenal glands and the sympathetic ganglion cells – both parts of the autonomic nervous system concerned among other things with the control of the circulation. The early entry of nicotine into these structures, as well as into the brain and into the cells of the heart itself, account for the rapid onset of circulatory changes associated with smoking a cigarette.

The reasons for the preferential uptake of nicotine by the nervous system probably include its high lipid concentration, its abundant blood flow and possibly its ability to take up certain substances from the blood-stream, even against a concentration gradient, by active enzymatic processes. Areas of the body less richly supplied with these attributes take up correspondingly less nicotine.

However, the high lipid solubility of free nicotine means that it can diffuse out of cells as readily as it can enter them, while the constant stream of blood which carries nicotine to brain cells is equally capable of carrying it away. And in fact the speed of exit of nicotine from the brain is almost as dramatic as its speed of entry. In the mouse, for instance, the peak brain concentration of nicotine may be reached within one minute of injection, but within five minutes the amount falls to 50 per cent of maximum and only 1 per cent is left after sixty minutes. The distribution of nicotine between different regions of the brain also varies over time. Thus it may be noteworthy that 10 minutes after injection the concentration of nicotine in the hippocampus, a cerebral structure intimately concerned with emotion, learning, and memory, may be 30 per cent higher than in the rest of the brain. In general, nicotine seems first to be taken up into the grey matter of the brain (containing mainly nerve cells) and later to be distributed to the white matter (consisting mainly of nerve fibres) before finally disappearing from the brain.

The time relations of the passage of nicotine in and out of the brain have largely been studied in small mammals, in whom the circulation time is undoubtedly shorter than in man. However, there is every reason to suppose that the same general pattern applies in humans and that, in man as in mouse, any nicotine entering the lungs is concentrated in the brain within a matter of minutes, and soon thereafter starts to leave it.

As mentioned previously, the smoking of a cigarette does not deliver nicotine in a steady stream to the smoker; rather, he receives a series of intermittent 'shots' or 'slugs' (boli) of nicotine coinciding with each inhaled puff (Russell 1978b). Of course, this discrete configuration does not last for long as the nicotine boli become mixed by the churning of the heart and travel in and out of organs along tortuous vascular channels. Nevertheless, the intermittent nature of nicotine presentation by smoking, coupled with the almost instantaneous uptake of nearly all the nicotine presented, ensure that, in the first passage of nicotine round the body after each puff, the tissues are briefly exposed to a relatively high concentration – much higher than if the same amount of nicotine were first mixed evenly with the whole blood volume. The tissues receiving the highest concentrations are those with the quickest and most direct blood supply – and these, in particular, include the brain cells.

This entrance of nicotine into the tissues as intermittent highly concentrated waves appears to be of great importance in determining its actions. The response of cells stimulated in this way is different from the response obtained if the same total amount is delivered in an evenly diluted form. It has been shown in animals that if one wishes to simulate the effects of inhaled puffs of cigarette smoke by means of intravenous injection of nicotine, it is necessary to give multiple, small, separate, quickly injected shots, rather than giving the same dose smoothly (Armitage, Hall, and Sellers 1969).

Metabolism and excretion of nicotine

The detailed biochemistry of nicotine metabolism need not concern us here. Nevertheless, it must be said that metabolism is relatively rapid. Several organs of the body contain enzymes which break nicotine down into many pharmacologically inactive substances, mainly cotinine and nicotine–N–oxide. The chief organ of metabolism is the liver, though some metabolism occurs in other organs, including the lung – but not the brain. The ability of individual subjects to form the different metabolites varies considerably and there may also be differences between the sexes (Beckett, Gorrod, and Jenner 1971). In general, habitual smokers are more efficient at metabolizing nicotine than non-smokers, and cotinine may begin to appear in the blood within minutes from the start of smoking.

It has been suggested that nicotine taken in the form of swallowed tablets might provide levels of the drug adequate to replace smoking (Jarvik, Glick, and Nakamura 1970). However, nicotine absorbed from the gastrointestinal tract enters blood vessels which lead the blood through the liver before it reaches the general circulation. Much of the ingested nicotine is thus inactivated by hepatic metabolism before it can be distributed around the body and any nicotine emerging from the liver is already mixed and diluted in a considerable pool of blood. Because of this, it is possible to swallow a potentially lethal dose of nicotine without serious ill effects, and small children who have eaten cigarettes containing several milligrams of nicotine have survived unharmed. For similar reasons, swallowed tobacco or nicotine does not give rise to peaks and troughs of nicotine concentration in the blood. The relative inefficacy of a swallowed dose has been demonstrated by Armitage (1973) who reported that 1 mg/kg of nicotine injected into the cat duodenum raised blood pressure by a much smaller amount than the comparatively minute dose from a single puff of smoke administered to the lungs. Russell and Feyerabend (1980: 39) found 'no detectable elevation of plasma nicotine' when a volunteer subject took 8 mg of the drug by mouth. Plasma nicotine levels comparable to those found after the smoking of two cigarettes were not achieved until the oral dose reached a massive 44 mg – equivalent to the standard nicotine delivery of around thirty cigarettes.

Nicotine excretion occurs largely through the kidney. As the blood passes through the kidney tubules, nicotine and its metabolites diffuse into the urine. If the urine is acid, nicotine is not easily reabsorbed into the circulation and some nicotine is removed unaltered from the body. When the urine is alkaline, however, much of the free nicotine is reabsorbed. If smokers seek to maintain relatively constant blood nicotine levels (or at least to prevent these levels falling below some critical value) the greater renal excretion of nicotine under acid conditions would be expected to lead to an increased frequency of smoking. The evidence relating to this question is considered at greater length in Chapter 4.

MECHANISMS OF ACTION

The particular mode of nicotine's circumnavigation of the body has been discussed because it is important in determining the actions the drug exerts. If nicotine were not absorbed quickly from the lungs, people would not take it in the form of smoke; if it were not taken up into the brain, it would not exert its potent psychopharmacological effects; if it were not rapidly metabolized and excreted, it would probably not be taken in such often-repeated doses. We now turn to consider the mechanisms which underlie the effects of nicotine on the body.

Nicotine and acetylcholine

The nicotine molecule has several remarkable features pertinent to its actions in man and other animals. Foremost among those is its structural similarity to the vital body chemical acetylcholine (ACh) (*Figure 7*). ACh is a chemical neurotransmitter, a substance which conveys information from one nerve cell to another. When a nerve is stimulated, the excitation is initially propagated along the nerve fibre in the form of an electrical impulse. At the point of junction of the first nerve fibre with the next nerve cell, however, there is an infinitesimal gap, called the synaptic cleft. On arrival at this point, the nerve impulse is momentarily extinguished. In its stead, the neurotransmitter ACh is liberated from storage vesicles in the nerve ending into the synaptic cleft. On the second nerve are special chemical receptors for ACh and when enough ACh has been released to excite a critical number of these receptors, electrical changes occur which initiate a further electrical impulse. This impulse is then propagated in turn along the second nerve fibre. Each time synaptic contact is made in this way, the neurotransmitter is used as the messenger to pass on the information carried in the nerves.

Figure 7 The structure of nicotine and acetylcholine

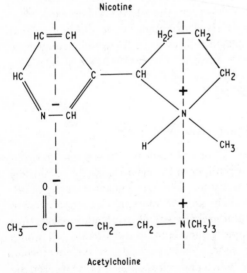

The positive and negative charges are the same distance apart in the two molecules.

In such manner, messages are carried from the body to the brain, from the brain to the body and between different parts of the brain and spinal cord. Many synaptic contacts are required to integrate information received continuously from the outside world and to coordinate the body's physiological and behavioural responses. Several other neurotransmitters are utilized by the nervous system besides ACh, but ACh is known to be involved in important systems including those concerned with physical and mental arousal, learning and memory, and several aspects of emotion. There are also other receptors for ACh in the body, apart from the ones at synapses. ACh receptors with slightly different characteristics are found at the junction between nerves and muscles and at the junctions between nerves and certain glands such as salivary and sweat glands.

In the synaptic arrangement of the nervous system, a vital role is played by the receptors for ACh. In order to pass on the nerve message correctly, they must respond specifically to ACh and not to other neurotransmitters or to chemicals with other functions that may be in the vicinity. The transmitter/receptor relationship has been described as similar to that between lock and key, the receptor being the lock which can only be opened by the particular neurotransmitter key.

One way in which the ACh receptor recognizes its key, the ACh molecule, is by the position of two electrical charges, one positive and one negative, located at certain sites on the molecule (*Figure 7*). The distance between these two charges is always the same and corresponds with two equally spaced and oppositely charged sites on the receptor. Since, in the physicochemical world, opposite charges attract one another, the ACh molecule is attracted to the ACh receptor and then fits snugly into it by virtue of their mutually satisfying configuration. Other molecules without the electrical and spatial characteristics of ACh simply pass the receptor by.

It is at this point that nicotine enters the scene, for in the nicotine molecule the positive charge on the ammonium head and the negative charge of the pyridine ring are just the same distance apart as they are in the ACh molecule. This structural similarity makes nicotine a perfect skeleton key to interact with ACh receptors. So specific is this fit of nicotine with certain ACh receptors that ACh receptors throughout the body are traditionally classified as nicotinic receptors (those that respond to nicotine) and muscarinic receptors (those that respond to another drug, muscarine, not present in tobacco though found in certain poisonous fungi).

The ability of nicotine to combine with ACh receptors means that it can exert actions like ACh at all synapses where nicotinic ACh receptors are present. Thus it can trigger impulses down post-synaptic nerve fibres, resulting in effects which otherwise only occur when ACh is released following stimulation of the pre-synaptic nerves. Synapses involving ACh are very widespread in the body, affecting systems ranging from the cardiovascular to the psychological and also interacting with other transmitter systems. Hence it is not surprising that nicotine too has multifarious actions.

The lock-and-key analogy of the transmitter/receptor interaction at the synapse does not tell the whole story. Events at the synapse are much more dynamic than this picture suggests because nerve impulses are not single events but come in multiple rapid succession. Electrical excitation of a nerve produces not just one impulse but a whole train of impulses. This multiplicity imposes the requirement at the synapse that the combination of transmitter with receptor must be quickly reversed between each impulse, leaving the receptor free to combine with the next packet of ACh released. In addition, the ACh released after interaction with the receptor and any extra, unused ACh must be removed from the site of action so that there is no interference with the quanta of ACh released by the next impulse.

These details of synaptic transmission are relevant to a second important property of the nicotine molecule. Although nicotine can combine with the ACh receptor, the resulting combination is much more enduring than the combination with ACh. It is so stable that some ACh receptors may still be occupied by nicotine when a fresh nerve impulse arrives at the synapse. If all the available receptors are occupied in this way by nicotine, the nerve impulse is blocked. In this case, instead of being stimulated, the eventual response mediated at the synapse will be inhibited or depressed.

Biphasic effects

This behaviour of nicotine at the synapse is one of the reasons for the biphasic effects which are a feature of its actions in the body. The initial combination of nicotine with the ACh receptor at first stimulates an ACh-like response, but the fixity of the drug/receptor combination then blocks any further response to ACh (or to more nicotine). The degree of stimulation versus block depends on the amount of nicotine present relative to the number of available ACh receptors: in general, small doses of nicotine produce a predominantly stimulant effect at synapses, larger doses produce a mainly depressant effect, while the effect of a lethal dose is to block nervous transmission altogether. For example, in the complex neural circuits involved in breathing, small doses of nicotine stimulate respiration, large doses of nicotine depress respiration, while a nicotine overdose causes complete arrest of respiration.

The duration of the effects of nicotine at a synapse obviously depend on how much nicotine is present – the dose administered. In a person smoking a cigarette, the time/dose relationship for the amount of nicotine reaching the central nervous system with each 'shot' of inhaled nicotine can be such as to allow the effect of nicotine at a synapse to come on and wear off between each puff. Depending on factors such as the size of the puff, the depth of inhalation and the individual sensitivity of the subject's receptors, a smoker can get a predominantly inhibitory or a predominantly excitatory effect – or indeed a mixture of both effects – from one cigarette. The ease with which nicotine can produce rapid, reversible, biphasic effects over a small dose range is a second remarkable characteristic which singles it out from most other drugs.

A third important property of the nicotine molecule has already been mentioned: its ability to penetrate into and become briefly concentrated in the brain and nervous tissue. Such a penetration is obviously a prerequisite for the nicotine to reveal the other two characteristics described above: that of being able to combine with ACh receptors, thus simulating ACh as a neurotransmitter, and that of locking to ACh receptors, thus also blocking ACh. The combination of these three features provides a basic mechanism by which nicotine exerts its widespread effects on the body, though it is probable that nicotine also has other modes of action, particularly in the brain.

Involvement of nicotine in integrated nervous activity

Many body functions are modulated by a system of dual controls. This is exemplified by the sympathetic and parasympathetic divisions of the nervous system which modulate autonomic functions such as heart rate, blood pressure and gastrointestinal motility. For example, stimulation of sympathetic nerves to the heart results in an increase in heart rate while stimulation of parasympathetic nerves to the heart decreases its rate. The heart rate at any one moment reflects the balance of sympathetic and parasympathetic nervous influences which are in turn controlled from autonomic centres in the brain.

Other more complex controls affecting thoughts and emotions, involving several neurotransmitters, also exist in the brain and influences from these affect the autonomic centres. These connections explain why the heart rate increases during emotions such as fear and rage (sympathetic stimulation) and why it decreases during the drowsy contentment after a meal (parasympathetic stimulation).

ACh acts as a neurotransmitter in both the sympathetic and parasympathetic nervous systems, and also in the brain. At these sites, for the reasons already discussed, nicotine is also active. In this arrangement lies a second reason for nicotine's ability to exert biphasic effects. In the case of the heart, nicotine can increase heart rate by stimulation of the sympathetic nervous system or by blockade of the parasympathetic system (allowing unopposed sympathetic activity). Similarly it can decrease heart rate either by stimulation of the parasympathetic nervous system or by inhibition of sympathetic nervous activity. Theoretically, it can change heart rate in either direction by purely stimulant effects, by purely blocking effects, or by a combination of both. The same is true for nicotine effects on other systems. The direction and degree of the effects observed in an individual will depend on a host of factors including the dose of nicotine and the relative degree of sympathetic or parasympathetic activity at the time the dose arrives at the relevant synapses.

Brain functions are modulated by a more complex multi-transmitter system, involving more than twenty different neurotransmitters. These include not only ACh and noradrenaline but also other compounds such as dopamine, serotonin and several different amino acids and polypeptides. These systems are so closely integrated that a change in any one of them affects the activity of several others. No synapse, for example, works in isolation. In some parts of the brain each single cell makes through its branches 100,000 synaptic connections with other nerve cells. Stimulation (or block) of these cells therefore has widespread repercussions, and any nervous activity represents the result of actions and interactions between large numbers of nerve cells, each with its own effects on various bodily functions.

Thus it is not surprising to find that nicotine has effects on neurotransmitter systems in the brain other than those involving acetylcholine. These effects are difficult to unravel, especially in man, but in animals it has been shown that nicotine affects release of the neurotransmitters dopamine, noradrenaline and serotonin. Exactly how it exerts its actions is in most cases not known: knowledge is limited by lack of understanding of the normal workings of the brain, let alone its workings in the presence of drugs. Needless to say the effects of nicotine are not the same in all individuals but are influenced by the mental as well as the physical make-up of the smoker – his personality, his emotional state at the time of smoking, and his environment.

At the risk of over-complicating the picture, it must finally be mentioned that there are both excitatory and inhibitory nervous pathways in the brain – systems both to initiate certain behaviours and their physiological concomitants and to inhibit these behaviours. For example, the impulse to flee from an enemy (via an excitatory pathway) may be countermanded by an impulse to stand ground (via an inhibitory pathway). Nicotine effects on these pathways can give rise to apparently paradoxical situations in which excitatory effects may stimulate inhibitory pathways or inhibitory effects block excitatory pathways (or vice versa) – yet another demonstration of nicotine's biphasic or dual effects.

Some of the actions of nicotine as obtained from smoking will be described in later chapters. It is known that nicotine can affect almost every system of the body, and these actions are obviously far from simple. As summarised by Domino:

> 'What is clear is that there is a mixture of stimulant and depressant properties at a variety of levels. These involve the central and peripheral nervous system, the cardiovascular and endocrine systems. This complex of effects is further intermingled with personality and other variables that result in the complicated behaviour . . . that is the phenomenon of tobacco smoking.'
>
> (Domino 1979: 142)

3 THE DEVELOPMENT OF SMOKING BEHAVIOUR

The development of cigarette-smoking behaviour is influenced by a complex interplay of positive and negative factors which diminish and increase in importance at different stages. Many of these factors are summarized diagrammatically in *Figure 8*. The figure also shows that the factors which are operative in starting smoking appear to be quite different from those which contribute to its continuation. Once started, the smoker becomes to a greater or lesser extent pharmacologically involved in smoking and may progress along a continuum from habit to dependence, although not all smokers necessarily proceed the whole way. Before discussing these aspects of established smoking, it is worth examining the influences which induce a person to start.

STARTING TO SMOKE

Much evidence suggests that starting to smoke is related to the influence of parents and peer group, and to the 'anticipation of adulthood' (Mausner and Platt 1971; Russell 1971). A survey of over 1500 adolescents, carried out in 1969 on behalf of the American Cancer Society, is a plentiful source of data on this point (Mausner and Platt 1971). The median age of first experimentation with cigarettes was twelve years, clearly identifying the time around puberty as the critical point for initiating the habit. The important role of parents, siblings and peers was also apparent. Smokers constituted 32 per cent of the teenage children of mothers who smoked, compared with only 23 per cent of the children of non-smoking mothers. Having a father who smoked influenced the likelihood of teenage smoking to a similar extent. The importance of having an elder brother or sister who smoked was greater. Smoking was found in only 20 per cent of teenagers whose elder brothers or

Figure 8 Factors affecting different stages in the development of smoking

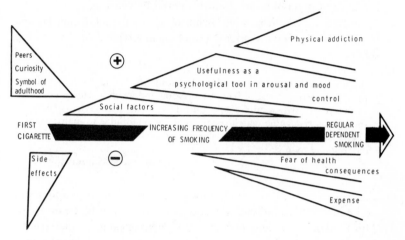

This figure first appeared in Stepney (1980c). Reproduced by permission of the editor and publishers of the *British Journal of Diseases of the Chest.*

sisters did *not* smoke, but in 43 per cent of teenagers whose older siblings did. The teenagers interviewed thought, on average, that 72 per cent of adults smoked (when the true figure was little over 40 per cent). This provided a clear indication of the extent to which smoking and adulthood were associated in the children's minds.

The greatest influence in starting smoking, however, appears to come from friends of similar age. Fifty-six per cent of smokers in Mausner and Platt's study said that their friends also smoked, compared with only 14 per cent in the case of non-smokers. The important effect of peer groups on the age of starting smoking has also been pointed out by Eysenck and Eaves (1980) in their analysis of twin and family studies, and by Bewley, Bland, and Harris (1974) in their work on Derbyshire school children.

The effect on childhood smoking of the behaviour of parents, peers and siblings is presumably mediated partly through increased exposure to cigarettes, and partly through the influences of imitation and example. However, constitutional and genetically determined factors are no doubt also relevant (Chapter 6). For example, Cherry and Kiernan (1976) have shown in a sample of UK schoolchildren that personality differences predate the onset of smoking. Individual differences may also determine an adolescent's orientation towards the kind of psychological rewards offered by smoking.

McArthur, Waldron, and Dickinson quote the following passage from a study which investigated smoking in a typical American high school:

> 'Law and the mores deny high school students the right to enjoy the pleasures derived from tobacco, gambling and alcohol. However, the mystery with which adults surround these areas of behaviour lends them a special value which seems to act as a stimulus to many young people who desire to experience the supposed thrill of pleasures their elders deny them.'
>
> (McArthur, Waldron, and Dickinson 1958: 269)

Transgressing the restrictions imposed by law and taboo is a source of excitement – both individually and within the clique of the initiated. This kind of excitement, of course, does not appeal to all adolescents. Not surprisingly, those to whom it does appeal are also more likely to indulge in other risk-taking behaviours and to find other sources of conflict with authority. In their review of the literature on smoking in childhood, Mausner and Platt (1971: 6) cite evidence that those boys and girls who begin to smoke 'are more rebellious than non-smokers, have poor relations with authority figures, date frequently, drive early and use alcohol, and tend to have accidents when they drive'. Russell (1971) reviews a number of studies which considered the onset of smoking in English adolescents. The factors associated with smoking are substantially the same as those found by Mausner and Platt. Russell (1971: 10) characterizes the environment from which the young smoker originates as one involving 'chasing girls, going to cafes, cinemas and dances, spending money on clothes and pop records'. He contrasts these activities with the less precocious pastimes of the likely non-smoker – homework, reading, watching television, or hobbies like woodwork, cycling, and looking after pets. In the United States, non-smoking is associated with the achievement and work-orientated 'American core culture', of which the following comment (from the father of a non-smoker) is supposedly typical:

> 'I know that Andy has a clean mind. He does not smoke, he does not loiter on the street with gangs, he has been brought up to look for the finer things in life and only by hard work and perseverance can they be achieved and enjoyed.'
>
> (McArthur, Waldron, and Dickinson 1958: 268)

Amongst girls, the precocity of the smoker is strikingly demonstrated in terms of sexual activity. Russell quotes figures from a 1965 survey showing that over 90 per cent of teenage girls who smoked over 20 cigarettes per day had had sexual intercourse, compared with only 16 per cent in the rest of the sample.

Both English and American studies have shown that early smoking is related to lower levels of perceived (and real) academic achievement (e.g. Bewley and Bland 1977). Russell accounts for this association by suggesting that children who perform poorly at school compensate by finding status outside school and in the company of those older than themselves. At this stage, the image of the smoker as mature, tough and sophisticated is undoubtedly attractive. An adolescent's first experience of cigarette smoking is described in Ian McEwan's *First Love, Last Rites*:

> 'Raymond was fifteen then, a year older than I was. . . . It was Raymond who initiated me into the secrets of adult life (but) the world he showed me never really suited him. So when Raymond produced cigarettes, it was I who learned to inhale and smoke deeply, to blow smoke rings and to cup my hands round the match like a film star, while Raymond choked and fumbled.'
>
> (McEwan 1976: 10)

The rewards derived from the first few cigarettes are obtained in spite (and not because) of nicotine, since initial experience with smoking usually involves unpleasant feelings of dizziness and nausea. (Bewley, Bland, and Harris (1974) report that 32 per cent of boys were sick, and only 21 per cent said they enjoyed their first cigarette.) Over the period during which tolerance is developing, smoking is repeated because the factors which led to the smoking of the first cigarette still operate. In addition, the fact that so many people smoke with apparent enjoyment suggests to the neophyte that the unpleasant effects must be purely temporary. With repeated exposure, the smoker comes to find that smoking is a useful accomplishment, especially in difficult social situations. It provides something to do with the hands; the giving and receiving of cigarettes aids in the establishment of new friendships and improves the cohesiveness of social groups. These factors can be expected to be of importance at a critical period in the adolescent's development of personal relationships, especially those involving the opposite sex.

The importance of the image of the smoker, and the usefulness of smoking in regulating social interaction, does not end with adolescence. There is evidence that adults continue to regard smoking as indicative of a series of favourable personality traits. In a study by

Weir (cited in Mausner and Platt 1971) subjects were shown two photographs of a man. In one, the man was smoking; in the other the cigarette had been removed by retouching the photograph. Subjects were asked to characterize the model by choosing adjectives from a check list. The presence of the cigarette produced a marked increase in the choice of adjectives such as adventurous, rugged, daring, energetic, and individualistic, and a significant decrease in the use of the descriptors awkward, timid, shy, gentle, and quiet. Smoking also plays a part in defining the self-image. The majority of adult smokers think that a photograph of themselves without a cigarette would not show 'the real me', whilst a picture of them with a cigarette would. In a further study, 200 female students were asked to choose people they would like to spend time with whilst engaged in three different kinds of activity – social, university, and work. There was a strong tendency for smokers to choose the company of other smokers, and for non-smokers to choose to be with non-smokers, even though the individuals chosen for each activity were different.

The influence of family and friends, of the cultural stereotype of 'the smoker', and of the social rewards of smoking, therefore seem to be of importance in initiating the habit in those predisposed by certain personality factors, and of continuing importance in maintaining it. However, as smoking continues, the effects of nicotine begin to overlap social factors in reinforcing the behaviour (*Figure 8*). The smoker quickly learns to appreciate the rewarding effects of nicotine as he develops tolerance to its unpleasant effects and becomes adept at manipulating the dosage. Pharmacological factors thus become of increasing importance relative to social factors in maintaining smoking behaviour. There are two main views of the way in which these pharmacological factors may operate. The first, the *addiction model*, holds that the smoker's brain and body become so adapted to the presence of nicotine that he cannot function properly without it. The progression from habit to dependence is discussed in the remaining sections of this chapter. The second view, the *psychological tool model*, suggests that the dose-dependent, stimulant-depressant actions of nicotine allow the smoker to use it as a means of manipulating his psychological state under many environmental conditions. This view is discussed in Chapter 5. The two views are not mutually exclusive and both effects of nicotine may interact in varying degrees with each other, and with social influences and constitutional needs, to determine not only whether an individual smokes but also the way in which he smokes.

SMOKING AS A HABIT

Man is not alone in being a creature of habit. The ethologist Konrad Lorenz (1961) observed that his water shrews became so used to jumping over a stone on their regular run that they continued to jump at that spot even when the obstruction had been removed. It is perhaps remarkable, however, that humans, possessed of a behavioural repertoire unparalleled in its versatility and sophistication, should choose to repeat endlessly certain acts which seem at best meaningless and at worst self-destructive. Marcel Proust remarked that the strength of a habit is generally in proportion to its absurdity; there are many who would agree.

Whatever else smoking may be, in many smokers it is certainly a habit – a behaviour governed by a learned disposition to act in a certain way, the tendency having been acquired by frequent repetition of the act. A great variety of behaviours fall into this category – washing before meals, shaking hands, reading before bed-time, sucking one's thumb, having a drink after work, eating cornflakes for breakfast. Where does smoking fit into this range of activities?

Other than repetition, there is no single element which all habits share and which distinguishes them from all other behaviours. Rather, as with the famous example of games (Wittgenstein 1972), habits are linked by a complex pattern of similarities – a series of 'family resemblances' (*Figure 9*). Certain habits (gum chewing, nail biting, the Greek 'worry beads') are alike in that they involve oral and manual manipulation. Others – like sweet-eating and adding sugar and salt to the diet – are food-based and taste-orientated. The habitual practice of certain sports (e.g. skiing, parachuting), together with gambling and delinquency, involve repetitive thrill-seeking behaviour, but other habits do not. Certain habits require a social context, but many (such as the hobbies which involve collecting) are primarily individual.

The range of habits which are drug-related forms a continuum of pharmacological involvement from tea and coffee (containing mild central nervous system stimulants), through alcohol (a CNS depressant) and the 'soft' drugs like cannabis, to drugs conventionally thought of as powerfully addictive such as the opiates. Although it would be difficult to argue that people inject heroin to be sociable, because they like the feel of the needle or because they have nothing to do with their hands, the use of narcotics is in some ways analogous to the habitual but non-pharmacological thrill-seeking behaviours.

Taste, sociability and oral-manipulative satisfactions clearly play a role in the consumption of tobacco, alcohol, tea, and coffee and the central position these behaviours occupy within the family network of habits shows their many-sided nature (*Figure 9*).

The strength of a habit, and its seriousness (determined by the severity of its individual, social and medical consequences) are independent of its pharmacological or non-pharmacological basis. Thus over-eating and under-eating (anorexia nervosa) and certain

Figure 9 The classification of habits by family resemblance

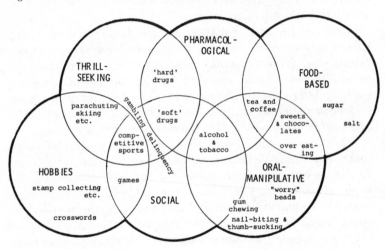

This figure first appeared in Stepney (1979c). Reproduced by kind permission of the editor of *World Medicine*.

forms of gambling can be as compulsive as drug addiction, as destructive to the individual, and as difficult to treat. The health consequences of over-eating or of incorrect diet can be as serious as those of drinking and smoking; and it would be as difficult to wean Western man from eating too much and from adding sugar and salt to his diet as it is to persuade him to refrain from drinking and smoking. The social acceptability of a habit is sometimes related to the apparent seriousness of its consequences. Thus taking heroin for 'kicks' is not socially acceptable. On the other hand, cigarette smoking, over-eating and over-drinking are still relatively acceptable, although potentially harmful, whilst the social use of marijuana, not proven to be of any greater harm, is not. The distinction between legal and illegal habits tends to co-vary with that of social acceptability, but to be sometimes behind and sometimes in advance of it.

It has been suggested that drug-based habits are uniquely characterized by the development of tolerance – a phenomenon in which successively larger doses are required to produce the same desired effects. Other habits, however, demonstrate similar features. For the confirmed gambler, it seems that the amount of stake or risk involved must be increased to produce the same thrill of uncertainty or euphoria of winning. A similar phenomenon is observed in certain aspects of delinquency, in which those involved seem to find themselves on a gradient of escalating damage and violence, whilst those who derive their excitement from challenging authority may progress from the home to the school to the police in their search to find a sufficiently arousing source of confrontation. The development of tolerance is in fact a very general feature of the family of habits. For the confirmed athlete no speed is fast enough, for the stamp collector no specimen rare enough, for the anorexic no weight low enough, for the businessman no bank balance large enough. Neither are the drug-related habits unique in their escapist function. Non-drug habits too may begin as a temporary refuge from everyday pressures only to become a permanent retreat from reality.

The view that habits which do not involve an obvious external pharmacological agent may be functionally equivalent (and indeed similar also in process) to those which do, is finding more frequent expression. The identification may be made lightheartedly as in the description by Patrick O'Donovan of existence without *The Times*:

> 'Within the sort of communities that used to take *The Times* for granted as a sort of daily fix, there are already signs of withdrawal symptoms. There are other noble daily papers that are acting as substitute drugs, like Methadone, to the great essential one upon which the establishment of Britain was hooked and yet *The Guardian*, which appears to have become a chief surrogate, does not quite satisfy the old and specialised and ingrained and incurable desires.'
>
> (*The Observer* January 1979)

A similar identification also takes place in a more serious context. At the recent Berlin conference on the bases of addiction, Bejerot and Bejerot argued that addictive conditioning may occur to pleasurable experiences arising from sources other than drugs. They regarded gambling, kleptomania, pyromania, anorexia nervosa – even compulsive nail biting – as 'closely related conditions' (Bejerot and Bejerot 1978: 90).

For many, the urge to over-eat seems as powerful as the urge to smoke, drink alcohol, or inject a narcotic. It is therefore interesting that recent work by Margules *et al.* (1978) suggests a physiological link between abnormal eating habits and mechanisms of opiate addiction. Levels of the naturally occurring opiate beta-endorphin were found to be twice as high in the pituitary glands of genetically obese mice and rats as in those of lean litter-mate controls. Small doses of the drug naloxone (which blocks opiate effects) selectively abolished over-eating in the obese animals, whilst leaving the behaviour of lean ones unaffected. Based on these findings, one of the authors of the study drew a parallel between compulsive eating and opiate addiction:

'Obese individuals show certain characteristics also shown in opiate dependence including excess consumption, dysphoria upon withdrawal and a powerful tendency toward relapse. There is a suggestion here of an opiate-like dependence on food. Such dependencies may be associated with excess production of an endogenous substance with opiate-like activity such as beta-endorphin.'
(Margules *et al.* 1978: Footnote 7)

Aldous Huxley anticipated just such a questioning of the difference between internal and external agents of addiction when he wrote in *The Devils of Loudun* of those who became 'adrenaline addicts, deliberately indulging their ugliest passions for the sake of the "kick" they derive from their psychically stimulated endocrines' (Huxley 1970: 19). More recently, certain correspondents who covered front-line fighting in Vietnam have come to be regarded as 'war junkies' with a compulsive desire to return to areas of conflict (Herr 1978). Extreme danger, self-starvation, sleep deprivation and rigorous physical asceticism may all be used to bring the brain into a biochemical (and the mind into a 'transcendent') state analogous to that following the use of drugs.

While certain non-drug habits show the features of psychological dependence, tolerance, and withdrawal normally associated with the repeated consumption of a drug, the other side of the coin is that use of even the most 'habit-forming' drugs does not invariably produce these features.

The social and personal context in which a drug is used seem to be as important as the drug's pharmacology in determining the effects it will have. This applies equally to the 'positive' effects of drug use (the sensations which one has to *learn* to interpret as pleasurable) and to its negative consequences. Even the narcotic analgesics do not invariably produce such pleasurable effects that it is difficult to avoid repetitive use. Most normal, pain-free individuals find the initial effects of subcutaneous opioids unpleasant, and Lindesmith (1965) reports that those unused to heroin rate a placebo as more pleasurable than small doses of the drug.

Patients given narcotics regularly for the relief of pain often develop 'significant physical dependence', but 'the overwhelming majority do not develop a psychological dependence, do not become compulsive users, and discontinue the drug when the medical condition is relieved' (Goodman and Gilman 1970: 278). The importance of the context in which a particular drug is taken is also illustrated by the report that only a small minority of the American GIs who used narcotics while they were in south-east Asia (and who themselves considered they were 'addicted') continued to use the drugs when they returned to the United States (Robins, Helzer, and Davis 1975). Prior to the Vietnamese war only 2 per cent of the servicemen had ever used heroin. One third of the sample admitted they had used it whilst in Vietnam and half of the users were addicted by the criterion of physical dependence. Yet ten months after return from Vietnam, use of heroin was back at pre-war levels, with fewer than 1 per cent of ex-servicemen continuing as daily users of narcotics.

Work such as that of Robins, Helzer, and Davis, involving the follow-up of large numbers of randomly selected drug users, has emphasized that samples identified through arrest or treatment may be atypical of the larger population. Addiction is then seen not as the inevitable consequence of habitual exposure to a drug but as a relatively infrequent (and indeed deviant) response:

'Temporary or occasional use, by contrast, is quite common. When heroin is available and peer group attitudes favour experimentation, most adolescents will try the drug. Many will reject it after one or two trials; others will use it for a period of time and discontinue when circumstances change; and only a few will evolve into typical long-term addicts. In fractional terms, perhaps less than one person out of fifty becomes a chronic addict. The actual frequency of addiction of course depends upon age, degree of exposure, and other conditions – but even in the most vulnerable group the incidence of persistent, life-destroying narcotics addiction appears to be surprisingly low.'

(Dole 1978: 41)

SMOKING AS A COMPULSION

Smoking, in common with some other behaviours, may become habitual; in common with some habitual behaviours it may become compulsive. It is common for those with compulsive disorders to recognize that the nature of their compulsion is foolish (or, in the case of smoking, for example, dangerous) but for this rational appreciation of the consequences to have no power to prevent the behaviour. Thus someone compulsively washing their hands, compiling lists, or avoiding the cracks between paving stones may recognize that their behaviour is entirely irrelevant to the demands of hygiene, memory, and locomotion, and yet be unable to refrain from it.

The essential ingredients of a psychiatrically recognized obsession are first the existence of a sense of compulsion overriding an internal resistance, and, second, the feeling that something disastrous will occur if the compulsive action is not undertaken. The obsessive rumination is obviously absent from compulsive smoking but the 'overriding of an internal resistance' may well be there, and the repeated overcoming of an expressed (and presumably sincerely meant) intention to stop smoking by the 'need' to have another cigarette certainly seems to have an analogy in other forms of compulsive behaviour.

There is a minority of occasional smokers who claim that a pleasure is no longer a pleasure when it becomes a habit. (These light smokers might therefore, paradoxically, be called the most indulgent of all.) There is room for dispute about this, but it is clear that the smokers – again a minority – for whom smoking is compulsive can no longer be considered as 'smoking for pleasure'. The most extreme examples of compulsive smokers are those who continue to smoke even though suffering from a progressive disease clearly related to smoking and whose prognosis would be greatly improved if they stopped. For example, certain patients with peripheral vascular disease will undergo successively more severe amputations rather than give up smoking.

The compulsive nature of some smoking is also demonstrated when smokers will go without food to obtain cigarettes and may even, at times of great social dislocation (as in Berlin at the end of the last war) prostitute themselves for tobacco. Under less extreme conditions, compulsive smoking takes the form simply of maintained (or possibly accelerating) high rates of cigarette consumption. McArthur and his colleagues in the Harvard study distinguished amongst their sample of 250 subjects a small group of compulsive smokers who were also 'compulsive fiddlers, desk-arrangers; people who allayed their tensions through fussy activities, of which smoking could understandably become one' (McArthur, Waldron, and Dickinson 1958: 271). When participants in the study were psychiatrically assessed, moderate smoking was found to be associated with the rating of 'Strong Basic Personality' whilst heavy smoking was linked with the 'Weak Basic Personality'. The authors commented that whilst it was not true that everyone who smoked more than a pack a day over his adult life showed evidence of a poorly integrated personality, it was true that poorly integrated people were much more commonly found among the heaviest smokers:

'These people may often be emotionally constricted types for whom there is great gain in simple "flight into behaviour" or they may be restless, active men, for whom smoking is just one more impulsive activity. It would also seem that anxious people can seize on smoking as a tension reducer if they have already, for other reasons, been orientated toward it. In short, the habit, once well available, increases in strength if it serves well the person's emotional economy.'

(McArthur, Waldron, and Dickinson 1958: 272)

SMOKING AS AN ADDICTION

'Cigarette smoking is probably the most addictive and dependence-producing object-specific self-administered gratification known to man.'

(Russell 1976b: 1)

The preceding sections have indicated that any distinctions between behaviours described as habitual, compulsive or addictive are far from clear-cut; each may merge into the others. The great majority of smokers (i.e. all who inhale) repeatedly take into their bodies quantities of nicotine large enough to produce psychological effects. Smoking therefore takes its place amongst other behaviours involving the use of drugs, and the conclusion that smoking is essentially a form of nicotine self-administration is difficult to avoid. But to what extent is continued smoking simply an expression of nicotine addiction?

The World Health Organisation in 1964 (Madden 1979) recommended that the term 'drug addiction' be replaced by 'drug dependence', defined as a compulsion to take a drug in order to experience its mental effects and sometimes to avoid the discomfort of its absence. The term addiction is still used internationally, however, as testified by the titles of specialist journals in the field (*The British*

Journal of Addiction, Addictive Behaviors, The International Journal of the Addictions) and in this country by the Addiction Research Unit of the London Institute of Psychiatry. In this book we therefore follow current practice and use the terms 'addiction' and 'dependence' inter-changeably.

The development of addiction or dependence is characterized by the central features of pleasure or reward, tolerance, and withdrawal effects. These features will now be considered with reference to the actions of nicotine.

Pleasure and reward

Probably the most important single factor in the whole smoking phenomenon is that smoking is pleasurable to smokers; they like doing it. It may not be pleasurable to all smokers at all times, but at least at some stage it gives enough pleasure to override the concomitant unpleasant sensations. The degree to which smokers report pleasure varies in different studies, but in an American Cancer Society survey, 87.5 per cent of regular smokers reported that they found smoking pleasurable, while a Leading Article in the *British Medical Journal* (1968, 1: 73) states: 'all confirmed smokers know that smoking is pleasurable'.

The pleasure of smoking may arise from all sorts of different sources, some of which have already been discussed. But the most important reason is likely to be that nicotine elicits a psychological response by exerting a particular pharmacological action on the brain. The nature of this action is not well understood but it may involve activity in certain brain systems which appear to have the function of signalling a feeling of pleasure or reward. These systems seem to be intimately involved not only in signalling pleasure, but also with the development of dependence or addiction to drugs.

The idea of 'pleasure centres' in the brain originated rather fortuitously from the work of Olds and Milner (reviewed in Olds 1962) who were investigating arousal systems in rats. The rats were fully conscious and unrestrained but had tiny electrodes implanted at various sites in their brains. A minute electrical current could be applied to the electrodes to provide gentle local stimulation to the underlying brain site. Olds and Milner noticed that some of their rats seemed to be attracted to the corner of the enclosure where they received the stimulation. Intrigued by this observation, the investigators decided they would allow the rats to control their own stimulation, and they arranged a system whereby the rats could press a lever which automatically caused a small current to pass through the implanted electrode.

By situating the electrodes in different areas in the brain, they found certain sites where the rats 'liked' the feeling so much that they would stimulate themselves at the rate of 2000 times an hour for hours on end until they fell down in an exhausted stupor. On waking up, they would immediately start stimulating themselves again. Furthermore, the rats were so motivated to obtain the stimulation that they would perform complex tasks to obtain the rewarding 'shots' of pleasure. In other areas of the brain, electrical stimulation was found to be extremely aversive. These second sites were termed 'punishment centres' and if the electrodes were implanted here the animals would again perform complicated actions, and even refuse food when they were hungry, in order to turn off or avoid the stimulus.

These positive and negative effects of brain stimulation have been found in all species of animals tested, including man. All the active sites are situated in or connected with the limbic system, an interconnected series of nerve cells and fibres concerned with the feeling and expression of emotions. The limbic system is also closely involved with learning and memory and with both the endocrine system and the peripheral autonomic nervous system. Through the limbic system, feelings and emotions are integrated with memory of previous experiences on the one hand and with the appropriate bodily responses on the other.

The anatomical arrangement of the pleasure and punishment systems has been fairly well mapped out in several species of animals. Their normal function is thought to be to reward behaviours that are good for survival of the individual or the species, such as eating or mating, and to punish actions which are unfavourable. The punishment system seems to be particularly important in various types of learning, not only in learning to avoid noxious stimuli but also in suppressing incorrect responses during the process of learning, the extinction of learned responses if they become inappropriate, and habituation to repeated stimuli. The two systems operating together constitute a useful evolutionary device to promote the seeking of rewarding behaviour and the avoidance of punishing behaviour.

At a more subtle level, these systems are probably concerned with mood control. It has been suggested that depression and elation may result from alterations in the relative activity of pleasure and punishment systems, and that drugs which affect mood may do so by acting on these pathways. Ecstatic moments may be evoked by certain drugs such as heroin, whose takers say that an intravenous injection may be more thrilling than an orgasm. Nicotine would be envisaged to act at a more mundane but more enduring level, altering the balance between the systems just enough to weight the scales in favour of reward.

Understanding of the reward and punishment systems is very incomplete. Nevertheless, much work has been done on the neuro-transmitters utilized in these systems. It appears from animal studies that at least three neurotransmitters are involved. The reward systems are probably subserved by noradrenaline or dopamine or both, while an inbuilt braking system, which signals satiety, may be operated via serotonin. Drugs which act like noradrenaline or dopamine (for example, amphetamines) enhance self-stimulation behaviour in animals and lower the threshold to the electrical current required to elicit self-stimulation. The punishment systems seem to involve acetylcholine, and drugs acting like ACh stimulate avoidance behaviour.

From what is known about the interaction of nicotine with ACh receptors, one would expect it to affect (in a biphasic manner) avoidance and other behaviours subserved by the punishment pathways. This supposition appears to be true, and nicotine in dif-ferent doses can both enhance and impair various types of learning in both animals and man. Effects on learning are discussed later, but they do not seem to be directly concerned with the pleasures or rewards of smoking. However, if certain doses of nicotine can inhibit ACh synapses in punishment pathways, these doses should have definite effects in allaying unpleasant emotions, such as anxiety, fear, boredom, frustration, and anger. Situations which give rise to these emotions are in fact situations in which many smokers feel the need to light a cigarette; when they do they tend to take deep puffs, probably obtaining a relatively high dose of nicotine, which would be expected to have an inhibitory effect.

However, a more positive action than merely the inhibition of punishment pathways seems necessary to explain the manifest pleasure that some smokers obtain from a cigarette. J.H. Burn (1961) suggested that the pleasure of smoking derives in part from the release of noradrenaline from its store in the brain. This idea was supported by Jarvik (1970: 190) who wrote: 'Nicotine produces reinforcing effects by stimulating reward mechanisms in the brain, very likely by causing or facilitating the release of norepinephrine (noradrenaline) at these centres'. There is now considerable evidence to support these ideas. Stein and Wise (1969) showed that pleasure centres could be stimulated by noradrenaline and blocked by noradrenaline receptor blockers in rats, and Hall and Turner (1972) demonstrated that nicotine and cigarette smoke increase the release of noradrenaline from the brain in rats, cats, and monkeys, particularly from areas of the limbic system involved in reward pathways. Furthermore, in certain doses nicotine facilitates self-stimulation behaviour in rats. A closely related neurotransmitter, dopamine, seems to have similar actions on pleasure mechanisms and this too can be released in the animal brain by nicotine. In addition, it is highly likely that some reward functions are mediated by an endogenous opioid peptide such as enkephalin (Stein 1978), and it is possible that nicotine is also involved in the release of this substance.

These findings strongly suggest that nicotine can stimulate reward systems in the brain and that the mechanism is likely to be the release of noradrenaline and dopamine at appopriate sites. The particular attraction of nicotine may result from its dual effects on both pleasure and punishment mechanisms, and its biphasic actions on each, which allow it to produce very subtle changes in the balance between pleasure and punishment. Unlike many pleasurable activities, it does not interfere with attention to or performance of other tasks, nor, as in overstimulation of the sympathetic system, does the pleasure often turn to anxiety. Furthermore, the type and degree of enjoyment, depending as it does on the dose of nicotine, can be manipulated and controlled by the smoker himself.

Further evidence that nicotine possesses intrinsic rewarding effects is provided by animal studies. It has been known for some time that, given the opportunity, animals will self-administer drugs, such as heroin, which humans find rewarding. Several investigations show that this behaviour also extends to nicotine.

Clark (1969) reported that rats will work, by pressing a lever, to obtain a dilute nicotine solution which they apparently prefer to unadulterated drinking water when given a free choice. Rats which have been 'primed' with injections of nicotine will also lever-press to obtain continued injections of the drug. Similar behaviour has been recorded with rhesus monkeys; some animals require priming 'shots' of injected nicotine, others start spontaneously to self-administer the drug by pressing a lever (Deneau and Inoki 1967). The monkeys gave themselves total doses of between 0.7 and 1.7 milligrams per kilogram of bodyweight daily. When the nicotine dose per injection was increased, self-administration became less frequent, eventually ceasing altogether.

The self-administration of tobacco smoke has been studied in monkeys. Jarvik (1967) described how rhesus monkeys will start to puff at lighted cigarettes attached to their cages and will continue to 'smoke', apparently for the pleasure of it. When the monkeys were given a choice between tubes from which they could puff a variety of substances, they were found to prefer tobacco smoke to either warmed air or tobacco vapour. There was, however, no preference between smoke of different nicotine content.

In a further experiment, monkeys were trained to puff in order to obtain water. Once the puffing behaviour had been established, the monkey's preference for puffing smoke and air was investigated. Initially all four animals preferred smoke to air, but this preference could be reversed by administering the drug mecamylamine, which pharmacologically blocks the central effects of nicotine. This suggests that the monkeys were in fact smoking for nicotine and that once the possibility of obtaining the 'pleasant' effects caused by the drug was removed, they lost interest in the smoke. Since little nicotine is absorbed from cigarette smoke in the mouth, the inference is that the monkeys were in fact inhaling. This interpretation is supported by the more recent work of Ando and Yanagita (1981) who found blood nicotine levels in excess of 30 nanograms per millilitre (comparable with those found in human smokers) in two rhesus monkeys who smoked 'voluntarily' and without other reinforcement for two or more years.

Tolerance

Tolerance is a state of decreased responsiveness by the body to a previously administered drug, so that a larger dose is required to elicit an effect of the original magnitude. The development of tolerance, although it occurs with most drugs of addiction, is not in itself a sufficient condition for dependence. Tolerance exists to many drugs which do not produce dependence, and the degree of dependence is not necessarily related to the degree of tolerance. In the case of alcohol, many people are able to tolerate large doses without apparently coming to crave its regular use (Madden 1979). With nicotine, the range of tolerable dosage is smaller, but the dependence-producing potential is generally agreed to be greater (Russell 1978a).

Tolerance to some of the effects of nicotine develops fairly rapidly.

Several mechanisms are involved. Acute tolerance can readily be demonstrated in animal tissues: if a few equal doses of nicotine are applied in close succession, the later doses have less and less effect. The resistance of the tissues to later doses of nicotine in this case is probably due to the persistent occupation of ACh receptors by nicotine molecules, as explained previously. This mechanism may partially account for the observation that in regular smokers the rise in pulse rate produced by an early morning cigarette is greater than that following a cigarette taken after smoking all day.

A more lasting tolerance appears to develop in regular smokers as a result of some type of tissue adaptation to a nicotine-impregnated environment. The mechanisms underlying tissue adaptation to drugs are poorly understood. However, the body is expert at homeostasis, the maintenance of a relatively constant internal environment in the face of external change, and the effects of external influence tend to be immediately opposed by internal compensatory devices. Thus if some extraneous factor, such as nicotine, repeatedly stimulates the vomiting centre in the brain, the body responds by making the vomiting centre less sensitive to nicotine. This change may result from an alteration in the balance of excitatory and inhibitory nervous influences that normally act on the vomiting centre, or from changes in the sensitivity of cells in the vomiting centre itself, or from some combination of the two. In any case it can be demonstrated in both man and animals that a dose of nicotine which initially causes vomiting loses this effect after chronic exposure. The development of some degree of tolerance to the irritant and nauseous effects seems to be a prerequisite for continued smoking.

At the behavioural level, development of tolerance to nicotine has been demonstrated in animals (Jarvik 1973). The effect of nicotine on the spontaneous activity of mice decreases with repeated injections of the drug. Multiple doses of nicotine over a period of time (such as would be experienced by the smoker) produce a greater degree of tolerance than a single larger dose. Moreover, the tolerance to nicotine is long-lasting, the effect of one eight-day period of administration being measurable sixty days later.

A third type of tolerance is achieved by an increase in the efficiency of nicotine metabolism, which develops after a few weeks of smoking or nicotine administration. This is due to stimulation of metabolic enzymes in the liver. Smokers metabolize not only nicotine, but also other drugs degraded by the same enzymes, more quickly than non-smokers.

The degree of drug tolerance developed by these and probably other mechanisms is not uniform throughout all the body systems. The brain seems to remain relatively sensitive to nicotine. In most confirmed smokers, a cigarette not only keeps withdrawal effects at bay but also in itself gives satisfaction and still has demonstrable effects on mental function, though it no longer causes nausea, vomiting or coughing. That different systems should have differing degrees of tolerance to drugs is well known. For example, the brain becomes tolerant to the euphoric effects of morphine, but the gut retains much of its sensitivity to the constipating effects.

Not only does the brain retain much of its sensitivity to nicotine, but the degree of tolerance developed by other systems, though definite, is only slight in terms of the extra dose that can be taken with impunity. Thus small-cigar smokers may feel sick after smoking a bigger cigar and cigarette smokers may feel sick after smoking a cigarette that is stronger than the type to which they are accustomed, or even after smoking more than the accustomed number of their usual cigarettes. In contrast, tolerance to morphine and heroin can build up to such an extent that the addict may eventually be taking a dose which is several times greater than that which would kill a subject not inured to such drugs. Similarly, the alcoholic, in order to function at all, may come to require an amount of spirits that would cause the teetotaller to fall, dead drunk, under the table.

This gross escalation of dosage is not seen with nicotine. Many cigarette smokers eventually graduate to between twenty and forty cigarettes a day but remain fairly constant for years at a level in this range. It would, of course, be a physical impossibility to smoke much more than a cigarette every fifteen minutes of the waking day (about sixty a day), but smokers could easily obtain more nicotine by inhaling more deeply, puffing more frequently, changing to stronger cigarettes, switching to cigars or becoming inhaling pipe-smokers. There is no evidence that a confirmed smoker makes this progression. Since people smoke for nicotine's actions on the brain, and since they can still obtain these actions after they have become tolerant to other effects, there is presumably no need for further escalation. Furthermore, since the rewarding effects of nicotine probably derive from a combination of stimulant and inhibitory actions, and most smokers require both of these effects, they may be forced into maintaining a medium level of dosage. Any great increase in dose would be likely to lead to a predominance of inhibitory (as well as unpleasant) effects and would simultaneously deprive the smoker of the stimulant effect.

Withdrawal effects

An important stage in the development of drug dependence is the move from taking the drug in order to feel better to taking it in order to avoid feeling worse. In some subjects and with some drugs, the motivation to obtain the rewarding effects becomes to a varying degree displaced by the motivation to avoid the withdrawal effects. Such a shift has been described in the development of alcoholism (Royal College of Psychiatrists 1979), and it is well known that the real thrill from 'mainlining' narcotics such as heroin may only last for a few weeks or months; after that confirmed addicts take narcotics to ward off the abstinence syndrome.

The causes of withdrawal symptoms are closely related to those of tolerance and are equally poorly understood. In many ways withdrawal symptoms seem to reflect an overswing of the homeostatic compensating mechanisms that enable tolerance to occur (*Figure 10*). Dependence-producing drugs that cause sedative or depressant effects on the nervous system (alcohol, sleeping pills, tranquillizers, heroin, morphine) trigger opposing excitatory mechanisms which allow the subject, as he becomes tolerant, to keep awake in the presence of increasing doses of the drug. These mechanisms may

Figure 10 The development of tolerance and withdrawal effects with repeated administration of a drug

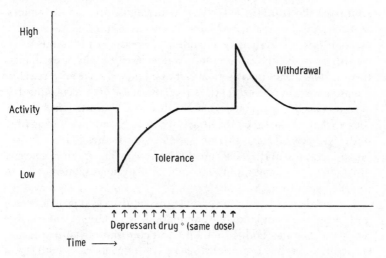

* Similar changes would occur with a stimulant drug, but in the opposite direction.

involve increased sensitivity or numbers of receptors at excitatory synapses in the brain and autonomic nervous system, an increased output of excitatory neurotransmitters (including acetylcholine and noradrenaline) and/or a decreased output of inhibitory neurotransmitters. An adjustment thus occurs so that the subject has chronically increased activity in his excitatory systems which tends to balance the depressant actions of the drug. On sudden withdrawal of the drug, the increased excitatory activity is no longer counteracted. The subject is now exposed to its full force and suffers symptoms due to unbuffered excess excitatory activity in all the nervous systems previously depressed by the drug. The symptoms are largely the opposites of those produced by the drug: calmness and tranquility are replaced by anxiety and panic, along with sweating, palpitations, and restlessness; constipation is replaced by diarrhoea, accompanied by cramping abdominal pains; the tendency to sleep is replaced by exaggerated brain activity as evidenced by insomnia, hallucinations, and convulsions. Excess salivation, streaming eyes, dilated pupils, 'gooseflesh', and muscle tremor are other signs of autonomic overactivity associated with sudden withdrawal of depressant drugs. The severity of the symptoms is associated with the degree of tolerance which the subject has built up, and all the symptoms can immediately be alleviated by an appropriate dose of the original drug. It is small wonder that the addicted subject develops a craving for another dose.

By contrast, the homeostatic response to drugs which have stimulant effects on the nervous system, for example amphetamines and cocaine, is decreased activity in excitatory systems. The mechanisms involved may include a decrease in the numbers or sensitivity of excitatory receptors, a decreased output of excitatory transmitters, or an increased output of inhibitory transmitters. This reaction tends to counteract the stimulant effects of the drug and also accounts for the symptoms when the drug is withdrawn. In this case the excitement caused by the drug is replaced by lethargy and apathy in the withdrawal stage; elation is replaced by depression; the raised blood pressure and heart rate by an overswing in the opposite direction. Again, the symptoms and signs respond immediately to replacement of the drug.

The abstinence syndrome of a depressant drug is thus characterized by agitation and that of a stimulant drug by fatigue and inertia. Since nicotine has both stimulant and depressant actions, it is not surprising that the nicotine abstinence syndrome includes both types of effects (Larson, Haag, and Silvette 1961; Larson and Silvette 1975;

Knapp, Bliss, and Wells 1963). Giving up smoking can cause anxiety, restlessness, sleep disturbance, irritability, sweating, and tremor – all symptoms which suggest rebound from depressant effects of nicotine. On the other hand, the abstinent smoker may complain of difficulty in concentration, listlessness, and depression and he can also be shown to have an abnormally low blood pressure and heart rate, while his electroencephalogram may give evidence of decreased alertness. These symptoms and signs suggest rebound from the stimulant effects of nicotine. The gain in weight experienced by some on cessation of smoking may also be partially due to rebound from stimulant effects on metabolic processes and general bodily activity. Most abstaining smokers develop their own pattern of withdrawal symptoms. Though not dangerous to life, these symptoms can be intense and severe.

Prominent among abstinence symptoms in some deprived smokers are craving and depression. The craving for nicotine is similar to that for other addictive drugs but it can last a surprisingly long time. It appears to reach its height at 24–48 hours and to decline steadily thereafter (Shiffman 1979), but in many smokers the craving can last for a year or even longer, far outlasting the more acute symptoms and signs such as irritability and cardiovascular changes (Larson and Silvette 1975). The degree and duration of the craving seem to bear little relation to previous cigarette consumption (usually between twenty and forty a day) or duration of smoking (usually some years) and are probably not closely related to the blood nicotine concentrations attained while smoking, which is very variable even among dependent smokers. There is some evidence that the homeostatic adjustments which take place as an adaptation to smoking take rather a long time to reverse. For example, the excretion of noradrenaline is greater in smokers than non-smokers and is still elevated for at least fifteen days after stopping smoking (Turnbull and Kelvin 1971): it does not appear to have been measured after this time.

The depression sometimes associated with smoking deprivation may be qualitatively similar to that seen in certain types of psychotic depression in which languor, apathy, and a feeling of the pointlessness of life are prominent, mingled with feelings of guilt and unworthiness. It has been said that smoking, though it gives pleasure, does not add to the joy of living: stopping smoking, however, may certainly detract from the enjoyment of life. As mentioned above, nicotine appears to stimulate pleasure systems in the brain, perhaps through the mediation of noradrenaline release, and seems in this way to be closely related to mood control. The dependent smoker may come to rely on nicotine to sustain his normal mood (Burn 1961). Deprivation may deny him this sustenance and thus lead to depression, along with reward-seeking behaviour in the form of craving. On the other hand it must also be said that anxiety, irritability, and depression might be expected to follow the loss of psychological rewards from any 'loved' object (car, house, job, wife, or lover, for example) to which a person was long accustomed and which had come to form a central part of his self-image and his support in facing the world.

Nevertheless, evidence indicates that nicotine has intrinsic rewarding actions, that it leads to tolerance, and that deprivation can produce withdrawal symptoms. Nicotine therefore possesses all the hallmarks of a drug of addiction. This observation has led to the description of cigarette smoking as an addictive behaviour. The *addiction model* as applied to smoking is illustrated in *Figure 11*. This model suggests that the motivation to continue the behaviour, once it is established, is to offset withdrawal symptoms brought about by the fall in tissue nicotine levels as the effect of each cigarette wears off. As

Figure 11 The addiction model of smoking

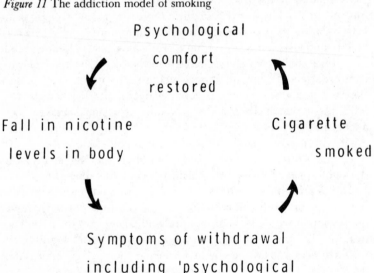

Psychological
comfort
restored

Fall in nicotine
levels in body

Cigarette
smoked

Symptoms of withdrawal
including 'psychological
discomfort'

This figure first appeared in Stepney (1980c). Reproduced by permission of the editor and publishers of *British Journal of Diseases of the Chest*.

we have seen, nicotine enters the brain within seconds of starting to smoke, but within 20–30 minutes of the cigarette being finished, most of the nicotine has left the brain. At about this time, the 20-to-30-a-day smoker feels the need for the next cigarette. As Russell (1971) noted, the smoker who inhales a cigarette every half hour ensures the maintenance of a high level of nicotine in his brain. It is suggested that a pharmacological need for nicotine – a drug addiction – seems to take over once a smoker is inhaling about 20 cigarettes a day.

In the individual, however, the degree to which smoking behaviour becomes a nicotine addiction is no doubt influenced, as with other pharmacological and non-pharmacological habits, by a variety of environmental and constitutional factors. It must also be noted that there are intriguing cases (relatively few but nevertheless disturbing for a straightforward addiction view of smoking) of heavy smokers who quit the habit suddenly and apparently without experiencing withdrawal symptoms. In addition, many smokers are able to refrain from smoking for relatively long periods, for practical or religious reasons, without apparently experiencing hardship – coal miners who cannot smoke at the pit face and orthodox Jews who do not smoke on the Sabbath are examples. It is unclear how the experience of these groups of people could be incorporated into a conventional addiction view of smoking.

4 SELF-REGULATION
OF NICOTINE INTAKE

If smokers are addicted to nicotine, it should be possible to design experiments to show two things:

1. That the nicotine smokers usually get from cigarettes can be replaced by nicotine from some other source.
2. That cigarettes of different 'strengths' are smoked differently. More specifically, it should be possible to show that smokers given cigarettes of reduced nicotine delivery smoke them more intensively and that smokers given stronger cigarettes smoke them less intensively, so that their usual levels of nicotine intake are maintained.

ALTERNATIVE SOURCES OF NICOTINE

Nicotine by injection

In 1942 Lennox Johnston, a Wallasey general practitioner, injected himself and other subjects with between 1/750 and 1/500 of a grain of nicotine. He claimed that this amount produced sensations equivalent to those following one deep inhalation from a cigarette. Non-smokers found the sensations queer, but smokers found them pleasant and, after repeated injections, did not feel inclined to smoke for a while afterwards. This seemed to show that nicotine which was injected could substitute for that normally derived from smoking. However, both Johnston and his patients knew what was being injected and the result of the experiment was therefore not free from the possible influence of conscious or unconscious expectations. Nevertheless, Johnston was sufficiently impressed with the evidence to write a book portraying smoking as gratuitous nicotine self-poisoning, and became a fervent opponent of the habit (Johnston 1957).

It was not until some years later that a controlled experiment along similar lines took place – this time at the University of Michigan Medical School (Lucchesi, Schuster, and Emley 1967). Smokers received a slow intravenous infusion of either nicotine solution or saline solution. The subjects performed a variety of psychological tests such as reaction time and time estimation, and blood pressure and the electrocardiogram were measured. Subjects thought that the interest of the experimenters was confined to these variables and they did not know that they were sometimes receiving nicotine. The smokers were allowed to smoke as and when they wished and were not aware that their smoking behaviour was being studied. The injection of 6 mg of nicotine over six hours produced no significant effect, but the injection of 22 mg (equivalent to the nicotine delivery of seventeen medium-strength cigarettes) was accompanied by a 30 per cent drop in the number of cigarettes smoked. There was also a significant increase in the amount of tobacco left unsmoked, showing that the cigarettes which were consumed were being smoked less fully.

Aware that the nicotine derived from smoking is not a steady intake over a period of hours, the investigators tried to approximate smoking more closely by injecting 1 mg of nicotine over a period of fourteen minutes on eight occasions over the six-hour period. This administration regime produced a decrease in the number of cigarettes smoked in three out of four subjects. The results of the experiment might have been still more impressive had the injection schedule even more accurately approximated the puff-by-puff peaks in nicotine-laden blood following each inhalation from a cigarette. If it is the effects of the peaks of heavily nicotinated blood which are responsible for the peculiarly pleasurable effects of smoking, no form of nicotine administration which did not produce such a pattern could be expected to substitute for the cigarette.

Kumar *et al.* (1977) therefore attempted to mimic smoking more precisely by administering the drug in five-second 'shots' (imitating the effect of a single puff), at a rate of one per minute. The experiment, which was carried out at the Institute of Psychiatry in London, involved twelve subjects who smoked between twenty-five and sixty cigarettes daily. Subjects knew that in one of the experimental conditions they would receive nicotine intravenously, but did not know that the purpose of the experiment was to investigate the effect this would have on their smoking behaviour.

The results of the experiment caused considerable surprise, not least amongst the experimenters themselves. The intravenous injections of nicotine did not depress levels of smoking, measured either by the number of puffs or the volume of smoke taken. There are a number of possible explanations for the apparent failure of the nicotine injections to substitute for smoking. It is possible that the nicotine, although injected into the saline infusion in 'shots' did not reach the smokers in that form. The heart rate and the electro-encephalographic measures taken showed that nicotine reached the smoker, but do not confirm that the method of administration did in fact mimic that accompanying smoking. However, even if the nicotine was administered in the form of a slow infusion, the results of the present experiment should have been similar to those found by Lucchesi, Schuster, and Emley, who showed an effect on measures of smoking cruder than those employed by Kumar *et al.*

A second possibility is that the unusual kind of smoking offered to subjects in the experiment (puffing through a cigarette holder at a constantly lit and continuously replaced cigarette) differed sufficiently from 'normal' smoking to have affected the outcome. It is also quite likely that the subjects' knowledge that nicotine was being administered affected the way they smoked. The pattern of puffing on the cigarettes following the intravenous infusion was very different from that shown by the same subjects in an earlier experiment following 'doses' of nicotine administered as inhaled smoke. In the injection experiment the volume of smoke per puff was approximately half that found in the earlier study and the number of puffs was considerably greater. This low-volume, rapid puffing suggests nervousness and may well have swamped any effects due to the injected nicotine itself.

Nicotine tablets

Oral administration offers a possible source of nicotine which is an alternative both to smoking and intravenous injection. However, we have already reviewed evidence suggesting that absorption of orally administered nicotine is relatively slow and inefficient. In view of what has already been said about the importance of mimicking the effects of smoking, it is a strategy which is not likely to be of any use in replacing the cigarette. It is therefore not surprising that Jarvik, Glick, and Nakamura (1970) failed to demonstrate a convincing effect. Seventeen heavy smokers were given 50 mg of nicotine tartrate daily in 10 mg capsules. In the control condition placebo capsules containing no drug were administered. The average cigarette consumption on 'placebo days' was 24.1 cigarettes, and on 'nicotine days' 23.4 cigarettes. The difference, although statistically significant – and therefore reliably an effect of the drug – was obviously extremely small.

Nicotine chewing gum

A further alternative source is gum which releases nicotine slowly as it is chewed over 20–30 minutes. The preparation is designed to maintain an alkaline pH in the mouth to maximize absorption through the buccal mucosa. There are several reports that this gum may be a helpful aid in maintaining abstinence from cigarettes and some smokers who have successfully given up the habit have in turn become dependent on the gum. Schneider *et al.* (1977) report several case studies which illustrate this phenomenon. A spicy flavour masks the taste and irritation of the nicotine, and enables the effectiveness of the gum to be compared with that of a 'placebo' containing none of the drug. A certain 'Mr A' was apparently able to distinguish the placebo from the active gum and was also able to differentiate, on the basis of strength, gums containing 1, 2, and 4 mg of nicotine. 'Mr A' successfully used the different gums available to control his symptoms, gradually reducing his reliance on this substitute source of nicotine as his craving diminished over a two-week period. A further subject experienced no withdrawal symptoms when switched from cigarettes to the nicotine gum, but rapidly returned to smoking when the nicotine gum was replaced after two weeks by the placebo.

However, a controlled experimental investigation carried out on forty subjects from the Maudsley Hospital smoking clinic produced equivocal evidence on the effectiveness of nicotine gum as an aid in short-term cigarette withdrawal (Russell *et al.* 1976a). In an initial period, *before* the subjects started actively trying to give up the habit, the number of cigarettes smoked was reduced by 37 per cent when nicotine gum was used. This decline in consumption seems impressive, but was only 6 per cent greater than the 31 per cent reduction accompanying use of the placebo gum. It therefore seemed that the major source of the gum effect was due not to nicotine but simply to the fact that chewing provided smokers with something to do with their mouths which largely precluded smoking. When subjects actively tried to give up, the small difference in the number of cigarettes smoked between the placebo and nicotine conditions all but disappeared.

However, counting the number of cigarettes smoked is only one way of measuring smoking. The amount of a cigarette smoked, the number of puffs taken from it, the volume of smoke drawn into the mouth, and the depth to which that smoke is inhaled, are all aspects of smoking behaviour which reflect the intensity of smoking and therefore contribute to total 'smoke exposure'. A useful way of estimating the overall intensity of smoking is to measure changes in the level of carbon monoxide (combined with haemoglobin to form carboxyhaemoglobin) in the smoker's blood. Carbon monoxide is a product of tobacco combustion, and is absorbed by the body only if the smoke is inhaled. Changes in carbon monoxide intake are therefore a good index of changes in the intake by the smoker of nicotine, and possibly also tar (Ashton, Stepney, and Thompson 1981).

Carbon monoxide levels in the subjects in the Maudsley experiment were significantly less with the nicotine chewing gum than when the placebo preparation was being used. It was therefore inferred that smokers were inhaling less from the cigarettes they were smoking, presumably because some at least of their requirement for nicotine was being met from an alternative source. The fact that three (out of forty) subjects were reported as becoming dependent on the nicotine gum reinforces this view.

In a subsequent publication, Russell *et al.* (1977) were able directly to compare the intake of nicotine from chewing gum and the intake from smoking. The average level of nicotine in the blood plasma of subjects chewing the 4 mg gum at hourly intervals was only very slightly less than blood levels following smoking. Nicotine gum can therefore substitute for cigarettes in terms of overall absorption of nicotine into the body, though not, of course, for the puff-by-puff peaks following each inhalation (*Figure 6*). However, subjects' ratings of their 'satisfaction' with the gum and the extent to which they 'missed' cigarettes were not related to blood nicotine levels. The relationship between the effects of withdrawal from smoking and blood levels of nicotine is therefore obviously not straightforward, and the experimenters concluded that the capacity of the gum to act as a substitute for smoking was not necessarily related to its capacity to provide an overall blood level of nicotine.

A further study (Turner *et al.* 1977) failed to find any effect of chewing nicotine gum on number of cigarettes smoked, pattern of inhalation, or amount of the cigarette consumed. The use of nicotine gum whilst smoking resulted merely in smokers having higher blood nicotine levels than when they smoked without the gum. The long-term efficacy of nicotine gum as an aid in stopping smoking is considered in the section of Chapter 8 covering smoking cessation techniques.

CIGARETTES OF DIFFERENT 'STRENGTHS'

The most frequently used method of investigating the importance of nicotine in the smoking habit has naturally enough been to consider cigarettes themselves. By altering cigarette composition and design in a great variety of ways (some of which are listed in *Figure 30* and discussed in Chapter 9) it is possible to manipulate the amount of nicotine (and tar) 'delivered' by the cigarette when smoked to the standard specifications of a smoking machine.

Twenty to thirty experiments have investigated smoking be-haviour when smokers are presented with cigarettes of different standard nicotine delivery. The assumption behind such experiments is that if the smoker is seeking some optimum and stable level of nicotine intake then any alteration in the availability of nicotine from a cigarette will lead to some compensatory adaptation in smoking behaviour.

What does happen when smokers used to cigarettes of a relatively high nicotine yield are given cigarettes of a lower standard delivery? Does the number of cigarettes smoked increase? Do smokers take more puffs and inhale the smoke more deeply? And are these changes in behaviour sufficient to restore nicotine intake to the smokers' habitual levels?

It is now fairly clear that smokers who are switched to lower nicotine cigarettes during the course of an experiment *do* increase the number of cigarettes smoked (Stepney 1980a). The increase in consumption, however, is not as large as might have been expected. The results of eighteen comparisons between brands are shown in *Figure 12*. The graph shows the relationship between changes in nicotine yield and changes in cigarette consumption. There is a good deal of scatter in the points plotted on the graph. Nevertheless, a trend is clearly apparent: the greater the reduction in standard nicotine yield, the greater the increase in the number of cigarettes smoked. The increases in consumption, however, are relatively small. A 10 per cent reduction in standard delivery would be expected to produce a rise in consumption of only 1 per cent; a 50 per cent reduction in yield a rise of just under 10 per cent.

A reduction in nicotine delivery of 50 per cent is roughly that

Figure 12 Increase in cigarette consumption related to change in nicotine yields: data from experiments

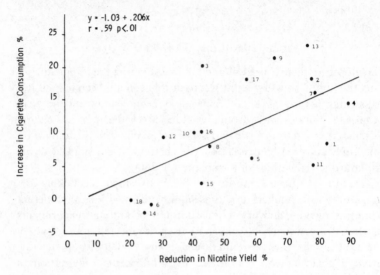

r = coefficient of correlation; the regression equation defines the slope and position of the line which best fits the experimental data.

The numbered points refer to the following studies:

1   Finnegan, Larson, and Haag (1945)
2   Russell *et al.* (1973)
3   Turner, Sillett, and Ball (1974)
4   Turner, Sillett, and Ball (1974)
5   Guillerm *et al.* (1974)
6   Freedman and Fletcher (1976)
7–11 Goldfarb *et al.* (1976)
12   Forbes *et al.* (1976)
13   Schachter (1977)
14   Mangan and Golding (1978)
15   Creighton and Lewis (1978b)
16   Adams (1978)
17   Ashton, Stepney, and Thompson (1978c)
18   Guillerm and Radziszewski (1978)

This figure first appeared in Stepney (1980a). Reproduced by permission of the editor and publishers of the *British Journal of Addiction*.

experienced by a smoker changing from a middle tar/middle nicotine cigarette to one on the borderline of the government's low and low-to-middle tar categories. A 10 per cent increase in the number of low-tar cigarettes smoked would therefore be expected to follow such a change in brands. But can these results be used to draw conclusions about what is likely to happen to the ordinary cigarette smoker changing brands?

Of the studies included in *Figure 12*, that of Freedman and Fletcher (1976) involved a cigarette composed partly of the tobacco substitute known as NSM, whilst in the experiment of Finnegan *et al.* (1945) nicotine was added to tobacco naturally low in nicotine content. The remaining studies, however, used either commercially available, or closely similar, brands, i.e. ones in which the nicotine delivery was varied by tobacco blending, filtration, and ventilation. It may be assumed that the subjects in the experiments represented a cross-section of the smoking population. Two studies were undertaken in France, five in the USA, one in Canada, and the remainder in Britain. Nevertheless, the changes of brand took place within the rather artificial context of an experiment, and were for a limited period only (though the period on each brand varied from several hours to several months in different experiments). The subjects who took part were not generally people who had expressed a desire to switch to a low-nicotine brand, and, in some cases, they would not have known for certain that the cigarettes they were smoking were designed to differ in this respect. The results may therefore not be directly applicable to brand-switching which occurs outside the confines of an experiment.

However, all smokers have to some extent been unwittingly involved in an 'experiment' over the last ten to thirty years. Over this period the nicotine delivery of cigarettes has been gradually but very considerably reduced, from an average of around 2.1 mg in 1965 to approximately 1.4 mg in 1975. *Figure 13* shows the stages in which this was accomplished. The figures for nicotine represent the *sales-weighted* standard nicotine yield, thus taking into account the different popularity of brands with different yields. Over this period of declining delivery, the number of cigarettes consumed per adult smoker quite dramatically and equally steadily rose. The figures for the ten-year period 1965–75 (during which nicotine delivery fell by 35 per cent) show an increased cigarette consumption per smoker of 18 per cent in men and 31 per cent in women.

There are obviously a large number of reasons which might explain rising cigarette consumption without reference to changes in nicotine yield. Changing attitudes towards smoking have had an effect – especially in the case of women, amongst whom smoking has become increasingly accepted. A reduction in the real price of cigarettes (i.e. the price related to general living standards) may also have played a

Figure 13 Sales weighted nicotine delivery and annual consumption of cigarettes 1965–75

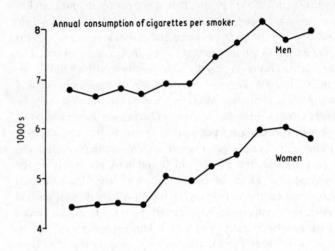

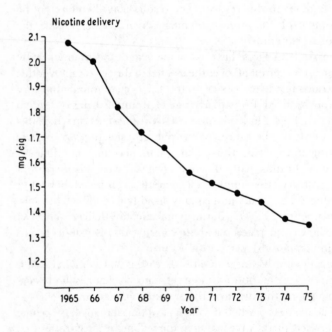

Source: Lee (1976): Tables 7, 17M, and 17W

part. Moreover, there is evidence that people giving up have been drawn proportionately more from light than from heavy smokers. Hammond (1980) reported the results of a survey which followed over one million smokers from the period 1965 to 1972. Of those who smoked fewer than ten cigarettes per day in 1965, 40–50 per cent were ex-smokers in 1972; this compares with only 20 per cent of those who smoked forty or more. Assuming smokers in Britain followed a similar pattern, such changes in the *composition* of the smoking population may have produced a misleading impression of changes in the consumption levels of persisting smokers. The fact that an increasingly large number of cigarettes are being smoked by children under the age of 16 (who are not counted as smokers in the surveys) may also have inflated consumption figures. Nevertheless, the association over a period of years between declining nicotine delivery and an increase in cigarette consumption is consistent with the view (based on experimental evidence) that people are smoking more cigarettes because they are getting less nicotine from each one they smoke.

The major problem with this line of reasoning, however, is that cigarettes which differ in nicotine delivery also differ in many other ways. Hundreds of different constituents of tobacco smoke have been identified, and nicotine is only one element amongst a great variety. Many of these other constituents will be affected by any of the alterations in cigarette design which are used to manipulate nicotine delivery. Low-nicotine cigarettes will very probably also have a different carbon monoxide yield, for example, and those constituents which affect the taste and flavour of the cigarette and the feel of the smoke as it hits the back of the throat (the 'scratch') will also be present in reduced concentrations.

Many of the substances which affect taste, flavour and 'scratch' are included in the group of chemicals which are collectively known as cigarette 'tar'. Tar is of great importance in terms of the health consequences of smoking, since various constituents of the tar phase of the smoke are implicated in the causation of cancer – hence the concerted effort on the part of government health agencies and the medical profession to persuade those who cannot stop smoking completely to switch to lower-tar brands. It has been thought that tar is probably not important in terms of the motivation to smoke, since as far as we know it has no psychological action. It was therefore suggested that smokers who complained that low-tar products lacked taste were in fact *really* complaining at their lack of nicotine.

One published study which independently varied the tar and nicotine yields of experimental brands showed that the number of cigarettes smoked was related to nicotine delivery but was unaffected by tar (Goldfarb *et al.* 1976). However, the possible role of tar, and associated taste factors, ought perhaps not to be dismissed. There is evidence emerging from more recent experiments, in which tar and nicotine deliveries have been independently manipulated, which suggests that the smoker's response to a given cigarette cannot be explained on the basis of nicotine yield alone (Stepney 1981).

The fact remains that the great majority of cigarette brands (both those commercially available and those used for experiments on smoking behaviour) have had nicotine and tar deliveries which are very closely related. High nicotine cigarettes are also high in tar delivery, and low nicotine cigarettes low in tar. For commercially available brands the correlation between nicotine and tar yield has been in excess of 0.9. Any increase in the number of lower-delivery cigarettes smoked could have been due as much to the desire for more taste, flavour, or 'scratch' as to the desire for more nicotine. Until it is possible to confirm and extend the findings of studies in which tar and nicotine levels are independently manipulated, it will be difficult to establish the true reasons for the changes in smoking behaviour which have been observed in brand-switching experiments.

This problem of interpretation applies as much to studies which have investigated the effect of reduced nicotine delivery on number of puffs, puff volume, depth of inhalation, and so on, as to those which have studied simply the number of cigarettes consumed.

There is nevertheless broad agreement about the way in which cigarettes of reduced delivery are smoked. The number of puffs taken from the cigarette rises, the puffs are of longer average duration, a greater volume of smoke is taken from each puff, and the smoke is inhaled more deeply. Lower-delivery cigarettes are also smoked to a shorter butt length, and the time taken to smoke them is usually less (e.g. Ashton and Watson 1970; Frith 1971a; Turner, Sillett, and Ball 1974; Guillerm and Radziszewski 1978; Adams 1978; Creighton and Lewis 1978b; Stepney 1979a). In short, cigarettes which deliver less tar and nicotine than those which a subject is used to smoking are smoked more intensively and more efficiently; less smoke 'goes to waste'. Conversely, cigarettes which deliver an unusually large amount of tar and nicotine – i.e. cigarettes which are 'stronger' – are smoked less intensively. The cigarettes take longer to smoke, fewer and smaller puffs are taken, and a longer length of tobacco is left unsmoked in the cigarette butt.

The results obtained by Ashton and Watson (1970), in what was probably the earliest study of its kind, are typical. Cigarettes of two standard deliveries were compared, one yielding 2.1 mg of nicotine on machine smoking and the other 1 mg. The lower delivery cigarette was smoked at a faster rate – 1.7 puffs per minute compared with 1.0 puff per minute; an average of roughly four puffs more was taken from the low yielding cigarette, and the time taken to smoke it was over a minute less. Because of these alterations in smoking style, the rate of intake of nicotine from the two brands was virtually the same, and the total dose obtained from the two cigarettes was also very similar. Smokers obtained rather less nicotine than expected on the basis of machine-yield from the higher delivery cigarette (1.5 mg instead of 2.1 mg) and rather more than expected from the lower yielding brand (1.3 mg compared with 1 mg). In terms of the standard specifications of puff volume, number, and duration used by the smoking machine to obtain the standard yield of the cigarettes, the human smokers had 'undersmoked' the stronger brand and 'oversmoked' the weaker one.

In the study just discussed, smoking behaviour was measured over a short period of time, while only a single cigarette was being smoked. The measures of nicotine intake were also indirect, being based on the technique of 'butt analysis'. (The amount of nicotine which is retained by a cigarette filter is proportional to the amount of nicotine which passes through the filter into the mouth of the smoker. By measuring the amount of nicotine trapped by the filter it is therefore possible, once the efficiency of the filter is known, to calculate the smoker's mouth-level nicotine intake.) This is not the same as the actual nicotine dose obtained by the smoker, since not all the nicotine taken into the mouth is eventually absorbed into the body – the amount which is absorbed depends on the depth and duration of inhalation.

A more recent investigation (Ashton, Stepney, and Thompson 1979b) addressed the question which lay behind the original study in a more sophisticated and detailed way. Twelve habitual smokers were studied whilst smoking their usual medium-delivery cigarettes (average nicotine yield 1.4 mg; tar 18 mg) and whilst smoking two experimental brands – one with a rather higher nicotine and tar delivery (1.8 mg nicotine; 27 mg tar), the other with a lower tar and nicotine yield (0.6 mg nicotine; 7 mg tar). Differences between the experimental brands in terms of the number of cigarettes smoked, and the intensity of smoking, were in the expected direction, although not always statistically significant. The main variables of interest, however, were those relating to the actual intake of nicotine from the different cigarettes.

The most direct way of finding out how much nicotine someone is getting from a cigarette is to measure the nicotine concentration in

Figure 14 Expected and observed nicotine intake in a brand-switching experiment

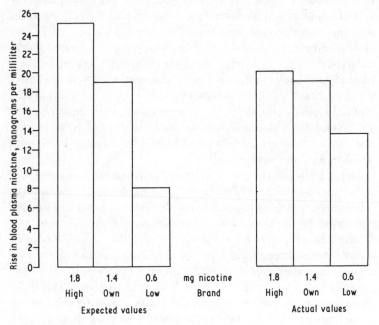

Source: Ashton, Stepney, and Thompson (1979b).

their blood before and after smoking. When this was done, the difference in actual nicotine intake between the high and low delivery cigarettes was found to be very much smaller than would be expected on the basis of the difference in machine-smoked nicotine yields (*Figure 14*). The columns to the left of the figure show the nicotine rise which would have been obtained from the high and low delivery cigarettes if each had been smoked in the same way as the smokers smoked their own brand. To the right the columns represent the average rise in blood nicotine actually observed.

Nicotine intake was also estimated on the basis of the amount of nicotine (and its principal metabolite, cotinine) excreted in the urine, and by butt analysis, as previously described. Taken together, the results showed that human smokers do not behave like smoking machines. In fact they compensated for about two-thirds of the between-brand differences in standard delivery. Compensation, although not complete, is therefore considerable.

This evidence is relevant to the debate about 'safer smoking', and we will return to it in the final chapter. Government policy, aimed at reducing the tar and nicotine intake of the average smoker, is (or was) based on the assumption that differences between brands in terms of standard delivery will be reflected in differences in the actual intake of tar and nicotine by the smoker. The experimental evidence related to brand switching suggests that someone who changes from a medium delivery cigarette to one yielding half the amount of nicotine and tar *will* be exposed to less nicotine and tar, but that the reduction in exposure is likely to be nearer a quarter than a half.

The practical implications of experiments investigating the behavioural regulation of nicotine intake are therefore important. The value of such experiments in throwing light on the question of smoking motivation is probably less – for the reason already mentioned. It may be assumed that the lower delivery cigarettes were more intensively smoked in an attempt to boost their yield of nicotine – and not simply because they tasted weaker and had less sensory impact – but proof that this is the correct explanation awaits the full analysis of experiments in which tar and nicotine yields are independently varied.

PATTERNS OF SMOKING

Much can be learned about behaviour simply by systematically observing and recording as it occurs. This way of investigating behaviour contrasts with and complements the orthodox experimental approach involving active intervention to control and manipulate variables.

The crudest record of smoking behaviour involves noting the number of cigarettes smoked over a given interval. After a period of getting used to the idea of making such notes, records can adequately be made by subjects themselves. *Figure 15* shows the number of cigarettes smoked each day over the period of a week, and each hour over the period of two days – one a working day, the other a rest day. The subjects who took part in this Cambridge study were sixty-seven medium and low-tar smokers of between five and fifty cigarettes per day. Three subjects were involved in shifts, working irregular hours and days; the remainder following the usual pattern of work and leisure time.

The notable feature of the average smoking pattern of this group is its consistency. There is the expected peak in the number of cigarettes

Figure 15 Pattern of cigarette consumption through the day and week

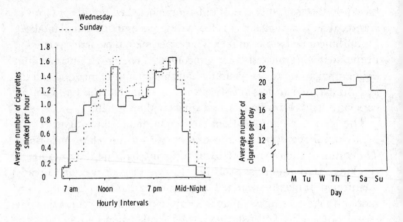

smoked on the Saturday, but even taking account of this the level of consumption is remarkably stable through the week. There is also little variation in smoking through the period of a day, although the after-lunch cigarette is reflected in a rise in consumption in the early afternoon, and the hours between 7 and 10 pm are also ones of heavier-than-average consumption. Wednesday and Sunday show similar patterns of smoking, though the generally later time of waking on Sunday skews the distribution slightly to the left.

Details of the average cigarette consumption of a group does not provide information about the variability of a particular individual's smoking pattern. Reference to the records of individual subjects, however, showed that smokers spaced their cigarettes regularly throughout the day, smoking one each hour or each two hours in the case of the light smokers, and three or four each hour in the heaviest smokers. There was no evidence that the light smokers confined their smoking to the afternoon and evening; some smokers seem to start later in the morning than others, though all but one subject had at least one cigarette before mid-day. The impressive regularity with which even light smokers consume cigarettes needs to be taken into account in any explanation of the tobacco habit. Whatever the smoker gets from a cigarette he clearly needs to get at regular intervals, day by day and hour by hour. Such a regular pattern of tobacco use has obvious implications for the view of smoking as nicotine addiction.

The sample of subjects who recorded their pattern of smoking deliberately did not include any people who smoked fewer than five cigarettes per day. It is therefore not possible to draw any conclusions on the basis of this information about the rarity or otherwise of the genuinely 'uncommitted' smoker – the person who smokes one cigarette a day after dinner or who smokes only at parties, for example. In 1975, 9 per cent of male cigarette smokers (and 14 per cent of women) were reported to smoke fewer than five cigarettes per day (Lee 1976: Table 22). The regularity with which these men and women smoked (and their degree of apparent dependence on the habit), however, is not known.

The smoking profile

Patterns of smoking behaviour can be analysed also at the level of the individual cigarette. A study conducted at Newcastle University set out to investigate whether individuals had a characteristic and consistent way of smoking (Ashton *et al.* 1979a). Subjects attended the laboratory on five occasions, at weekly intervals, to take part in an experiment investigating the physiological (heart rate, blood pressure and electroencephalographic) changes following smoking. Unknown to the subjects, their smoking behaviour was monitored through a one-way mirror by an observer who activated an event marker at the beginning and end of each puff. This allowed measurement of the duration of each puff, the interval between puffs and the distribution of puffs through the smoking of the cigarette. Using this information it is possible to plot smoking profiles for each subject and each cigarette.

Typical profiles are shown in *Figure 16 a–c*. The duration of each puff is represented graphically by the length of the stippled rectangles and numerically by the values (in seconds) above each rectangle. The

Figure 16a–c Puffing profiles on different occasions in three subjects

R.G. PUFF FREQUENCY AND DURATION

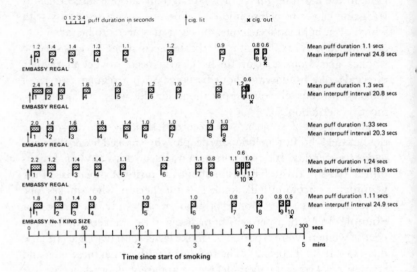

O.S. PUFF FREQUENCY AND DURATION

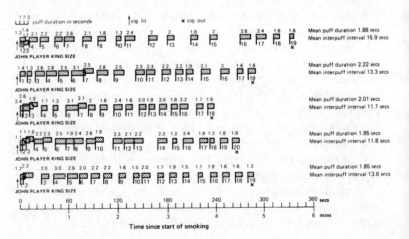

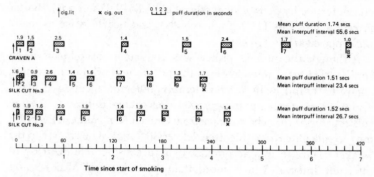

Each rectangle represents one puff; the puff duration is given above in seconds. The interval between puffs is shown by the distance between the numbered vertical lines, measured along the bottom scale.

(a) Subject smoked Embassy Regal, 1.3 mg nicotine, and Embassy No 1 King Size, 1.47 mg

(b) Subject smoked John Player King Size, 1.4 mg nicotine.

(c) Subject smoked Craven A, 1.3 mg nicotine, and Silk Cut No. 3, 0.7 mg.

Source: Ashton *et al.* (1979a). Reproduced by kind permission of Elsevier/N. Holland Biomedical Press.

interval between puffs is shown by the distance between the numbered vertical lines, measured along the bottom scale.

All three subjects showed a clustering of puffs at the start of smoking and lengthening intervals between puffs as smoking progressed. (This suggests that smokers perhaps seek a rapid build-up of nicotine at the start of smoking, and then maintain the levels they have achieved through the rest of the cigarette.) Apart from this similarity, each smoker had his or her own characteristic puffing profile which was remarkably unchanged from occasion to occasion when cigarettes of similar nicotine delivery were smoked under the same conditions. There were great differences, however, between the puffing profiles of different individuals smoking similar cigarettes under the same conditions. For example, in the subject in *Figure 16a*, who smoked Embassy Regal (nicotine delivery 1.3 mg) on four occasions and Embassy No. 1 King Size (nicotine delivery 1.47 mg) on one occasion, the mean puff duration varied little between 1.1 and 1.3 seconds; the mean interval between puffs ranged from 18.9 to 24.4 seconds, and the number of puffs per cigarette remained between 9 and 11. In contrast, the subject shown in *Figure 16b*, who smoked on all occasions a cigarette similar in nicotine delivery to those of the previous subject (John Player King Size, nicotine delivery 1.4 mg) had a totally dissimilar but equally consistent puffing profile, characterized by puffs of longer duration (1.85–2.22 seconds), shorter interpuff intervals (11.7–15.9 seconds), and nearly twice as many puffs per cigarette (18–20).

Although the puffing profile was consistent for subjects when similar cigarettes were smoked, the one subject who changed to a cigarette brand with a considerably different nicotine delivery appeared to alter her puffing profile. This change is illustrated in the subject (*Figure 16c*) who changed from Craven A (nicotine delivery 1.3 mg) to Silk Cut No. 3 (nicotine delivery 0.7 mg). The change to the weaker cigarette was accompanied by a considerable decrease in interpuff interval which more than halved (from 55.6 sec. on Craven A to 23.4 and 36.7 sec. on Silk Cut No. 3), an increase in the number of puffs per cigarette from 8 to 10, and a shortening of the time taken to smoke the cigarette from nearly 7 minutes to approximately 4 minutes. The apparent adaptation of the puffing profile to the different nicotine delivery may have resulted in a similar amount of nicotine being taken by the subject from both brands of cigarette.

In addition to measuring puff frequency and duration, and the spacing of puffs along the 'tobacco rod', it is often possible to obtain a measure of the volume of smoke taken in each puff. This is done by having subjects smoke a cigarette through a small holder which enables the amount of pressure (or 'suck') used to draw the smoke to be measured, together with its rate of flow (Creighton, Noble, and Whewell 1979). If pressure and flow are recorded at intervals during the taking of each puff, a record of the 'shape' of the puff may be obtained. Smokers tend to have a characteristic puff shape – some taking the greatest volume of smoke at the beginning, some gradually building up towards the end of the puff, others showing intermediate patterns.

It may be thought that such microscopic examination of smoking behaviour is of only academic interest. However, valuable information has in fact emerged from such studies. For example, female smokers differ from male smokers in detailed aspects of puffing behaviour. Thus not only do women take more puffs, of a smaller volume, but the peak flow rates of their puffs are lower, and the 'rising edge' of the puff profile sharper (Creighton and Lewis 1978a). The amount of nicotine obtained from a cigarette, relative to the amount of tar, depends on the puffing pattern and puff shape, and it is presumably differences in these variables which are responsible for

Figure 17 The relationship between puff and inhalation profiles in two smokers

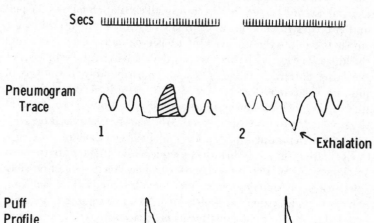

Source: Rawbone *et al.* (1978: 179). Reproduced by permission of Churchill Livingstone.

the lower tar-to-nicotine ratios obtained by female smokers. Assuming that smokers smoke to obtain nicotine, but that the most serious health consequences of smoking stem from the intake of tar, any attempt to make smoking 'safer' would aim to reduce the amount of tar obtained per unit of nicotine. If male smokers could be persuaded (or trained) to smoke more like women, they would be moving in the right direction.

We have so far assumed that all the smoke taken during a puff is eventually inhaled, and indeed this is what happens with the great majority of smokers. The depth and duration of inhalation, however, may vary considerably – as may the precise positioning of the puff within the breathing cycle. Rawbone *et al.* (1978) have shown how these aspects of smoking behaviour may be investigated. The taking of puffs from a cigarette is recorded at the same time as movements of the chest wall are measured by a pneumogram (a mercury strain gauge held across the upper part of the chest). *Figure 17* shows the relationship between a single puff and the pattern of chest wall movement which follows it. In the first record, inhalation (marked by a larger than usual movement of the chest wall) rapidly succeeds the taking of a puff. The area of the shaded portion of the trace can be calculated, providing an index of smoke exposure.

In the second record, however, a small exhalation follows the puff and precedes inhalation, indicating that only a proportion of the smoke taken into the smoker's mouth is eventually being drawn into the lungs. The former pattern is typical of the majority of subjects, but the latter pattern is found in a few – most notably in smokers of high-tar cigarettes (Rawbone *et al.* 1978). If it is generally the case that smokers of high-tar cigarettes actually inhale only a proportion of the smoke drawn from the cigarette, the health risks associated with smoking such products may be less than had been thought.

Evaluating the likely health consequences of different patterns of smoking is therefore complex, and we will be able to suggest possibly safer ways of smoking only after detailed analysis of smoking behaviour. The extent to which an individual smoker is actually exposed to the harmful constituents of tobacco smoke depends both on the nature of the product smoked and on the *way* it is smoked. The patterning of smoking – in terms of frequency and in the detailed aspects of puffing and inhalation – is a critical variable, and the complex interaction between the tobacco product and the smoker is perhaps best summarized by saying that what the smoker does to the cigarette is as important as what the cigarette does to the smoker.

CUES TO SMOKING

Although smokers in general show considerable regularity in the frequency with which they consume cigarettes (*Figure 15*), this is not always the case. Some people smoke more when working alone, others when in company, for example. This has prompted psychologists to consider the events which initiate smoking in a particular context. What are the cues which determine smoking frequency? What prompts the lighting of the next cigarette now, rather than half an hour ago, or half an hour hence?

In social contexts, a form of contagion seems to operate, though this effect may be more important for light than for heavy smokers. Glad and Adesso (1976) observed the behaviour of 140 subjects who were asked to wait in a room in which confederates of the experimenters either smoked or refrained from smoking. The company of smokers significantly increased the incidence of smoking, though the effect was greater amongst subjects smoking fewer than ten cigarettes per day than among those smoking more than fifteen. There is also evidence that light and heavy smokers respond differently simply to the prominence with which cigarettes are displayed. In an experiment involving two conditions, Herman (1974) placed a pack of cigarettes either directly under the main source of illumination in a room (high salience) or in shadow (low salience) and observed smokers' behaviour. Light smokers lit up in an average of five minutes when their attention was directed to the cigarettes by the obvious 'external' cue, but took fifteen minutes in the low salience condition. Heavy smokers, motivated, it was argued, more by *internal* cues (the 'need' for nicotine) lit up in six minutes in both conditions. Apparently, a similar sort of difference distinguishes obese from normal-weight eaters, though here the roles of internal and external cues are reversed. 'Food addicted' obese people eat when they *see* food; non-obese people eat when they are hungry.

'The brain in the bladder'

One of the most intriguing things about smoking is the way in which it increases in social contexts, and with stress. Various ideas have been put forward to account for this association. Smoking is perhaps of greater value as something to do (even though irrelevant) when all *other* behaviours are inappropriate. Then there is the evidence (which we shall consider in Chapter 5) that smoking, probably through the effects of nicotine, alters the physiological and psychological response to stress. Recently, Schachter has suggested that a cue to smoking behaviour may be provided indirectly by the acidity of the urine. As previously noted (Chapter 2), more nicotine is excreted by the body when the urine is acid than when it is alkaline. Under acidic conditions, therefore, the level of nicotine in the blood would be expected to fall more rapidly, and the frequency with which blood nicotine levels needed to be 'topped up' should be greater. Hence, it is suggested, people smoke more often. The theory that a falling blood level of nicotine is the cue that 'signals' further smoking of course assumes that smokers are dependent on a fairly stable level of blood nicotine – and we have seen evidence which casts doubt on this. Nevertheless, to the extent that the 'urine hypothesis' is supported, the view that smoking is a nicotine addiction will be supported too.

In a series of experiments (Schachter, Kozlowski, and Silverstein 1977a), Schachter and his colleagues showed firstly that artificial acidification of the urine led to an increased frequency of smoking. Over a period of days subjects were given either vitamin C or

'Acidulin' to acidify their urine, or a cornstarch placebo. The number of cigarettes smoked was approximately 20 per cent greater on the acidification days, compared to the placebo condition. Secondly, on the days when subjects had attended parties their bed-time urine was more acid than usual, and, as predicted, they had smoked more cigarettes than on days when they had not attended parties. Their rate of smoking (allowing for the fact that on 'social days' subjects were awake longer) was 7 per cent greater (Silverstein, Kozlowski, and Schachter 1977). Thirdly, subjects in a high-stress experiment (involving painful electric shocks) had more acid urine, smoked more cigarettes and took a greater number of puffs from their cigarettes than subjects in a low-stress version of the same experiment (Schachter *et al.* 1977b).

These three experiments showed a clear association between acid urine and increased cigarette consumption. However, for variables to be associated does not prove a causal connection between them. It could be that party-going and stress increase urine acidity and, entirely independently, increase smoking frequency also. Schachter *et al.* therefore required a further experiment to strengthen their assertion that the acidity of the urine caused the increased smoking. They therefore repeated the stress experiment, but on this occasion prevented the acidification of the urine by giving the subjects sodium bicarbonate. This time, the high-stress group did *not* have more acid urine and they did not smoke more than the low-stress group.

It is still possible to argue that the increased cigarette smoking caused the increased urine acidity, rather than vice versa. This possibility was not excluded, as it could have been, either by performing the stressful electric shock experiments on a group of non-smokers – to see whether high stress produced acid urine in the absence of smoking – or, more simply, by instructing a number of unstressed smokers to smoke more, and seeing whether that alone affected urine acidity. However, in a further study, in which stress was 'naturally' induced by various academic activities such as giving lectures and sitting examinations, both smokers and non-smokers were found to have more acid urine than on occasions when they were not stressed. Assuming similar mechanisms operated in the electric shock stress-experiment, we would be justified in concluding that the acidification of the urine was the cause and not the effect of the increased smoking.

The development of the urine-acidity hypothesis hinges on the claim that, with nicotine intake constant, blood nicotine levels will vary according to urine acidity. Schachter *et al.* provided no direct evidence that this is in fact the case. However, since their experiments were published, Feyerabend and Russell (1978) have reported a study in which blood levels of nicotine were measured whilst urine acidity was manipulated. Blood nicotine concentrations following cigarette smoking and the chewing of nicotine gum were found to be 30–60 per cent higher when the urine was alkaline than when it was acidified. Under acidic control, eighteen to thirty times more nicotine appeared in the urine than under alkaline conditions. Thus, although the precise mechanism mediating the relationship between urine acidity and blood levels still remains to be established, the reality of the relationship has been demonstrated. 'This elegant juxtaposition of facts makes almost irresistible the conclusion that the smoker's mind is in the bladder' (Schachter 1978: 218). Nevertheless, a number of problems remain.

If a falling blood nicotine level due to the increased excretion of nicotine is such a good cue for increased smoking, why is a rising level of blood nicotine (due to the chewing of gum, or nicotine injection, or nicotine tablets) apparently not a good cue for *decreased* smoking? A second point is that although Schachter's experiments show an increase in the number of cigarettes smoked (and, in one instance, also an increased number of puffs taken from cigarettes), they do not demonstrate that the intake of *nicotine* actually rose. As has been mentioned, the smoker can adjust his intake of nicotine by changing the duration of each puff, the distribution of puffs along the length of the cigarette, the velocity and volume of each puff, the depth to which smoke is inhaled, and the length of time smoke is held in the mouth, larynx, and lungs. Changes in any of these variables, especially those related to inhalation, critically affect the nicotine dose taken from a cigarette. In the absence of a direct measure of nicotine intake it is difficult to conclude that urine acidification, even though it increased the number of cigarettes smoked, actually led smokers to compensate by taking in more nicotine.

A further difficulty with the urine-acidity theory is the relatively slow time-scale over which the suggested changes operate. The acidification of urine due to stress or due to party-going presumably takes place over a long period – yet nowhere is there the suggestion that the effect on cigarette consumption is comparably delayed. If urine acidity and cigarette consumption were to change equally slowly it might be expected that the peak period for cigarette consumption would be well after the start of a party (perhaps even after it had finished) or after a stressful experience. Yet it is usually found that with the first drink of a party, or after, for example, a traffic accident, the urge to have a cigarette is immediate rather than delayed. The evidence that nicotine can be of immediate psychological value in aiding an individual's response to a variety of environmental demands is considered in the next chapter.

5 SMOKING AS A PSYCHOLOGICAL TOOL

Evidence derived from patterns of smoking behaviour – and in particular from the regularity with which cigarettes are consumed – suggests that smoking might be equivalent to nicotine addiction. The existence of a form of withdrawal syndrome is consistent with this idea. However, experiments designed to support this view have not been conclusive. In some measure this is probably due to difficulties in design (as in the case of the brand-switching studies which largely confound the importance of nicotine with that of tar), though practical difficulties (for example in finding a method of nicotine administration equivalent to smoking) have obviously also contributed.

There exists an alternative approach to the question of smoking motivation – one which remains compatible with the idea that nicotine is of central importance in the habit, but which does not suggest that smokers are addicted to nicotine in the conventional sense. This alternative view may be described as the *psychological tool* model. This view gains support from the results of experiments which suggest that smoking can have beneficial short-term psychological effects, maintaining levels of performance in the face of monotony and fatigue, increasing the selectivity of attention, and attenuating the effects of stress.

The model is consistent with the view that nicotine plays a vital part in the cigarette habit (since the beneficial psychological effects are attributable to nicotine) and does not preclude consideration of the habit as a dependence disorder. If smoking is a convenient way of manipulating psychological state, one can imagine a situation in which smokers might become reliant on this 'short-cut' method of psychological control. On this view, however, the motivation to continue smoking would not be the need to stave off the consequences of nicotine deprivation, as in the addiction model, but the desire to experience the psychological effects of smoking which continue to be rewarding in their own right. This approach to smoking has been less fully represented in the literature than the addiction view, although the evidence available at the time was reviewed by Eysenck (1973) and an interesting example of the explicit use of the psychological tool concept is provided by Myrsten *et al.* (1975).

In connection with these two approaches, we may first consider what smokers themselves say about the reasons why they smoke. Some are quite prepared to say that they are addicted; that smoking, although it might once have given them pleasure, no longer does, but that it is necessary to stave off 'craving'. Others will give reasons for smoking in terms which suggest they find it of value in combating boredom and fatigue, in reducing tension, and so on. This variety of response gives face validity to both views of smoking maintenance – but it also perhaps suggests that each view is right about some smokers and wrong about others. There is no *a priori* reason to suppose that one explanation will be sufficient to provide a satisfactory account of the motivation of all smokers. It may also be the case that both views are right about all smokers but that the extent to which each applies varies according to the individual concerned.

Various attempts have been made to design questionnaires which will measure the strength of different sorts of motivation. Tomkins (1966) distinguished between smokers who used cigarettes primarily for relaxation and enjoyment ('positive affect' smokers), those who smoked to reduce feelings of distress ('negative affect' smoking), and those in whom smoking was habitual or addictive. These basic distinctions were elaborated (Ikard, Green, and Horn 1969; Russell, Peto, and Patel 1974) and a rather different smoking typology has been developed by McKennell (1973).

For interest, a copy of one of these questionnaires (based on Russell, Peto, and Patel 1974) is included, together with instructions on how to score the answers, as an appendix. Broadly speaking, the forty items can be grouped into seven factors, each measuring an aspect of smoking motivation. The *addictive* (and possibly also the *automatic*) factor can be considered as attempting to measure the kind of dependence on nicotine hypothesized in the *addiction model* of smoking, whilst the *sedative* and *stimulant* (and possibly also the *indulgent*) factors correspond to the psychological rewards of smoking envisaged in the *psychological tool* model. The *psychosocial* and *sensorimotor* factors cover aspects of the smoking act largely unrelated to nicotine.

CONTROL OF AROUSAL

One of the most important factors in determining a person's psychological state is his degree of arousal, since this controls both his behavioural response and his emotional reaction to any environmental stimulus. Basic to the psychological tool model is the suggestion that smoking confers psychological benefits by allowing the smoker to modulate his degree of arousal (*Figure 18*). In order to examine this hypothesis it is necessary to outline briefly the physiological mechanisms underlying arousal and also to consider how the level of arousal can be measured.

Physiological mechanisms of arousal

There appear to be two systems in the brain that control arousal in man and higher animals. The first is a non-specific system which determines the general degree of responsiveness of the whole brain and body. This system governs consciousness and its activity determines whether the subject is asleep, awake, or at any intermediate level of awareness. It operates through the reticular formation, a bundle of nerve fibres and cells, which connect the sense organs to the cerebral cortex, and the cortex to all parts of the body necessary for responding to a sensory stimulus. There is good evidence that the neurotransmitter for many of the important pathways in this system is ACh (Abel 1974). Thus nicotine would be expected to act on this general arousal system.

The second arousal system in the brain is more specific and goal-directed. It is concerned with drive and emotion and to a large extent determines the quality and strength of response to environmental stimuli. Its 'setting' may be a determinant of personality (Gray 1970). It is also important in allowing selective attention to relevant stimuli and in the closely related functions of learning and memory. The anatomical basis of this arousal mechanism is the limbic system, which has been mentioned before in relation to reward and punishment centres. Among the neurotransmitters involved are noradrenaline and dopamine, both of which can be influenced by nicotine.

The two arousal systems interact with each other, both influencing the level of arousal and hence the response to stimuli. The general arousal system can be said to provide the background level of arousal while the goal-directed system focuses the attention on the factors relevant at a particular moment. At certain levels of activity, however, the two systems appear to be mutually inhibitory, activity in one tending to reduce activity in the other. This is the basis for the 'two arousal' hypothesis put forward by Routtenberg (1968). Such an arrangement no doubt has survival value. For example, overactivity in the general arousal system would mean that the individual would react non-selectively to any stimulus and be so 'jumpy' that he would

Figure 18 Smoking as a psychological tool

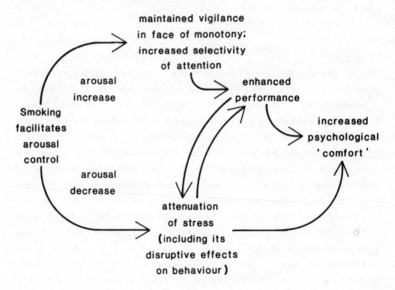

This figure first appeared in Stepney (1980c). Reproduced by permission of the editor and publishers of the *British Journal of Diseases of the Chest*.

not be able to differentiate the important from the unimportant. Selective attention to relevant stimuli would be achieved by the inhibitory action of the limbic system. Similarly, excessive emotional arousal from the limbic system could detract from performance in tasks demanding a high level of general activity. In this case the general arousal system would inhibit selective and emotional limbic activity. There is probably an optimal level of activity in both arousal systems for the performance of each particular task.

Measurement of arousal

At first sight the measurement of arousal seems simple enough. Arousal can be envisaged as a dimension with sleep at one end and hyperactivity at the other, with drowsiness, boredom, alert interest, etc., as intervening stages. A stimulant drug (such as amphetamine) shifts an organism towards the high-arousal end of the continuum, and a depressant drug (for example, a barbiturate) shifts it towards the low arousal end and will, in a large enough dose, result in sleep (Claridge 1970). This, basically, is the concept of arousal as physical activation and it can be measured in its crudest form in animal experiments by, for example, counting the number of squares on a large grid into which an animal moves in a given period of time, or by measuring the distance 'travelled' on a running wheel.

However, the relationship of performance to arousal is more complicated. If, for example, reaction time is taken as a measure of alertness, it is found that the speed of response becomes faster as the subject becomes less drowsy, but at a certain point, which one can think of as the beginning of over-arousal, the speed of response begins to slow. Such considerations led to the formulation of the 'Yerkes-Dodson law' which holds that the quality of performance relates in an inverted U-shaped function to arousal level. Thus performance is poor when subjects are under-aroused, and also when they are over-aroused, with the optimum level of arousal lying somewhere in the middle (*Figure 19*).

A stimulant drug may enhance performance when an animal is at the low-arousal end of the dimension. However, if the animal is already moderately or highly aroused, the effect of the drug will be to push it over the 'hump' of the performance/arousal curve, and actually impair performance. A similar dual effect on performance is possible with a depressant drug; the performance of the highly aroused subject may, paradoxically, be improved, even though arousal level is reduced. This situation is further complicated by the fact that the particular level of arousal which is the optimum for performance on a given task depends on the nature of the task itself. Thus, in general, complicated tasks (especially those involving fine motor co-ordination) are performed optimally at relatively low levels of arousal. Less demanding tasks are performed better at higher levels. Peak performance on a particular task presumably reflects an optimal balance of activity in the general and limbic arousal systems.

Performance on various psychological tests can be used as a

Figure 19 The arousal dimension

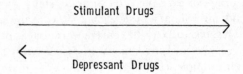

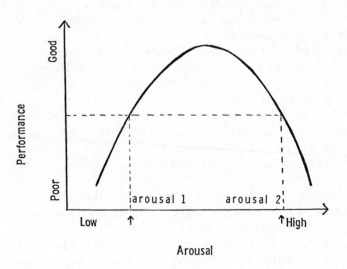

Arousal

measure of arousal in man; but in view of the inverted-U relationship between arousal and performance, any given level of performance (except the optimum itself) can be the result of two different levels of arousal (*Figure 19*). The problem can be partially resolved if it is possible to measure performance at a given level of arousal, and then shift the subject's arousal. Assume for the moment that arousal is increased. Then, if the subject's performance is impaired relative to the previous occasion, we can conclude that he is now somewhere on the downward curve of the function; if performance improves we can conclude he is somewhere on the upward slope (Corcoran 1965). This solution presupposes that we can shift arousal in a known direction, and this obviously requires that we have a measure of arousal (or change in arousal) which is independent of the performance itself.

The concept of arousal has therefore been extended to incorporate physiological activation. Two sets of measures have been found useful in this respect. One set concerns the activity of the autonomic nervous system. Here variables such as heart rate, blood pressure, and sweating (indicated by changes in skin resistance) have been measured. The other set of variables involves the attempt to measure changes in the activity of the brain. It is this second set of measures which has most relevance to the psychological effects of smoking.

Various aspects of the electroencephalogram (EEG) – which records electrical activity in the brain from electrodes placed on the scalp – have been widely used as an index of brain activity. These EEG measures are not without problems. Their precise relationship with autonomic and behavioural measures of arousal is often unclear, and experiments involving drugs and surgical interference in the brain have shown that it is possible to dissociate EEG and behavioural arousal (Lacey 1967). It is possible, for example, to find an EEG characteristic of sleep when an animal is simultaneously showing a high degree of behavioural activity. Similarly, stimuli which produce arousal as measured by one set of criteria do not always produce similar changes on other indices of arousal. Thus some drugs can simultaneously increase autonomic arousal as reflected in heart rate while producing sedative effects on the brain. Nevertheless, in intact animals the EEG varies systematically with behavioural and subjective changes in arousal and is probably the best measure available at present of stimulant and depressant effects of drugs which act on the brain.

When a subject is drowsy, there is a tendency for electrical activity in the brain to occur in regular 'bursts', as groups of cells discharge together. This gives the EEG a high-amplitude, low frequency wave-form (see *Figure 20*) in which much of the activity occurs in the 8–12 cycles per second range. Activity of this frequency is termed 'alpha'. As the subject becomes more alert, the dominant frequency of alpha activity becomes faster, the total amount of alpha present in the EEG tends to decrease, and other waves of faster frequency become more prominent – a process known as desynchronization. A regular, high-amplitude, and low-frequency pattern is thus characteristic of low arousal states and a desynchronized pattern of high arousal states. Desynchronized electrical activity in the brain can be

Figure 20 Changes in EEG activity found during the transition from a relaxed state to one of mental concentration.

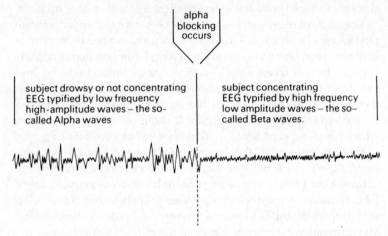

Source: Einon (1974: 39). Reproduced by permission of The Open University (©1974 The Open University Press).

produced behaviourally (by getting someone to concentrate on a problem, for example), by providing alerting sensory stimulation, or by the use of stimulant drugs; alpha activity is induced by relaxation and by sedative drugs.

Other EEG measures can also be used as an index of arousal. One such measure is the 'expectancy wave' or Contingent Negative Variation (CNV). This is a slow negative potential, recorded from scalp electrodes, which occurs in the few seconds between an alerting stimulus and one to which the subject is required to respond. The magnitude of this negative shift is increased by stimulant drugs and decreased by depressant drugs (Ashton *et al.* 1974).

Biphasic effects of nicotine and smoking

One of the speedy and powerful actions of nicotine on the brain is a clear-cut alerting effect. Domino (1979) found that within 30 seconds of a single intravenous injection of very small doses of nicotine (0.005–0.01 mg per kilogram body weight) a sleeping cat awoke and became alert, showing increased arousal both in behaviour and in EEG activity. However, the brief awakening lasted only 3 minutes, after which the cat lapsed into sleep again. Moreover, the post-nicotine sleep was deeper than before and was followed after about 20 minutes by an intense period of sleep of the type usually associated with dreaming. Such effects were not seen when control injections of saline solution were substituted for nicotine. Furthermore, the nicotine effects could be blocked by a drug (mecamylamine) which opposes the action of nicotine on ACh receptors in the brain. These findings, which have been confirmed in other studies, suggest that the effects are due to an action of nicotine on arousal systems in the brain utilizing ACh as a transmitter.

Hall (1970) also demonstrated arousal in sleeping cats following the intravenous injection over 20 minutes of small doses of nicotine. He further observed that the same changes occurred after the introduction of puffs of cigarette smoke into the lungs or application of cigarette smoke to the nostrils. Armitage, Hall and Sellers (1969) showed in anaesthetized cats that the stimulant effect of nicotine on the EEG was associated with an increased output of ACh from the cerebral cortex, again suggesting an arousal mechanism involving ACh. When larger doses of nicotine were given, some cats showed a slowing of EEG activity and a fall in brain ACh output, reflecting the characteristic biphasic stimulant-depressant effect of nicotine. This biphasic effect is not confined to cats but has also been shown in the EEG and behaviour of dogs, chickens, rabbits, mice, rats, and monkeys.

In man, nicotine or smoking can produce similar alerting effects. Many studies have shown that smoking is followed by EEG changes typical of arousal (Knott and Venables 1977). Murphree, Pfeiffer, and Price (1967) and Lambiase and Serra (1957) studied the effect of smoking cigars or cigarettes. Although the extent of the smoking effect depended very much on the baseline state of the subject, the characteristic change was one of decreased alpha activity.

Conversely, smoking abstinence has been reported to reduce arousal. Ulett and Itil (1969) looked at the EEG of 20-a-day smokers deprived of cigarettes for 24 hours and found a pronounced increase in slow-frequency activity. This state was reversed when smoking was resumed. Such findings led to the suggestion that some smokers use the nicotine in cigarettes to stimulate brain activity. Furthermore, the people who eventually become smokers may be those whose 'natural' level of brain excitation is low.

The arousing effects on brain activity induced by smoking have been associated with enhanced vigilance and attention and faster reaction time, and Knott and Venables (1977) have suggested that the dominant alpha frequency may be a major factor in controlling the rate at which the brain functions as an information processor. A possible link between the EEG effects noted here and the influence of smoking on various measures of performance, which will be discussed later, is therefore clear.

For every smoker who says that cigarettes are a valuable stimulant, there is another who claims that the advantages of smoking lie in apparently the opposite direction. Not surprisingly in view of nicotine's biphasic actions, depressant effects on brain activity can also be demonstrated in man in certain situations. Mangan and Golding (1978) showed that the effect of smoking could be stimulant or depressant depending on the environment. Their experiment involved two conditions. In one condition subjects were stressed by being subjected at random intervals to uncomfortably loud bursts of 'white' noise. In the second condition subjects simply relaxed while lying on a bed in a quiet room. The lack of available stimulation in this condition led the experimenters to term it 'mild sensory isolation'. The main part of the experiment lasted for 15 minutes, during the middle 5 minutes of which subjects either smoked a cigarette, pretended to smoke an unlit cigarette, or did nothing.

Several variables including EEG frequency were measured. The EEG traces were analysed in terms of 'per cent alpha' – i.e., the proportion of total EEG activity which fell within that particular waveband. In the relaxation condition, per cent alpha fell by around 25 per cent in the subjects who were smoking normally, but remained at roughly baseline level in those who were not smoking at all. The decline in alpha activity represented an alerting effect (*Figure 21a*).

In the stress condition, smoking had entirely the opposite effect, increasing per cent alpha by approximately 15 per cent relative to baseline, whilst the non-smoking group showed a slight reduction in alpha activity (*Figure 21b*). The effect of smoking in this context was therefore apparently to decrease arousal. The 'activity control' (provided by the 'sham smoking' of an unlit cigarette) had an effect on arousal which was relatively small and short-lived. This demonstrates that the act of smoking itself – the manipulation of the cigarette, the lip contact, the puffing and so on – is not sufficient to produce the effects on arousal which follow the inhalation of tobacco smoke, and it is likely that the constituent of tobacco smoke which alters arousal is nicotine. The view that smoking may in some sense normalize arousal, increasing it in conditions of boredom, and decreasing it under stress, therefore finds support.

Figure 21 Deviation from baseline alpha activity in three groups under conditions of (a) relaxation and (b) stress

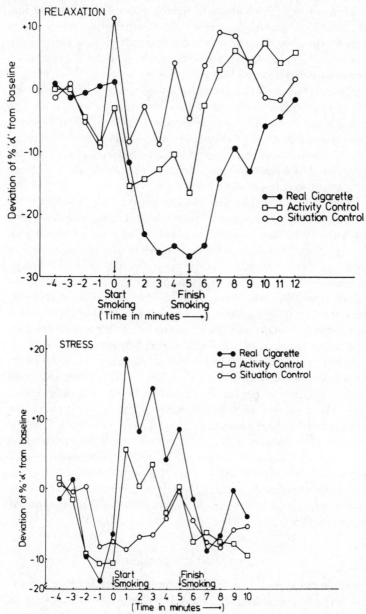

Source: Mangan and Golding (1978: 100). Reproduced by permission of Churchill Livingstone.

Further evidence that smoking and nicotine have biphasic effects on brain activity, depending on context, comes from studies of the Contingent Negative Variation. Ashton *et al.* (1978a) showed that when subjects smoked cigarettes in their natural manner, consistent increases in CNV magnitude (i.e. stimulant effects) were seen in some subjects whilst in others, under the same conditions, consistently depressant effects were observed.

The direction of effect depended on dosage; smokers with a relatively low rate of nicotine intake showed a stimulant effect while those who took a larger dose per minute obtained a depressant effect. A further finding was that the dose chosen by each smoker, as reflected in the way he smoked, was related to personality. Subjects who were more extraverted took smaller stimulant doses while those who were more introverted took larger depressant ones.

In a further study, nicotine was administered not by smoking but by intravenous injection (Ashton *et al.* 1980). The nicotine doses used fell within the range which it is possible to obtain by smoking an average cigarette. It was found that in each individual nicotine could produce either a stimulant or a depressant effect depending on the dose administered. Small doses of intravenous nicotine had a stimulant effect on the CNV and larger amounts a depressant effect. All subjects showed this type of biphasic dose-response curve, but each had his own individual shape and slope of curve so that the dosage at which stimulation changed to depression varied between subjects.

The bidirectional effects found in these studies are consistent with the known actions of nicotine. Furthermore, it appears that each smoker can, by varying his smoking style, figuratively slide up and down his nicotine dose-response curve to obtain the stimulant or depressant effect he requires in the prevailing circumstances. There is evidence that smokers adjust their dosage in this way in different situations. Ashton and Watson (1970) showed that smokers took significantly fewer puffs and less nicotine from a standard cigarette while concentrating on a driving simulator task than when relaxing. Thus nicotine dosage, circumstances, and personality are all involved in the complex biphasic effect of smoking on arousal.

ENHANCEMENT OF PERFORMANCE

Attention has already been drawn to the interaction between arousal and performance (*Figure 19*). Evaluating the effects of smoking on performance involves further difficulties. In drug studies it is desirable to compare the results with some form of placebo – an inactive tablet or capsule made up to look exactly like the drug – since performance can be affected simply by the idea that a drug of any kind is being administered. For example in one experiment (cited in Claridge 1970), subjects were given white capsules on their first attendance and pink capsules on their second. They were told that the white capsules would induce sleepiness and that the pink ones were stimulant. Both were in fact placebos. The 'depressant' placebo led to feelings of drowsiness, a decrease in heart rate and blood pressure and an increase in reaction time – all typical effects of a genuine depressant drug. The 'stimulant' placebo, on all these measures, had entirely the opposite effect. It is to take account of the possibility of such reactions that a placebo control condition is used.

In an ideal experiment, subjects would experience both the drug and the placebo. Thus any variability in the results due to the differences between subjects can be taken account of by comparing each subject with himself. For some subjects, the drug condition would precede the placebo; for others the order would reverse. Again ideally, neither subject nor experimenter would be able to tell on which occasion the drug was given. Such a 'double blind' procedure aims to eliminate any effects due to the expectations of either subject or experimenter.

With smoking, there is no real possibility of a genuine placebo condition. Nicotine-free herbal and lettuce-leaf (even rose-petal) cigarettes do exist, but smokers judge them to be nothing like tobacco. There is therefore little possibility of the subject being 'blind' as to whether or not he is actually receiving nicotine. Hull (1924) realized that this was a problem and found an ingenious solution. He used an elaborate system of deception which involved administering tobacco smoke or a control 'dose' of warmed air to blindfolded subjects in a room in which the experimenter himself smoked tobacco to provide the appropriate background aroma. Hull's experiment involved the use of a pipe, from which smoke or warmed air was drawn into the mouth, but not inhaled. The placebo was thus obtained, but only at the cost of making the smoking highly abnormal. The difficulty in finding an adequate placebo condition is less of a problem when nicotine is administered by some means other than smoking; this is one way around the problem.

A second major set of difficulties arises from the question of whether a within- or a between-subjects design is the more appropriate. Should we compare smokers smoking with smokers not smoking, or should we compare smokers smoking with non-smokers? The problem with the former approach is that smokers who are not smoking are, in a sense, deprived smokers. Any difference found between the performance of the two groups might therefore be due not to the positive advantages which smoking confers, but to the disadvantages of smoking abstinence. (In any very short-term experiment, the effect of withdrawal from nicotine is likely to be slight, but its influence cannot be discounted in any longer lasting experiment.) Unfortunately, comparing smokers with non-smokers also raises difficulties since smokers and non-smokers differ in respects other than their smoking. As will be more fully discussed, smokers are on average more extravert than non-smokers, and possibly more neurotic. These differences, which may follow from smoking, or may predispose to it, are likely themselves to influence performance and so be confounded with any effects due to smoking. Research on the psychological effects of smoking is therefore difficult. Nevertheless, there is now evidence from a variety of sources showing that smoking and nicotine can enhance performance in certain circumstances.

Vigilance

In short-term reaction time tasks, smoking may either increase or decrease the speed of response (Ashton *et al.* 1972) depending on such factors as dose, task difficulty, and individual characteristics. However, under conditions requiring vigilance and sustained attention, smokers smoking have often been found to perform better, not only in relation to smokers not smoking, but in comparison also with groups of non-smokers. Increased efficiency has been demonstrated in reaction speed and in the accuracy with which stimuli are detected. A likely explanation for such results is that smoking alleviates boredom and facilitates concentration at least partly through stimulant actions of nicotine on arousal systems.

Figure 22 shows the results of an experiment (Wesnes and Warburton 1978) in which subjects' performance in signal detection is plotted against time. The task required subjects to detect and respond to brief pauses in the otherwise continuous movement of a clock hand. In an attempt to maintain levels of motivation, subjects were paid for correctly detecting the discontinuous movements. The performance of subjects smoking (at 20, 40, and 60 minutes into the task) was maintained at a relatively high level, whilst that of the non-smokers and deprived smokers deteriorated with time. The

Figure 22 Effects of cigarette smoking on visual vigilance

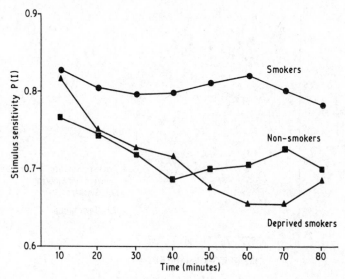

Source: Wesnes and Warburton (1978: 133). Reproduced by permission of Churchill Livingstone.

difference between the smoking group and the other two groups was statistically significant.

A similar result had been reported earlier by Tarrière and Hartemann (1964) who studied the effect of smoking on performance in a task designed to simulate car driving. The signal detection skill of a group of twenty-four smokers, smoking and not smoking, was compared with that of non-smokers. The results of the experiment (*Figure 23*) were similar to those on the clock task. The percentage of signals which subjects failed to detect increased with time in the non-smoking and smoking-deprived groups, but remained relatively constant in the smoking condition.

In a different kind of experiment, Frankenhaeuser *et al.* (1971) showed that the reaction time of a group of light smokers remained at roughly the same level over an 80-minute period during which three cigarettes were smoked. The same subjects without cigarettes showed slower reactions with time (*Figure 24*). Frankenhaeuser *et al.* argue that abstinence effects are unlikely to have played a major part in this impairment. Nevertheless, eighty minutes of a reaction-time experiment would probably be enough to make most smokers feel like

Figure 23 Visual vigilance in smokers, non-smokers, and deprived smokers

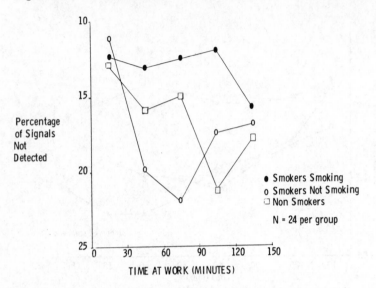

Source: based on Tarrière and Hartemann (1964: 526). Reproduced by permission of the authors, and the publishers of *Ergonomics*.

smoking. The importance of smoking deprivation in longer-term vigilance tasks is demonstrated by Heimstra *et al.* (1967) who found no enhancement of performance due to smoking in a six hour vigilance and tracking task, but a significant *impairment* in deprived smokers.

Interaction with alcohol

Myrsten and Andersson (1975) produced evidence that smoking can counter impaired performance due to alcohol intoxication. The experiment took place in a 'relaxed social setting' in which experimenters and subjects had dinner together. In one condition subjects smoked a total of five cigarettes in the course of the evening. In the other, they abstained from tobacco. With alcohol and tobacco combined, subjects had a faster heart rate, higher blood pressure, and excreted more adrenaline. They were also less steady on their feet, experienced more hand tremor, and had higher ratings of subjective intoxication. Nevertheless, the subjects had faster reaction times and

Figure 24 Successive mean scores in visual reaction time under smoking and control conditions

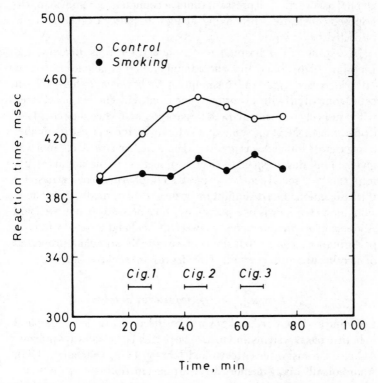

The first point represents the mean of two 'pre-cigarette' measures. A longer reaction time indicates poorer performance.
Source: Frankenhaeuser *et al.* (1971: 4). Reproduced by permission of Springer Verlag.

performed better on a test of mental arithmetic when they smoked and drank than when they drank without smoking.

The association between smoking and alcohol consumption has been well documented in both normal and clinical populations. Smokers trying to give up, for example, report that one of the times they have greatest difficulty in not smoking is when drinking. The association could be due to taste factors; tobacco and alcoholic drinks might happen to go particularly well together, like pork and apple sauce. Alternatively, since both drinking and smoking are to some extent social habits, their association on this basis alone would be understandable. On the other hand, if it is assumed that most smokers normally smoke less than they would like to, the effect of alcohol as a cortical depressant could account for the removal of self-imposed constraints on smoking, along with those on other normally inhibited behaviours.

In a study of five hospitalized alcoholics, Griffiths, Bigelow, and Liebson (1976) found that the administration of ethanol in orange juice increased cigarette consumption by between 26 and 117 per cent, compared with an orange juice control. The effect occurred when subjects were not allowed to socialize, and when they could not drink and smoke at the same time. Moreover, the increase in number of cigarettes smoked was greater when a higher dose of ethanol was given. This dose-response effect, together with the apparent unimportance of social context, suggests some pharmacological basis for the association. The disinhibition by alcohol of normally constrained smoking behaviour is one possibility. But the study of Myrsten and Andersson on the interaction between alcohol and tobacco effects on performance suggests that smokers may use the stimulant properties of nicotine to counter certain of the depressant effects of alcohol.

Learning, memory, and selective attention

Learning and memory are known to be affected by the level of arousal in both arousal systems and to involve particularly pathways utilizing ACh as a transmitter (Alpern and Jackson 1978; Drachman 1978). Anatomically many memory and learning functions are located in the hippocampus and other limbic structures (Isaacson and Pribram 1975). Since nicotine acts at ACh synapses and is also concentrated in the hippocampus, it might be expected to influence these processes.

There is considerable evidence that nicotine affects learning and memory in animals. For example, Flood *et al.* (1978) reported that nicotine improved memory consolidation and Alpern and Jackson (1978) observed complex dose-dependent biphasic effects of nicotine and other stimulants and depressants on various stages of the memory process in mice. Morrison and Armitage (1967) found in rats that nicotine could increase the rate of learning of reward or avoidance tasks, depending on the dose and time after injection. Often an initial depressant effect was followed by a more prolonged stimulant phase.

Nicotine and smoking appear also to affect learning and memory in humans. Andersson (1975) studied the effect of smoking on learning in a group of ten habitual smokers. The task involved memorizing lists of nonsense syllables which have few associations and are relatively unaffected by previous learning. The syllables were repeatedly projected one at a time on to a screen and the subjects were asked to respond by naming the next syllable which would appear. Smoking a single cigarette produced an initial drop in the number of correct responses, but after a forty-five minute break from the task performance was superior. It was suggested that smoking causes an increase in arousal which disrupts initial recall but improves memory consolidation.

Mangan and Golding (1978) investigated performance of a task requiring subjects to remember a series of word associations. In one condition the subjects smoked a cigarette immediately before the words were presented. Smoking had little effect on the speed with which subjects learned the correct associations, but recall after a thirty-minute rest was significantly improved. This apparent facilitatory effect of smoking on long-term memory was supported by the results of a second experiment, in which subjects were required to learn word lists. Smoking before learning improved recall of words at the beginning of the lists, but had no effect on words occurring later. Items presented first have longer to be consolidated into long-term memory than more recently presented words, and the fact that smoking seemed to improve recall only of the earlier items suggested that it enhanced learning by aiding consolidation.

Smokers often suggest that a cigarette is a valuable aid to concentration. Andersson and Hockey (1977) have shown how this impression might arise. Female smokers were studied on a serial word-recall task under either smoking or non-smoking conditions. Words were individually presented, and appeared in any one of the four corners of a screen. Overall, there was no difference in recall between the smoking and the non-smoking groups. Subjects had not been instructed to pay attention to the position of the words as they appeared. However, when asked to recall this apparently irrelevant information (a test of 'incidental learning') smokers were considerably less accurate. The effect of smoking, therefore, seemed to have been to narrow the subjects' focus of attention to the relevant aspects of the task, leaving other features of the situation unattended.

The ability of people to concentrate on the relevant aspects of a stimulus has also been studied using the 'Stroop' task (Wesnes and Warburton 1978). In this task subjects are initially required quickly to name the colour of a series of differently coloured patches. They are then asked to name the colour of the ink in which a series of colour names is written, the problem being that the colour of the ink is different from the colour that the word names. Thus the word 'green' is written in blue ink, for example. The difference between the time taken to name the colours in the two conditions is a measure of the interference caused by the conflict between the meaning of the word and its appearance. The effect of nicotine on the degree of Stroop interference was studied in a group of six smokers and six non-smokers. Nicotine was administered by buccal absorption from 1 and 2 mg tablets held in the mouth. Both doses of nicotine significantly reduced interference, compared to placebo, in both smokers and non-smokers.

ANXIETY AND AGGRESSION

If asked why they smoke, many people will reply in a way which suggests they use smoking to alleviate anxiety. In a questionnaire study (Frith 1971b) smokers were asked to record how much they would want to smoke under a range of different circumstances. Their answers suggested they needed to smoke under both relaxing conditions (after a meal, or having a quiet evening with friends, for example) and under stressful conditions (such as when waiting for an important job interview or watching an horrific film).

Perhaps surprisingly, little is known about people's smoking habits under natural conditions of low and high stress. In an unpublished report to the Tobacco Research Council by National Opinion Polls, smoking was reported as being more intensive under conditions of excitement but no quantitative account of the results was presented. The measurement of smoking style outside the laboratory is not without problems. It has to be surreptitious and yet detailed. Some form of event marker linked to a small concealed tape recorder can be used to record the number and duration of each puff, and the time taken to smoke the cigarette, and there is evidence that depth of inhalation can be estimated by eye. Within the laboratory (which unfortunately seems to be an abnormal smoking environment), smoking style can be more easily recorded and the effect of anxiety has been more extensively studied, although even here knowledge is limited.

Schachter *et al.* (1977b) who studied the effect of electric shock on smoking and urine acidity, recorded an increase in the number of cigarettes smoked under the high anxiety condition, whilst Mangan and Golding (1978) found an increase in the number and 'strength' of puffs when subjects were stressed by white noise. In brand-switching experiments reported by Ashton, Stepney, and Thompson (1978b, 1979b) analysis of nicotine retained by the filters of cigarettes smoked inside the laboratory and those smoked outside suggested that a greater nicotine dose was taken in the more stressful laboratory environment.

The evidence indicating more intensive smoking under short-term increases in anxiety is complemented by a number of non-laboratory studies which have shown that smoking is associated with longer-term stressful life events and high levels of personal anger and anxiety. Thomas (1973) followed a group of 600 medical students (whose initial psychological profile was obtained at the average age of twenty-three) through between ten and twenty-four years of professional life. Doctors who continued to smoke over the entire period of the study had experienced greater awareness of feelings of anger and anxiety on initial examination than those who were non-smokers. Those who had given up smoking in the course of the study were intermediate on these measures between doctors who had never smoked and those who continued to smoke.

In an ambitious project, Emery, Hilgendorf, and Irving (1968) aimed to elucidate the 'psychological dynamics' of smoking by interviewing a national sample of 2500 working English adults. The assumption was that tobacco (along with other objects or behaviours) is used to regulate emotional feelings and responses – either because the experience of emotion is itself unpleasant, because it intrudes into some 'ongoing commitment', or simply because the display of emotion, especially in English culture, is discouraged. It was further suggested that the use of tobacco would be related to four factors – exposure to stress, personal sensitivity to that exposure, the existence or absence of social supports that might reduce these effects, and the availability of alternative ways of regulating emotion.

The 2500 interviewees, divided into age and sex sub-groups, were assessed on their replies to 590 items on the interview schedule. The data were analysed by intercorrelating the 202 sub-scales to which the original interview items could be reduced.

Analysis of the situations in which smoking was thought appropriate yielded three factors. In decreasing order of importance, these were the need to concentrate, offset boredom, and relieve tension. Smoking was positively associated with a cluster of job-related items – job over-demanding, frustrating, busy – and negatively related to another set of items which included perception of the job as challenging, rushed, and creative. These patterns of response fitted the initial assumptions of the study reasonably well. On the other hand stress through lengthy separation from loved ones – caused by marriage difficulties, bereavement, etc. – was not related to smoking.

The investigators also chose particular dependent variables – such as heavy cigarette consumption or stress smoking – and attempted to trace a path of causal connexions (through attitudes, personality, and social background) which contributed to the behaviour. This method of 'linkage' produced a complex pattern of results, with different causal paths appearing in the different age and sex groups. Thus 'neuroticism' was positively related to stress smoking in middle-aged women, but not in older women. In the latter group (but in that group alone) identification with their father seemed a good predictor of heavy smoking. In older (but not in younger) males, heavy cigarette smoking was related to a large family background and to an indulgent and extravert personality. Pipe smoking in men over fifty years of age was linked with origins in a small family and higher social class, and also (via a different causal path) with long-term occupational and environmental stress. Pipe smoking, unlike cigarette smoking, was not related to emotionality. This finding led the authors to suggest that pipe smoking (with its 'series of small defensive behaviours behind which one can hide') is a valuable coping mechanism for the less emotionally reactive man, whilst cigarette smoking serves a similar function for the more emotionally labile individual.

These studies suggest that smoking can be used to attenuate emotional responses such as anxiety and anger, possibly through the depressant effects of nicotine on limbic arousal and punishment systems. Since such emotions may impair performance, it should be possible to show that nicotine or smoking prevents these disruptive effects. This question has been investigated in animals and man.

Hutchinson and Emley (1973) trained rats and monkeys to obtain food rewards by pressing a lever. Over the period of training, tone stimuli were occasionally paired with the delivery of an electric shock. The animals came to associate the tone with the shock, the tone therefore becoming a conditioned stressor. In the post-training period, presentation of the tone alone disrupted the food-acquisition response. Nicotine counteracted this stress-induced suppression of behaviour. Nelsen (1978) also found that nicotine could alter the response to stress in rats. 'Freezing', which normally occurs when a cat is present, was significantly reduced (compared with controls) in animals that had received repeated injections of nicotine. Nicotine's effectiveness in reducing this stress response was more marked in highly 'emotional' animals than in those of low emotionality. The same schedule of subcutaneous nicotine injections also reduced the disruption of goal-directed behaviour caused by electrical stimulation of the reticular formation.

Hall and Morrison (1973) provided evidence for a relationship between nicotine dependence and stress. Rats were trained to press a lever to avoid being given an electric shock in a stressful procedure in which the correct avoidance response was not 'signalled' to them. Animals given nicotine injections while learning the task performed more successfully than controls injected with a saline solution. However, when saline was substituted for nicotine, performance deteriorated to a level below that of the control animals. This showed that the rats given nicotine were dependent on it to sustain their high level of performance. However, the dependence occurred only under stressful conditions; in a low-stress version of the same experiment, in which successful avoidance of the electric shock was indicated, the substitution of saline for nicotine did not affect performance. This experiment suggested that nicotine could be of value to an organism, probably because of its effects on arousal, in the context of the demands of a specific environment.

Aggressive behaviour in animals can also be modified by nicotine. Berntson, Beattie, and Walker (1976) showed that nicotine, in appropriate doses, produces a selective decrease in predatory behaviour in the cat. In the squirrel monkey, animals which received nicotine responded to electric shocks with less of their customary biting-attack behaviour (Hutchinson and Emley 1973).

Such investigations with nicotine in animals may be relevant to nicotine and smoking effects in man. Hutchinson and Emley suggested that the human counterpart of biting behaviour in the squirrel monkey is the jaw-clenching and teeth-grinding which accompanies irritability and frustration. They noted that abstaining smokers showed an increased frequency of jaw-clenching and investigated the possibility that nicotine could modify this behaviour. Four non-smokers were chosen for an experiment in which the force and frequency of jaw-clenching was measured from records of electrical activity in the masseter muscle. Exposure at regular intervals to very loud tones (110 decibels) produced a pattern of jaw contractions immediately following each tone and preceding the next one. Administration of 5 mg of nicotine in drinking water fifteen minutes before the test considerably reduced this response, compared to the control condition in which distilled water was given. In view of the relative inefficiency of nicotine absorbed from the gut, this result is somewhat surprising. It is also possible that the effect, rather than

Figure 25 The reaction time of high- and low-arousal smokers

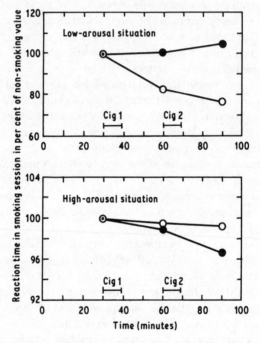

Mean reaction times are shown as a percentage of the values found in the non-smoking condition (values less than 100 indicate improved performance). Open circles represent low-arousal smokers; filled circles, high-arousal smokers.
Source: Myrsten *et al.* (1975). Reproduced by permission of the editors of *Perceptual and Motor Skills*.

being mediated through the action of nicotine on the brain, was due to decreased reflex activity in the masseter muscle, such as has been demonstrated in the case of the knee-jerk response (Domino 1973).

Nevertheless, several other studies have reported a relationship between smoking and aggression which suggests a central action of nicotine. For example, Heimstra (1973) found that during a six-hour vigilance task, subjects allowed to smoke did not increase their ratings of aggression while both smoking-deprived subjects and non-smokers did. Dunn (1978) investigated a group of students who were assigned to smoker, non-smoker and deprived smoker groups and played a complex perceptual motor game. Subjects scored points, which were displayed and which could later be converted to cash. The machine started by awarding points fairly, but then began randomly to cheat subjects. The situation in which the players found themselves was described as analogous to 'that of the hapless victim of the machine age whose coin fails to win him a drink from an automatic dispensing machine' (Dunn 1978: 20–21). In this instance, all three groups showed a comparable increase in anger. The performance proficiency shown by the smokers, however, unlike that of the non-smoking and deprived groups, did not deteriorate. Dunn concluded that, whilst smoking had no apparent effect under conditions conducive to good performance, it did confer an advantage under conditions likely to disrupt behaviour.

The relation between smoking and performance under stress was also studied by Myrsten *et al.* (1975). On the basis of questionnaire responses, eight subjects who smoked in situations of high arousal were selected, and eight who were low-arousal smokers. Both groups performed a task at two levels of complexity (and therefore at two levels of inferred stress) under both smoking and non-smoking conditions. The low-arousal smokers performed and felt better when smoking only when the task was set at a low level of complexity. The high-arousal smokers performed and felt better when smoking only at the high level of task complexity. Under non-smoking conditions both groups performed equally well at both task levels. The interaction between task complexity and the different smoking-motivation groups is shown for the reaction time measure in *Figure 25*. It was the result of this study which led Myrsten to formulate explicitly the notion of smoking as a psychological tool used to modify arousal level.

Ashton and Watson (1970) observed that smokers' puffing behaviour and nicotine intake depended on task demands. Nicotine intake increased during relaxation and decreased during a driving simulator task. It appeared that, while driving, smokers were striving for alerting effects of nicotine, and while relaxing for tranquillizing effects. It was therefore suggested (Ashton and Watson 1970: 3) that there exists an 'optimum' nicotine dose for a given activity and that smokers unconsciously modify their smoking patterns in an attempt to obtain this dose.

IMPLICATIONS

The available evidence presents a picture which is probably somewhat contradictory and which is certainly incomplete. Nevertheless, it is clear that nicotine in animals and nicotine and smoking in man can in certain circumstances facilitate performance, increase or decrease arousal, and combat the disruptive effects of aggression and stress on behaviour. In general, where smoking has been shown to affect mood and performance in man, the results of experiments correspond to what smokers themselves say about the reasons for, and effects of, smoking. The apparent usefulness of smoking as a psychological tool should therefore be taken into account in any comprehensive evaluation of the behaviour.

Acceptance of the psychological-tool model of smoking would have several implications for health education and smoking cessation techniques. First, the smoker might come to be seen not so much as an irrational addict, but as someone weighing genuine benefits (however small and short-lived) against the likelihood of serious long-term penalties. The second change in emphasis concerns the apparent importance of nicotine. If people smoke primarily for nicotine, it would be rational to pursue further the idea of maintaining the nicotine delivery of cigarettes whilst reducing that of tar and carbon monoxide, as has been suggested by Russell (1976a). Cigarettes delivering proportionately more nicotine, relative to tar, have been produced on an experimental basis, and commercially available cigarettes are also showing an 'improvement' in tar:nicotine ratio (Stepney 1979b). An attempt to provide nicotine from some source other than smoking may also be worthwhile. Nicotine chewing-gum and tablets have not met with great success, but the failure of existing tactics does not demonstrate that the general strategy is unreasonable. The American National Cancer Institute has recently expressed interest in the possibility of providing nicotine in the form of an aerosol spray and it is not inconceivable that the smoker's packet of cigarettes might one day be replaced by an inhaler. A recent report (Jacobson, Jacobson, and Phillip 1979) suggests that nicotine vapour inhaled from a 'non-combustible cigarette' could provide a practical alternative to the conventional product. Blood nicotine levels during normal smoking and during vapour inhalation were similar, and subjects reported themselves satisfied with this new method of nicotine administration. It has also been suggested (Russell, Jarvis, and Feyerabend 1980a) that nicotine obtained from snuff could provide an acceptable and safer substitute for the cigarette.

The idea of an alternative source of nicotine should not suggest that nicotine has a clean bill of health. It probably contributes to cardiovascular disease, and has recently been suggested as a co-carcinogen (Bock 1980). But if nicotine could be provided in an acceptable form without tar (implicated in respiratory disease) and without carbon monoxide (implicated in cardiovascular disease, and in damage to the foetus), the situation would surely be improved. With the possible exception of the Arabs' (far from wholehearted) abandonment of alcohol under the precepts of Islam, probably no society has ever voluntarily given up a widely-used psychotropic substance, and there is nothing in the history of prohibition to suggest it can unwillingly be made to do so. Any attempt to abolish smoking, without providing some alternative source of nicotine, would therefore be unlikely to succeed.

The third change of emphasis is that the question of why some people find it 'necessary' to smoke, while others do not, comes more to the fore. In response to this question there are two main views, one holding that differences in environment are crucial, the other, differences in constitution. If environmental factors are important, one would expect the habit to be of greatest use to those whose environment is most stressful. Some evidence that individuals subject to stress are more inclined to smoke has been reviewed in this chapter. Possibly, ways of counteracting environmental stress could be explored as a way of reducing smoking. A second approach is to examine more closely the constitutional view, which implies that smokers smoke because they are constitutionally different from non-smokers in ways that make the pharmacological effects of nicotine particularly valuable. In the next chapter constitutional differences between smokers and non-smokers, and their possible biological basis, are reviewed.

APPENDIX: THE SMOKING PATTERNS TEST

[The questionnaire is closely based on that developed by Russell, Peto, and Patel (1974). This particular version was supplied by Dr D. Taylor of Southampton University Psychology Department.]

Here are some statements about some of the reasons that people give for their smoking. Please indicate how much each statement applies to you by drawing a circle around the appropriate number.

Uncertain or not at all	0	Quite a bit	2
A little	1	Very much so	3

1	It is easier to talk and get on with other people when smoking.	0 1 2 3
2	I like smoking while I am busy and working hard.	0 1 2 3
3	Without a cigarette I don't know what to do with my hands.	0 1 2 3
4	I want to smoke most when I am comfortable and relaxed.	0 1 2 3
5	Part of the enjoyment of smoking comes from the steps I take to light up.	0 1 2 3
6	Smoking helps to keep me going when I'm tired.	0 1 2 3
7	I light up a cigarette whenever I talk on the telephone.	0 1 2 3
8	I think I look good with a cigarette.	0 1 2 3
9	I smoke more when I am unhappy.	0 1 2 3
10	I usually smoke a cigarette first thing in the morning.	0 1 2 3
11	I like a cigarette best when I am having a quiet rest.	0 1 2 3
12	I like to offer cigarettes as a way of making friends.	0 1 2 3
13	Part of the enjoyment of smoking is watching the smoke as I blow it out.	0 1 2 3
14	I often smoke without really enjoying it.	0 1 2 3
15	I smoke to keep my weight down.	0 1 2 3
16	I feel more attractive to the opposite sex when smoking.	0 1 2 3
17	I smoke automatically without even being aware of it.	0 1 2 3
18	I am very much aware of the fact when I am not smoking a cigarette.	0 1 2 3
19	I smoke more when I am worried about something.	0 1 2 3
20	I get a definite lift and feel more alert when smoking.	0 1 2 3
21	While smoking I feel more confident with other people.	0 1 2 3
22	After meals is the time I most enjoy smoking.	0 1 2 3
23	I smoke because I like the smell so much.	0 1 2 3
24	Smoking cheers me up.	0 1 2 3
25	When I have run out of cigarettes I find it almost unbearable until I can get them.	0 1 2 3
26	I light up a cigarette when I feel angry about something.	0 1 2 3
27	I light up a cigarette without realizing I already have one burning in the ashtray.	0 1 2 3
28	I feel I look more mature and sophisticated when smoking.	0 1 2 3
29	I usually only smoke when I have something to drink (tea, coffee, alcohol).	0 1 2 3
30	I smoke more when I am rushed and have lots to do.	0 1 2 3
31	Part of the enjoyment of smoking is having something to put in my mouth.	0 1 2 3
32	I am usually very careful not to run out of cigarettes.	0 1 2 3
33	I smoke to calm my nerves.	0 1 2 3
34	I find myself smoking without remembering lighting up.	0 1 2 3
35	Smoking helps me to think and concentrate.	0 1 2 3
36	I smoke much more when I am with other people.	0 1 2 3
37	Handling a cigarette is part of the enjoyment of smoking it.	0 1 2 3

38   I get a real gnawing hunger to smoke when I haven't
     smoked for a while.   0 1 2 3
39   I usually only smoke when I can really sit back and enjoy
     it.   0 1 2 3
40   I feel guilty about my smoking.   0 1 2 3

Please check that you have answered every item

If there is any other important reason for your smoking please write it down here:

The questions can be divided into seven categories: psycho-social (PS), sensory-motor (SM), indulgent (IN), sedative (SE), stimulant (ST), addictive (AD), and automatic (AU). Depending on their response, subjects score 0, 1, 2, or 3 for each of the questions included in each category; sum the scores to obtain an overall value for each category. The higher the score, the more important is the factor in terms of the individual's motivation to smoke. Since the number of questions included in each factor is not the same, the score on one factor is not always directly comparable with the score on another factor.

PS	1	8	12	16	21	28	36
SM	3	5	13	23	31	37	
IN	4	11	22	29	39		
SE	9	19	26	33			
ST	2	6	20	24	30	35	
AD	10	14	18	25	32	38	
AU	7	17	27	34			

Questions 15 and 40 are not related to any factor.

6 SMOKING AND PERSONALITY

Many environmental variables are related to smoking. Age, social class, occupation, work stress, and area of residence all have a clearly identifiable influence, and peer pressure is an important factor in starting the smoking habit (Chapters 1 and 3). However, smokers and non-smokers also differ significantly in certain characteristics known to have a genetic basis, such as body build, the ability to taste phenylthiourea, and possibly also blood group (Eysenck and Eaves 1980). These differences raise the question of how far genetic variables are related to smoking.

It has been known for some time from studies of twins (Fisher 1958; Friberg *et al.* 1959) that genetic identity increases the similarity of the smoking habit. Recently, Eysenck and Eaves (1980) have added to our knowledge in this area. In a study of over a thousand individuals, they confirmed earlier work on identical and non-identical twins. When classified into smokers and non-smokers, 74 per cent of identical twins, but only 50 per cent of non-identical twins, were found to have the same smoking status. Moreover, identical twins reared apart showed the same concordance in smoking habits as identical twins reared together, suggesting that genetic factors were a major determinant of smoking status. There was evidence too of an inherited factor influencing the amount smoked, the correlation for average reported cigarette consumption being greater for identical twins ($r = 0.52$) than for non-identical twins ($r = 0.30$).

This study also contributed new data on the genetics of smoking by correlating the smoking habits of family members of different degrees of relatedness, including the special case of foster-relationships. Eysenck and Eaves found, for example, a small but significant correlation ($r = 0.21$) between the cigarette consumption of parents and their natural children. In contrast, there was virtually no correlation between the smoking habits of foster children and their adoptive parents (r = −0.02), nor between those of foster children and siblings with whom they shared the same family environment but to whom they were not genetically related (r = 0.05). Thus inherited factors appear to play a part in determining who will smoke and how much they will smoke.

Smokers also differ from non-smokers in the way they behave. Matarazzo and Saslow (1960) found that smokers changed their jobs more frequently, married more often, were more likely to be divorced and also had more traffic accidents than non-smokers. Young smokers show lower academic achievement, more rebellion against authority, greater precocity in sexual behaviour, and drink more alcohol than non-smoking contemporaries (Mausner and Platt 1971; Russell 1971). Such behavioural differences, along with the pattern of statistical correlations in family studies, suggest that 'part of the genetic variation in the smoking habit is mediated through inherited differences which affect other more general aspects of behaviour, particularly individual differences in personality' (Eysenck and Eaves 1980: 283). Personality differences between smokers and non-smokers, and their possible relevance to the self-administration of nicotine by smoking, are discussed in this chapter.

EXTRAVERSION AND NEUROTICISM

In 1960, Eysenck *et al.* reported the results of a survey of smoking and personality commissioned by the UK Tobacco Manufacturers' Standing Committee. A sample of 2400 people was drawn from over 7000 initial contacts, covering light, medium, and heavy cigarette smokers, pipe smokers, ex-smokers, and non-smokers. (In other respects, however, the range of people studied was limited, the sample being drawn exclusively from males between the ages of 40 and 70.) Subjects were given a 31-item questionnaire covering the personality dimensions of Extraversion (Would you rate yourself a lively individual? Do you usually take the initiative in making new friends?, etc.) and Neuroticism (questions dealing with swings of mood and emotionality).

A positive correlation was found between smoking and extraversion. The average extraversion score increased as smoking became heavier (*Figure 26*): those smoking fewer than fifteen cigarettes a day had an average score of 7.13, and those smoking over twenty-four a day a score of 7.81. The most introverted group was formed by the

Figure 26 Extraversion scores in different groups of smokers and non smokers

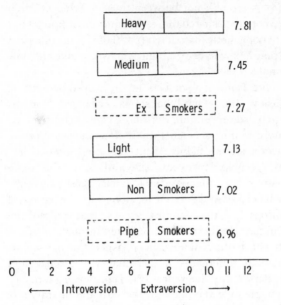

Each rectangle represents a range of scores covering approximately 70 per cent of the individuals within each group; the central line denotes the mean score of the group as a whole. Source: based on data published by Eysenck *et al.* (1960) and additional information contained in the April 1959 *Reports* by Mass-Observation Ltd.

pipe smokers (E = 6.96). Ex-smokers had an intermediate extraversion score of 7.27. However, although the average extraversion scores for the various smoking groups were reliably different, the size of the differences was extremely small. The large degree of overlap between the groups is represented schematically in *Figure 26*. Approximately 70 per cent of the individuals belonging to each group appear within the range of scores indicated by the length of each rectangle. It is apparent, for example, that there are a great many light smokers who are more extravert than the majority of heavy smokers. The between-group differences, although statistically significant, may therefore have little practical relevance. From the knowledge that a given individual has a particular extraversion score, one cannot predict with any degree of confidence whether or not he will be a smoker. Nevertheless, the fact remained that the *population* of smokers and non-smokers could be distinguished in terms of a particular aspect of personality.

Eysenck's study was one of the first to establish the positive association between smoking and extraversion, but it is by no means the only one. In the period 1956–70, twenty-five studies analysed this relationship, and all twenty-two which produced significant results pointed in the same direction. Smokers have been found to be more extravert than non-smokers in Britain, the United States and Australia, whether school students or adults and whether male or female (Smith 1970).

The unanimity of these findings contrasts with the conflicting conclusions resulting from the even larger number of studies which have considered the relationship between smoking and emotional stability (Smith 1970). Eysenck *et al.* (1960) found no evidence of a systematic relationship between smoking and neuroticism. Yet, typical of more recent work is the finding that current smokers scored higher on the free-floating and phobic anxiety scales of the Middlesex Hospital Questionnaire, and also showed evidence of hysterical personality traits (Haines, Imeson, and Meade 1980). Using a sample of American males (McRae, Costa and Bossé 1978), and a group of 200 Australian antenatal patients (Meares *et al.* 1971), a similar association was found between smoking and higher levels of anxiety and neuroticism. Nevertheless, many investigations have failed to confirm any such relationship. An association between smoking and lower emotional stability may exist amongst certain age groups or particular populations, but the existence of any more general link between smoking and emotionality is not proven.

The conclusion that extraversion and smoking are related poses a further question. Does a more extravert personality result in an individual taking up smoking, or is the greater extraversion itself the product of smoking? It is at least theoretically possible that smoking might lead to greater sociability, for example, and that greater social contact might result over a period of years in more extravert attitudes and patterns of behaviour.

In this context, the results of Cherry and Kiernan (1976) are of interest since they show that personality differences between smokers and non-smokers precede rather than follow the establishment of the cigarette habit. The UK National Survey of Health and Development has followed through childhood and into adult life a large group of people drawn from those born throughout Britain during a single week in March 1946. Nearly 3000 members of the study, who completed a personality questionnaire when they were sixteen, have subsequently (at ages twenty and twenty-five) been asked to provide details about their smoking habits. The likelihood that subjects had taken up smoking by the age of twenty-five was found to relate to both extraversion and neuroticism at the age of sixteen. The more extravert the individual, the more likely it was that he or she would become a smoker. The same applied to neuroticism; and those most likely to become smokers were those who had high scores on both dimensions. Since a proportion of the subjects who completed the questionnaire at age sixteen would already have started to smoke by that time, the conclusion that personality differences were present before smoking was established remained slightly uncertain until the data from those subjects who were not regular smokers by their seventeenth birthday were analysed separately. When this was done higher extraversion and neuroticism scores were still found to be predictive of subsequent smoking (*Figure 27*).

In addition to the major effects of personality on subsequent recruitment to smoking, certain relationships were established between extraversion and neuroticism and more detailed aspects of

Figure 27 Likelihood of becoming a smoker between the ages of 16 and 25, related to personality at age 16.

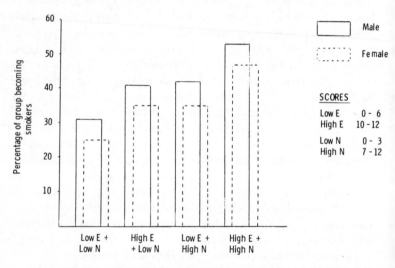

Values for subjects with intermediate E and N scores (not shown here) conform to the relationships indicated by the low and high scoring groups.

Source: fitted model based on observed proportions – see Cherry and Kiernan (1976: Table VIB).

smoking behaviour. Subjects were asked to rate their degree of inhalation as slight, moderate, or deep, and were also divided, on the basis of cigarette consumption, into three categories. For both men and women, the mean neuroticism score increased with depth of inhalation.

There is some doubt as to the accuracy with which smokers judge the extent of inhalation, and even as to the reliability of their estimates of cigarette consumption, not to mention the uncertainties which surround the measurement of personality. Nevertheless, on the basis of the association found between certain aspects of personality and smoking habits, it is tempting to speculate not only that certain personality types predispose to smoking, but also that different patterns of smoking may be related to different personality 'needs'. Thus the deep inhalation of the more neurotic smokers perhaps reflects their requirement for large sedative doses of nicotine.

The longitudinal study also provided evidence that personality variables were related to the likelihood of giving up smoking. Greater extraversion (and, in men, lower neuroticism) were predictive of greater success in quitting.

RISK-TAKING AND IMPULSIVITY

Williams (1973) investigated the relationship between smoking, risk-taking tendencies, and impulsivity in a sample of 400 American senior high school students. Smoking was positively associated with risk-taking in both boys and girls, and with impulsivity in boys. The method used to measure personality, as is usual, involved self-assessment. As with all such assessment, the question arises as to how accurately an individual perceives his or her own personality. Smokers may rate themselves as taking greater risks simply because such a self-image is attractive. Nevertheless, corroboration of sorts came from answers to a question about seat-belt usage – a simple risk-related piece of behaviour about which one might expect a reasonably honest report. Smokers were found to use seat belts significantly less than non-smokers. (This finding, incidentally, is supported by Eiser, Sutton, and Wober (1979) who found lower self-reported seat-belt use in a sample of 400 British smokers). In a similar exercise, patterns of drug use (including tobacco) were related by Kohn and Annis (1977) to a series of measures of 'desire for novelty'. The survey found that the proportion of smokers was greater among people with high scores on a scale measuring 'internal sensation-seeking' (indicating a liking for unusual fantasies, dreams and perceptual experiences) although there was apparently no relationship between smoking and the desire for externally-derived 'thrills'. However, Schubert (1965) had earlier found student smokers to be more thrill-seeking and less tolerant of routine than non-smokers; such a conclusion would be supported by the work of Coan (1973) who considered that, although there were no sharp differences between smokers and non-smokers, the former tended to be 'more liberal, more open to experience and more inclined to favor spontaneity' (Coan 1973: 86).

Eysenck and Eaves (1980) report that smokers are high on the personality dimension Psychoticism which reflects emotional coldness, egocentricity and hostility. The 'P' scale is a relatively recent introduction to Eysenck's stable of personality traits, and there are some doubts about its breeding. A large number of items used in the scale reflect the kind of risk-taking and impulsivity which might be considered characteristic of the extravert personality. Nevertheless, the association between smoking and high P scores is in agreement with previous findings.

Young smokers have generally been found to hold more non-conformist attitudes than non-smokers and to admit to more minor classroom misbehaviour and even potentially delinquent acts. However, the problems involved in interpreting such results were revealed by a recent study (Powell, Stewart, and Grylls 1979) which showed that smokers scored lower on a personality dimension (the 'lie scale') measuring the amount of socially-acceptable responding to a questionnaire. The investigators commented that the smokers were not preoccupied with presenting a good image of themselves. The *New Scientist*, however, used the data in the survey to conclude that smoking should not be considered in isolation since 'it appeared to be just one facet of a delinquent personality' (*New Scientist*, 28 February 1980: 655). An equally appropriate conclusion would have been that smokers were more honest than non-smokers, since there was no way of distinguishing whether the association between smoking and unfavourable personality traits had been due to dishonest concealment on the part of delinquent non-smokers or to the honest admissions of the smokers.

PERSONALITY AND SMOKING-RELATED DISEASE

The finding that smokers and non-smokers differ to a measurable extent in certain genetically-based characteristics, including personality, is relevant to the subject of smoking-related diseases. A full discussion of smoking and health is beyond the scope of this book (although certain actions of various smoke constituents on the body are described in Chapter 9). Here, the association between certain diseases and constitutional and personality factors will be briefly touched on; a fuller account has been mentioned already (Eysenck and Eaves 1980).

The statistical association between smoking and diseases such as lung cancer could arise because smoking is an aggravating factor or a cause of such diseases; this is a conclusion which is widely accepted. However, many people, not exclusively in the tobacco industry, have argued against this view (e.g. Fisher 1958; Burch 1974; Eysenck 1965). A correlation between smoking and disease does not itself prove a causal connection. It remains possible that other variables, present more frequently or more strongly in smokers than in non-smokers, underlie both the smoking and the disease.

Two such possibilities are discussed by Eysenck and Eaves (1980). The first is that people who are genetically predisposed to smoke are also genetically predisposed to certain diseases; the second, that people who are prone to smoke differ from non-smokers also in life-style (or 'rate of living') so that at any chronological age they are biologically older, and therefore more at risk. Both possibilities suggest that there may be differences, other than smoking habit, between people who suffer from certain diseases and those who do not. Evidence for differences in genetically-based characteristics (including personality dimensions, which have a constitutional basis and are obviously relevant to life-style) has therefore been sought.

With respect to lung cancer, there is some evidence of an inherited susceptibility to the disease. Eysenck and Eaves cite the work of Tokuhata, who investigated the first-degree relatives of 270 lung cancer patients and 270 matched controls. Lung cancer deaths among non-smoking first-degree relatives of the cancer patients were nearly four times as many as amongst the relatives of the controls, whilst there was no excess of deaths among the spouses of the cancer victims. The increased risk of cancer was therefore attributed to genetic relatedness rather than similarity of environment. The idea that personality may predispose to cancer is also not without support (Le Shan 1959). Coppen and Metcalfe (1963) reported that women with breast cancer had significantly higher extraversion scores than an age-matched group of patients without malignant disease, whilst Kissen and Eysenck (1962) found lower levels of neuroticism when they compared the scores of 116 male lung cancer patients with those of 123 hospitalized controls with no evidence of cancer.

There is also evidence of a genetic element in certain cardio-vascular diseases. This is illustrated by the work of DeFaire (1974, cited in Eysenck and Eaves 1980) who studied 197 same-sexed twin pairs. When one twin died of ischaemic heart disease, the health of the other member of the pair was investigated. In identical twins, 94 per cent of the survivors also showed evidence of ischaemic heart disease, but in non-identical twins only 74 per cent. There is also evidence that the prevalence of this type of heart disease is greater in people who have particular personality traits and patterns of behaviour, even when all other risk factors have been taken into account. Thus Rosenman (1979) reports that the 'Type A' person who is character-ized as ambitious, aggressive, competitive, hard driving, and goal directed, is particularly prone to coronary artery disease. Although the association has yet to be demonstrated, one might expect a person so described to be a smoker, and probably also someone of rather extravert personality.

The statistical association between smoking and disease may thus be the result of a complex interaction in which the contributions of smoking, personality, and genetic make-up are difficult to disentangle (*Figure 28*). This is especially true of cardiovascular disorders, where the association with smoking is only one of many factors correlated with occurrence of the disease. In the case of lung cancer, the alternative to the view that smoking is a direct cause of the disease is less plausible. Although smoking is neither a necessary nor a sufficient condition for lung cancer to occur, only around 10 per cent of lung cancer patients are non-smokers. It would be difficult to imagine any genetic or environmental cause – other than smoking

Figure 28 Possible factors in smoking-related disease

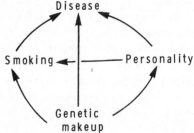

itself – which selected smokers with this degree of specificity. Further, the organ affected is the organ exposed to smoke, and we know that certain substances found in condensed smoke cause cancer when applied to animal tissue. It is highly likely that similar processes operate in the case of inhaled smoke and the human lung.

PERSONALITY AND NICOTINE EFFECTS

The effect of any psychotropic drug depends on many factors, including the situation in which the drug is administered and the personality of the user. As Claridge has written, 'A drug is just like any other stimulus applied to the organism, its purely pharmacological action interacting with the many other influences that are affecting behaviour at the same time' (Claridge 1970: 124).

These interactions are varied and complex. For example, the drug user's expectations are important. Thus subjects led to believe there will be a sedative effect may experience greater sleepiness after taking a placebo than after 200 mg pentobarbitone (Frankenhaeuser *et al.* 1964). Situational factors also play a role. Certain doses of amphetamine increase activity when mice are in a group but have no detectable effect on a single animal. Similarly, in man, a psychotropic drug often has less effect on behaviour when an individual is in the company of people who are not experiencing the same drug than when in a group of drug users (Claridge 1970). With respect to personality, emotionality and extraversion may interact in complicated ways in determining the action of a drug. Thus Claridge (1970) cites an experiment showing that subjects most susceptible to the effects of the depressant nitrous oxide are those with high scores on both extraversion and neuroticism. As a further example, McPeake and DiMascio (1965) found that the learning ability of anxious introverts was improved, whilst that of non-anxious extraverts was impaired by the neuroleptics chlorpromazine and trifluoroperazine.

Evidence that the effects of nicotine vary according to dose, situation, and personality has already been presented in Chapter 5. The mechanisms which may underlie these complicated interactions will now be considered, although it must be admitted that whilst certain personality characteristics can be described and measured, their basis is ill understood.

Eysenck has suggested that the biological difference between extraverts and introverts lies in their respective levels of cortical arousal:

'Under identical conditions of low sensory input and low autonomic involvement, extraverts will be characterised by low cortical arousal, introverts by high cortical arousal' (Eysenck 1973: 117). In line with this proposal, the EEGs of introverts are characterized by higher alpha frequencies and lower amplitudes, while those of extraverts tend to show the lower alpha frequencies and higher amplitudes associated with states of low arousal. Extraverts have poorer vigilance performance than introverts, habituate more quickly to repeated stimuli, and under some conditions are less susceptible to conditioning. Introverts and extraverts respond differently to stimulant and depressant drugs in line with the prediction.

Eysenck further proposed that differences in cortical arousal reflected differences in the intrinsic level of activity in the reticular activating system, which was thought to be highly active in introverts and less so in extraverts. Since it is not yet possible to correlate direct measurement of reticular activity with personality in man, this proposal remains hypothetical. Moreover, as discussed in Chapter 5, cortical arousal is now thought to depend on ascending activity in both the reticular and limbic arousal systems. These systems are connected by mutually inhibitory links, and a modification of Eysenck's hypothesis has been suggested by Gray (1970) who includes as a biological basis for introversion the activity of an inhibitory feedback loop comprising the reticular activating system, frontal cortex and two limbic structures, the medial septal area, and the hippocampus. An increase in reticular activating system activity is held to initiate inhibitory influences of three kinds through this loop: (1) on the reticular activating system itself, (2) on behavioural acts leading to punishment or frustrative non-reward, and (3) on sensory inputs. There is much experimental evidence for such a circuit in the brain of many animals (Isaacson and Pribram 1975). Gray suggests that the introvert has high reticular activity but also high inhibitory limbic activity. Among other things, this model helps to explain the greater susceptibility of the introvert to conditioning, which is envisaged as the result of his greater sensitivity to punishment. It is interesting from the point of view of nicotine actions that this model closely involves limbic punishment systems, and also that the inhibition of sensory input is part of the selective attention mechanism.

Eysenck (1973) suggested that the biological basis for neuroticism was the degree of autonomic activation, controlled by the limbic system. It was suggested that activity in this system was high in individuals with high neuroticism scores, giving them high drive and emotionality, and low in more stable individuals, who were correspondingly less emotional. Gray (1970) conceived of neuroticism as depending on the sensitivity of both reward and punishment systems. Subjects with high neuroticism scores were held to have greater sensitivity in both systems than those with low neuroticism scores. On the basis of sensitivity to reward and punishment, the relation between introversion and extraversion, neuroticism and stability (as envisaged by Gray) is illustrated in *Figure 29*. If nicotine, as discussed in Chapter 3, can in small doses stimulate pleasure systems and in larger doses inhibit punishment systems, the evidence that both extraverts and some neurotics tend to be smokers fits in with this scheme.

Present knowledge allows only fumbling attempts at explaining personality dimensions in physiological terms; a fuller explanation will have to await a clearer understanding of brain functions. The *psychological tool* model of smoking views nicotine as acting largely on arousal systems, while the *addiction model* attributes its effects mainly to its action on pleasure and punishment systems. It is interesting that research completely unrelated to nicotine has centred on the same systems as the biological bases of personality. Bearing in mind the biphasic actions of nicotine on these systems, one would expect it to be rewarding over the whole personality range.

For extraverts, who tend to be under-aroused under non-exacting conditions, the stimulant effects of nicotine would be of greatest value. The greater an individual's extraversion, the more frequently will prevailing environmental conditions be insufficiently stimulating to produce optimal arousal. This could account for the systematic association between greater extraversion and higher levels of cigarette consumption. The relatively high sensitivity of reward systems compared to punishment systems (*Figure 29*) would give extraverts the added motive of smoking for the stimulant effects of nicotine on reward systems. The possibility that extraverts derive two benefits from nicotine might explain why there is a slight preponderance of extraverts among smokers.

For introverts, who are relatively over-aroused under many conditions, the depressant effects of nicotine would be expected to be of greater value. This would require them to take slightly larger doses of nicotine, and evidence has been cited (Ashton *et al.* 1974) that they do so when allowed to smoke naturally. However, the effect of the same dose of nicotine appears to be opposite in introverts and

Figure 29 The relationship between personality and susceptibility to reward and punishment

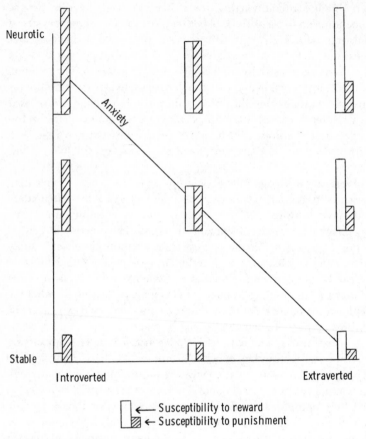

Source: Gray (1970: 263). Reproduced by permission of Pergamon Press Ltd.

extraverts. Eysenck and O'Connor (1979) showed that similar doses of nicotine, obtained from paced smoking, produced stimulant effects on the CNV (increased arousal) in extraverts and depressant effects (decreased arousal) in introverts. The depressant effects in introverts could have been due to stimulation of the inhibitory feedback loop which Gray has suggested is more active in introverts. According to Gray's ideas, introverts would have less reason than extraverts to smoke for stimulant effects on their reward systems because these are relatively insensitive; hence rather fewer introverts would be expected amongst smokers.

In the case of neuroticism, introverted neurotics would be expected to smoke for large depressant doses of nicotine to counteract excessive limbic activity and high sensitivity to punishment. Warburton and Wesnes (1978) found that nicotine improved the performance of neurotic subjects in a vigilance task, and there was also an indication that the more neurotic took larger doses. The relation of neuroticism to deeper reported cigarette inhalation, found by Cherry and Kiernan (1976), has already been noted. Stable subjects, with balanced sensitivity to punishment and reward, would appear to be the least likely to find nicotine rewarding, especially if they are in the middle range of the extraversion scale, and the ability to give up smoking appears to be positively associated with low neuroticism scores (Cherry and Kiernan 1976). It is likely that extraversion and neuroticism interact in determining the effects of nicotine as they do with other drugs.

It is difficult to suggest in physiological terms why smoking is apparently attractive to subjects with high Psychoticism scores. One of the hallmarks of schizophrenia, which can be reproduced in normal subjects by hallucinogenic drugs (such as LSD and cannabis) and amphetamine, is a defect of selective attention, possibly due to hippocampal dysfunction (Paton, Pertwee, and Tylden 1973; Miller 1979; Douglas 1975). Nicotine can improve selective attention, and one benefit of smoking in subjects with high Psychoticism scores may be an improvement in certain types of performance. It is likely also that the smoking of these subjects partly reflects non-pharmacological motives such as the expression of risk-taking tendencies, impulsivity, and non-conformist behaviour.

There may well be other as yet uncharted personality dimensions and undiscovered brain mechanisms upon which nicotine may act. Despite these uncertainties and complexities, the literature on smoking and personality justifies two conclusions relevant to smoking motivation. First, there is evidence that the effects of nicotine vary according to the personality (and situation) of the smoker. Secondly, there are small but statistically reliable personality differences between the population of smokers and the population of non-smokers. There is also evidence of an association, amongst smokers, between personality and the number of cigarettes smoked. These relationships have been demonstrated in the case of extraversion, and differences in smoking behaviour possibly also reflect other aspects of personality such as emotionality and psychoticism. However, the relationships between smoking and personality are complex and the population of smokers is extremely heterogeneous and little different from that of non-smokers. Nevertheless, the manifold effects of nicotine on brain and behaviour, and the interaction of these with individual differences, suggest that many smokers, in their own way, are engaged in manipulating their psychological state through the effects of smoking on arousal and reward and punishment systems.

7 INDIVIDUAL AND SOCIAL ATTITUDES TOWARDS SMOKING

There can be few smokers in the modern world who have not been exposed to information concerning the relationship between smoking, death, and disease. For nearly ten years there have been government health warnings on all packets of cigarettes sold in the UK and USA, and health education campaigns in the press and on television have been extensive, if not particularly effective in altering behaviour. Moreover, the majority of smokers appear to accept the evidence that smoking is hazardous to health. As early as 1963 Horn found that in the USA 50 per cent of smokers agreed cigarettes were responsible for lung cancer (with only 29 per cent rejecting smoking as a likely cause), whilst Pervin and Yatko (1965) reported that smokers knew as much as non-smokers about the relationship between smoking and cancer. In a survey conducted in the UK by National Opinion Polls in 1978, 66 per cent of smokers thought that smoking could help cause lung cancer. In the case of bronchitis and heart disease, the figures were 72 per cent and 52 per cent respectively (Russell and Feyerabend 1980). With regard to all three diseases, the proportion of smokers agreeing to the causal link was not greatly different from that of non-smokers. Given that smokers are currently aware of the relationship between smoking and ill-health, and that they have been aware of the relationship for many years, why are so many still smoking? We can attempt to explain continued smoking in the face of the evidence by reference to the concept of addiction, or in terms of the usefulness of nicotine in manipulating psychological state. But how does the smoker himself rationalize his behaviour? What are the processes involved?

COGNITIVE DISSONANCE

The concepts of cognitive consonance and dissonance emerged in the social psychology of the late 1950s as part of a larger attempt at understanding attitude formation and change and the relationship between attitudes and behaviour. The underlying idea was that people desire consistency amongst their attitudes and between their attitudes and their behaviour. Where inconsistency (dissonance) exists, the pressure for change should exist also.

In his book on cognitive dissonance, Festinger himself used the smoker as an example:

> 'let us now examine how dissonance may be reduced, using as an illustration the example of the habitual cigarette smoker who has learned that smoking is bad for his health. This knowledge is certainly dissonant with cognition that he continues to smoke. If the hypothesis that there will be pressures to reduce this dissonance is correct, what would the person involved be expected to do?
>
> 1. He might simply change his cognition about his behaviour by changing his actions; that is, he might stop smoking. If he no longer smokes, then his cognition of what he does will be consonant with the knowledge that smoking is bad for his health.
> 2. He might change his 'knowledge' about the effect of smoking. This sounds like a peculiar way to put it, but it expresses well what must happen. He might simply end up believing that smoking does not have any deleterious effects, or he might acquire so much 'knowledge' pointing to the good effects it has that the harmful aspects become negligible. If he can manage to change his knowledge in either of these ways, he will have reduced, or even eliminated, the dissonance between what he does, and what he knows.'
>
> (Festinger 1957: 5)

Not surprisingly, Festinger's use of this illustration has borne fruit in a number of experimental studies – conducted by those concerned with smoking and by those interested in the phenomenon of dissonance itself. Is there evidence that smokers actually employ any of the techniques which Festinger lists?

Although straightforward non-acceptance of the medical evidence linking smoking with disease is relatively rare, there is evidence of more subtle forms of denial. In a study conducted by Spelman and Ley (1966), smokers and non-smokers were asked to complete a multiple-choice questionnaire on the causes, symptoms, treatment, and prognosis of ten common diseases, including lung cancer. The smokers and non-smokers did not differ in their general medical knowledge of causes and symptoms and, with nine of the ten diseases, there was no difference either in their estimates of prognosis. However, with respect to lung cancer, heavy smokers (fifteen or more cigarettes per day) underestimated the poor prognosis for the disease.

Sixty per cent of the non-smokers and light smokers chose the answer giving the correct prognosis ('usually die within 2–3 years of cancer being diagnosed'), whilst only 35 per cent of heavy smokers did so. Thus even if the smokers correctly perceived their increased risk of contracting the disease, they were over-sanguine about their chances of survival.

Eiser, Sutton, and Wober (1979) have also reported findings which suggest that, although smokers broadly accept the health evidence, they differ from non-smokers in the detailed evaluation of the risks involved. Whilst 90 per cent of non-smokers believed that smoking was 'really as dangerous as they say' only 50 per cent of smokers agreed with this statement. Thirty per cent of non-smokers realized that smoking caused more deaths than road accidents, but only 14 per cent of smokers. Again, taking sex, age, and social class into account, smokers were less enthusiastic about anti-smoking campaigns, more assertive of the individual's right to put his own health at risk, and more likely to question the benefits of giving up.

There is therefore some reason to believe that smokers reduce dissonance by only qualified acceptance of the evidence linking smoking with disease. Another possible strategy listed by Festinger was the subjective enhancement of the value of smoking so as to balance its negative associations. There is clear evidence that smokers do place greater emphasis on the possibly compensatory benefits of smoking. In a series of experiments carried out on American college students by Mausner and Platt (1971), both smokers and non-smokers were asked to rate how much they valued certain 'outcomes' – such as being nervous, getting lung cancer, living longer, concentrating well, and getting along with friends. They were also asked to say how likely they thought it was that starting to smoke, continuing to smoke, or giving up smoking, would contribute to achieving these outcomes. Combining an individual's 'value' score with his 'expectancy' rating gave a measure of the usefulness to the individual (or 'subjective expected utility') of smoking or non-smoking.

The patterns of subjective utilities were broadly consistent with the reasons smokers gave for smoking. Thus subjects who smoked to relieve tension, for example, believed that stopping smoking would produce difficulties in tension-reduction. Differences in the subjective utility of continued smoking were also consistent with existing smoking status. Compared to non-smokers, smokers both valued the psychological effects of smoking more highly and had a greater expectation that smoking would achieve these effects. Smokers therefore had greater faith than non-smokers in the usefulness of continued smoking. However, inconsistent with their current status (but consistent with the widespread knowledge of the effects of cigarettes) was the fact that even the smokers rated giving up smoking more highly than continuing to smoke. The pressure for change therefore remained – despite the high value placed on the habit.

Questioning smokers shows that they are generally aware of the health risks. It would nevertheless make sense, in terms of dissonance reduction, if they tended where possible to avoid exposure to that information. Brock (1965) gave a group of smokers the opportunity to do this, and compared their response with that of a similar group of non-smokers. Subjects were asked to rank the titles of a series of magazine articles in the order in which they would be interested in reading them. There were two relevant titles in the list of thirteen. One read 'Smoking Leads to Lung Cancer', the other 'Smoking Does Not Lead to Lung Cancer'. In one condition subjects expected that they would actually have to read the articles; in the other condition they did not.

The experiment showed two things. When smokers expected that they would have to read the articles, they showed greater interest in the denial of the cancer link than in its assertion; that is, they expressed a preference for exposure to the material which might decrease dissonance. However, the smokers did not avoid exposure to the dissonance-increasing message, showing roughly the same level of interest in it as the non-smokers. In a second experiment, subjects were required to listen to a series of tape-recorded messages which were partially masked by static (Brock and Balloun 1967). They were asked to evaluate the sincerity and persuasiveness of the various talks, which they were told had been recorded on a small portable machine which was unfortunately liable to considerable electrical interference. By pressing a button, subjects were able momentarily to remove the offending static, and the amount of static removed was taken as a measure of the subjects' interest in the talks. Smokers were found to remove more static than non-smokers from a tape disputing the smoking-cancer link, and to remove less static than non-smokers from a message affirming the association. Amongst male subjects, the heavier cigarette smokers were less inclined than the lighter smokers to remove interference from the cancer message. The evidence therefore suggested that smokers, even if they were prepared to be exposed to disconcerting information, were not necessarily willing to attend conscientiously to it.

ATTITUDES TOWARDS ADDICTION

Although smokers will generally assent to the view that smoking is dangerous, there is evidence that subtle dissonance-reducing processes are at work. These fall short of outright denial of the link between smoking and ill health, but include misperception of the relative risks of smoking and of the prognosis for smoking-related disease. There is also evidence that smokers employ various strategies – such as attending more to information disputing the association with disease, and less to the anti-smoking message – which would diminish the impact of the health-education information they receive.

Another way of reconciling an inconsistency between beliefs and behaviour is to deny that the behaviour is engaged in of one's free will. In the case of the smoker, continuing the habit can be attributed to addiction, over which one has no control. The 'addict' is then absolved from responsibility for trying to give up.

In a survey of attitudes towards smoking to determine how readily people would describe smokers as cigarette addicts, the authors of the study noted that it would be surprising if the description – with all its 'junkie' connotations – was thought appropriate for people who participated in a 'lawful, economically legitimized and vastly popular activity like smoking' (Eiser, Sutton, and Wober 1977: 329). Nevertheless, 80 per cent of non-smokers thought smokers *were* addicted to cigarettes, and 50 per cent of smokers themselves agreed. This finding is interesting in its own right, but is also important in relation to attitudes towards giving up. The survey showed that people who labelled smokers as addicts considered smoking more difficult to give up than those who did not think this description was justified. This seems reasonable since it is part of the common conception of the addict that he should not be able easily to forsake the substance on which he has become 'hooked'. Amongst smokers themselves, those in the process of cutting down or giving up considered themselves less addicted than those not trying to control their habit. Of course, the views of smokers not currently giving up may have been based on previous unsuccessful attempts to quit, in which case their self-attribution of addiction might seem reasonable. However, the possibility that their lack of effort at giving up stemmed from their view of smoking as an irreversible addiction cannot be excluded. The close association between the concept of addiction and that of difficulty in giving up a habit therefore creates a problem for those who are concerned with reducing the prevalence of smoking.

It could be argued that the tendency for some medical authorities to label the use of cigarettes as an addiction may do a disservice to the smoker in a variety of ways. First, people who wish to give up smoking may be discouraged from the attempt by the apparent enormity of the task and their slim chance of success. In *The Guardian*, Russell wrote: 'Once a smoker – always a smoker. This is only a slight exaggeration. It is unlikely that more than one in four smokers succeeds in giving it up for good before the age of sixty' (Russell 1977). Although true, and perhaps designed to discourage people from starting the habit, such a statement is unlikely to help motivate smokers to give it up, especially since the smoker may find it an advantage to cast himself in the 'quasi-sick' role of addict (Lehrer 1978). According to Bernstein and McAlister (1976), expectation of success influences the outcome of attempts to quit. Encouraging smokers to believe that their likelihood of stopping is small may therefore tend to reduce the chances of those who make the attempt.

A second unfortunate consequence of the emphasis on addiction is that attention is drawn to the symptoms of withdrawal – making them seem inevitable and severe when the evidence suggests this is not always so. Many smokers have an unpleasant time when attempting to give up, and this should not be denied. However, emphasizing the withdrawal syndrome may encourage recent ex-smokers to look for symptoms, or lead them to exaggerate the ones they find. Moreover, the possibility of interpreting what is happening as evidence of withdrawal may tend to confirm the smoker's view of himself as an addict and legitimize abandoning what seems an unequal struggle.

Equating cigarette smoking with the use of addictive drugs like the opiates also has the disadvantage of making eventual dependence seem inevitable, even when viewed from the early stages of the habit. Russell, in interpreting the results of an earlier study, makes the somewhat startling claim that 'it requires no more than three or four casual cigarettes during adolescence virtually to ensure that a person will eventually become a regular dependent smoker. Only about 15 per cent of those who have more than *one cigarette* [my italics] avoid becoming regular smokers' (Russell 1971: 3). In the *Guardian* article we find the statement 'Not with alcohol, cannabis and possibly even heroin is the addiction so easily acquired.' Again the non-smoker is presumably being warned about the great dangers of ever getting at all involved with cigarettes, but the impact of the warning is enhanced perhaps at the cost of making those who have just started smoking believe that they can neither quit the habit nor prevent its inevitable escalation. In fact there are probably many people who experiment with smoking but do not become confirmed in the habit. Bewley *et al.* (1980) report that 70 per cent of fourteen to fifteen-year-old schoolchildren had tried smoking, yet only 25 per cent were smoking one or more cigarettes per week. Assuming the schoolchildren of the mid 1970s follow the pattern of previous generations, the proportion becoming regular smokers as adults will be far less than the proportion who experimented with smoking as teenagers.

The number of people able to smoke occasionally or intermittently has been put at only 2 per cent of adult smokers, a figure based on McKennell and Thomas's 1967 government survey of smoking habits (Russell 1971). However, a recent study of 1500 smokers attending the surgeries of twenty-eight London general practitioners suggested that this figure was an under-estimate (Russell *et al.* 1980b). Five per cent of men and 7 per cent of women smokers said they smoked on fewer than three days a week, and around 15 per cent claimed they did not smoke every day. The latest General Household Survey does not include data on the regularity of smoking, but provides information on consumption (Office of Population Censuses and Surveys 1980). A quarter of current smokers claimed they averaged fewer than ten cigarettes a day, whilst 62 per cent of women smokers and 48 per cent of men claimed to smoke fewer than twenty. Although smokers tend to under-report their consumption, these figures are probably not too inaccurate since data collected for the Tobacco Advisory Council, which are adjusted so that the total consumption claimed corresponds to the known sales of cigarettes, show that smokers in 1979 consumed an average of 19 cigarettes per day (Research Services Limited, personal communication). Russell *et al.* (1980b) suggest that pharmacological factors (presumably nicotine addiction) become predominant when consumption reaches roughly twenty cigarettes a day. It is then that regular dependent smoking becomes 'virtually inevitable'. By this criterion, therefore (and even allowing for under-reporting), the majority of current smokers do not fall into this category, and the rationale for labelling them as addicts is not convincing.

General opinion may perhaps be pessimistic about the smoker's ability to control this habit. Nevertheless, it is a disturbing fact that the majority of smokers apparently report that they want to give up, have tried, and have failed. In the 1978 National Opinion Poll survey, 59 per cent of current smokers said that they would like to give up smoking and 70 per cent said that they had actually tried – obviously unsuccessfully – to stop. The view that smoking is not really all that difficult to give up can account for these findings only by questioning the sincerity of those who claim actually to have tried. Interestingly, there is some evidence that 'trying' may not always represent a serious attempt. Kozlowski, Herman, and Frecker draw attention to the difference between what smokers say and what they actually do, and suggest that many smokers who claim to have tried to quit may not in fact have tried very hard. 'How better for a smoker to avoid the pesterings of a physician or other interviewer than to say (whether believing it or not) that he wants to and has even tried to give up cigarettes? And if the questioner asks if attempts to stop have been serious, who would want to confess to a half-hearted effort?' (Kozlowski, Herman, and Frecker 1980: 699). In a questionnaire study which involved more than 1500 current cigarette smokers (Russell 1978a), respondents were categorized according to whether they were high or low on dependence, and high or low on motivation to quit. On the basis of this classification, Russell divided his sample into 'consonant' and 'dissonant' smokers. Perhaps surprisingly, 67 per cent of the sample appeared in the consonant category composed of people (high or low on dependence) who were considered as having a low motivation to give up. Kozlowski's argument therefore seems to be largely supported by Russell's evidence, although the latter author came to substantially different conclusions. The importance of establishing how serious is the desire (and intention) to give up is shown by comparing the response to two slightly different questions. Although 69 per cent of Russell's sample said they would like to give up if they could do so easily, only half that number (35 per cent) wanted to give up 'quite strongly or very strongly'.

If the evidence of really wanting something is actually trying to get it, then perhaps relatively few really want to stop. In a study (cited by Kozlowski, Herman, and Frecker 1980) of parents of Philadelphia schoolchildren, nearly 5000 (out of 12,000) current smokers said they would be interested in stopping smoking if a clinic were arranged. Yet only 257 people attended an initial meeting and only 150 actually made use of the clinic. A further example is given by Jaffe (1978). Representatives of the New York State Psychiatric Institute arranged for an organization to conduct an anti-smoking clinic at work, in working time. Half of the 204 smokers contacted said they would like to stop smoking, but only 4 per cent attended the clinic. A similar experience is reported by Lehrer (1978). Of 42,000 people who wrote to the Israeli Ministry of Health for a booklet on stopping smoking, only 400 subsequently attended anti-smoking clinics. Moreover, those who did attend were something of a 'hard core'. Almost all smoked in excess of twenty cigarettes per day, and two-thirds said it would be very difficult to quit. This evidence agrees with that of Russell, Peto, and Patel (1974) who compared the pattern of smoking motivation in a group of 100 people attending a clinic with that found amongst 'normal' smokers. Although scores on stimulation, indulgent, and psychosocial factors did not distinguish the two groups, the clinic sample scored significantly higher on the factors indicating addictive, sedative, and habitual smoking. With cigarettes (as with heroin and alcohol) users seeking professional assistance represent a self-selected and atypical sample of the total population. Conclusions based on the experiences of those attending smoking clinics may therefore misrepresent the difficulties faced by the average smoker.

Even though smokers seem generally disinclined to seek professional help (and those who do are often unsuccessful), large numbers of those who do wish to stop have succeeded in doing so (Premack 1970). In the UK Government's 1978 General Household Survey, 27 per cent of the adult males interviewed claimed to be ex-smokers, and 14 per cent of adult females. Assuming their replies were honest, and the sample representative of the wider population, this would mean that roughly eight million people had broken the cigarette habit (Ball 1980). In the United States, it is estimated that one million people successfully give up smoking each year (Bernstein and McAlister 1976; Horn 1978), and that there are currently more than thirty million ex-smokers (Surgeon General 1979; World Health Organisation 1979). We do not know precisely how many of the ex-smokers attended one or other of the many kinds of anti-smoking clinic, nor what aids, if any, were used – but the aspiring non-smoker who is not content with 'willpower' alone has a great number from which to choose. The variety of smoking cessation techniques are considered in the next chapter. We now turn, however, from consideration of individual attitudes to smoking to the wider response of government and society.

THE ATTITUDE OF SOCIETY AND GOVERNMENT

'Those very people who once received you in an office solid with cigarette smoke, who smoked cigars over your dinner, who blew pipe smoke at you in the elevator, are beginning to be embarrassed by their habits'

(Mahler 1980: 11).

The individual has a responsibility for his own behaviour, but what attitude towards smoking should we have as a society? In particular, should the government play a role in disseminating information, discouraging smoking by legislation, and perhaps even in compelling abstinence? To mark World Health Day in 1980, the *British Medical Journal* conducted an editorial onslaught on government inaction and 'irresponsibility' which, it was argued, had failed to prevent a 'holocaust' in which between one-and-a-half and three million Britons had died unnecessarily. The article went on: 'Britain suffers more than almost any other country from smoking-related disease and her Government has no excuse for allowing this to continue' (*BMJ* 1980: 959). Sir George Young, a junior health minister in the UK Government, showed himself aware of the changing responsibilities of the politician when he addressed the Fourth World Conference on Smoking and Health: 'The traditional role of politicians has been to prevent an individual causing harm to another, but to allow him to do harm to himself. However, as modern society has made us all more interdependent, this attitude is now changing' (Young 1980: 123).

There is a school of thought which draws an analogy between drug abuse and epidemic disease (Bejerot and Bejerot 1978). On this view, drug abuse is transmissible and, once widespread, extremely difficult to eradicate. It can best be tackled not only by an attempt to 'cure' those who already have the 'disease' (which may be very difficult), but by a comprehensive strategy aimed – in traditional public health terms – at the susceptible individual, the environment, and the agent. With cigarette smoking, the three aims of the strategy can be seen as involving the education of the young non-smoker (so that he is resistant to 'infection'), changing governmental policy and social attitudes (so that the climate is one in which smoking will not thrive), and reducing the 'virulence' of smoking by making cigarettes less harmful.

It is in this context that the attitude of society and the actions of government are seen as important. It is also against this background that any progress, however slow, is seen as highly significant. Although the time-scale for such a population change should not be underestimated, once the spread of an epidemic is halted, its decline is often rapid. There are two encouraging signs. One is that smoking has been greatly reduced in social classes I and II. If it is true that what social classes I and II do today, the rest of the population does tomorrow, then an equivalent reduction in smoking prevalence in the bulk of the population may yet occur. The other encouragement comes from experience in Scandinavian countries in which governments have embarked on comprehensive anti-smoking programmes. There the proportion of the population smoking has been markedly reduced, especially amongst the young, to the extent that a 'non-smoking generation' is now conceivable (Bjartveit 1981). If the great majority of young people were to refrain from starting to smoke, the immediate impact on smoking prevalence would not be great, but the long-term consequences enormous.

What are the options open to government, and what are the limits to its action in a free society? There are several means by which the government can attempt to influence the prevalence of cigarette smoking. These include:

1   Raising tobacco duty, so increasing the price.
2   Legislating to limit the public areas in which it is permissible to smoke.
3   Restricting or forbidding the advertising and promotion of tobacco products.
4   Engaging in 'negative advertising' by spreading the arguments against smoking, requiring health warnings on cigarette packets, etc.
5   Helping smokers give up by increasing the provision of smoking withdrawal clinics and subsidizing anti-smoking aids.

All of of these approaches have been tried – at various times, and in a variety of countries – though often rather half-heartedly, and none has proven especially effective. However, the problem of assessing the extent to which each measure contributes to changes in smoking behaviour is difficult, since the factors never operate in isolation, and critics of existing policy can always fall back on the argument that government action has rarely been decisive or comprehensive enough to provide a fair test of the strategy.

Price

At present over half the price of a packet of UK cigarettes is tobacco tax. When VAT is taken into account, the proportion of the cost taken by the government is nearer two-thirds. The price of smoking may seem high, but in fact the cost of cigarettes has risen less fast than that of other goods and in real terms cigarettes are now 20 per cent cheaper than they were in the 1960s (*Which?* 1980).

There is evidence to suggest that price factors have had a great influence on certain limited aspects of smoking behaviour. The 7 pence surcharge on UK high-tar brands, introduced in 1978, seems virtually to have wiped out this particular form of smoking, and there is no doubt that the recent switch to 'king size' cigarettes has been brought about by changes in tobacco duty (since Britain joined the EEC) which have reduced the price advantage of smoking shorter cigarettes. The evidence that price has a large effect on overall consumption, however, is less clear. Although a recent *Which?* report claimed that the 6 pence price increase following the 1979 Budget reduced sales by 10 per cent, studies which have considered longer-term trends have shown less dramatic effects. An economist who studied cigarette sales in Finland over the period 1960–77 concluded that a 10 per cent increase in real price could be expected to reduce consumption by only 1 per cent. A much more significant factor seemed to be real disposable income, which had risen, and which tended to increase sales of cigarettes (Sehm 1979). It was estimated that a 10 per cent increase in consumer spending-power would increase cigarette sales by an equal amount. A Swiss study of tobacco consumption from 1950 to 1976 also concluded that real disposable income was the main predictor of sales. These findings would pose a problem for governments, since to reduce the amount of money available to consumers is obviously not a politically acceptable way of attempting to reduce smoking.

However, a recent British study originating from the Department of Economics at Essex University (Atkinson and Townsend 1977) provides evidence that price increases, although not of overriding importance, could play an important part in an overall strategy designed to reduce smoking by 40 per cent. Atkinson and Townsend estimate that a price increase of around 50 per cent would probably produce a fall in cigarette sales of 20 per cent, whilst a virtual doubling of the present cost would reduce smoking by 40 per cent. The 50 per cent price increase would have the modest effect of restoring the real price of cigarettes to the 1950 level. Nevertheless, Atkinson and Townsend suggest that any increase substantially greater than this would place an unreasonable burden on people in the lower socioeconomic groups amongst whom smoking is most prevalent and cigarette consumption heaviest. It must also be noted that the smoker may respond to a price increase by decreasing the number of cigarettes smoked whilst smoking each cigarette to a shorter butt length.

Restricting smoking

'Non-smoking should now be the norm on public transport, in places of entertainment, and at meetings – and the rules need to be enforced'
(British Medical Journal 1980: 960).

At present smoking is banned in theatres, churches, certain shops, cinemas, and offices, roughly two-thirds of train carriages, and on certain buses. In many other situations, smokers and non-smokers are segregated. The idea that local and national government should extend the ban on smoking to cover many more areas to which the public has free access obviously has attractions for the anti-smoking lobby, both in terms of reducing the social acceptability of smoking and in terms simply of restricting people's opportunities to smoke. There *is* an extent to which smoking is 'contagious'. One person lighting up will often be closely followed by others who had been reluctant to be the first to start, or who have suddenly been reminded of their 'need' to smoke. Forbidding much public smoking would probably reduce the frequency of such social imitation. However, although smoking undoubtedly could be driven into the position of an act committed only by consenting adults in private, the social costs of the measures required to do this would be great. If over 40 per cent of the adult population remain smokers, problems of enforcement would be considerable, and the fairness of the law brought into question. Our liberal respect for the rights of minorities (especially substantial and vocal ones) would suggest that the non-smoking majority could not go very far in restricting the activities of smokers. This would apply both to attempts motivated by the desire to diminish the nuisance to non-smokers and to those with the more altruistic purpose of helping the smoker help himself.

The pressure-group Action on Smoking and Health (ASH) argues, probably quite correctly, that the majority of people would favour somewhat more severe restrictions on smoking than we have at present. However, the limits of acceptability were clearly exceeded by California's 'Proposition Thirteen' – banning smoking in a wide range of public places – which was rejected in a referendum in 1978. Ex-President Carter has been quoted as saying that it is not the responsibility of government to tell a particular American citizen if he can or cannot smoke. With only 33 per cent of the population smoking cigarettes, the proportion of non-smokers in the United States (and especially in California) is greater than in Britain, where the tolerance for restrictions on smoking would probably be even less. However, one area where the public is traditionally tolerant of government 'interference' is in attempts to safeguard the welfare of children. The recent *Which?* report on smoking argues that present legislation forbidding the sale of cigarettes to those under sixteen years of age is not at all effective. In 1978 there were apparently only eleven prosecutions. Stricter enforcement of the law in this respect would meet with general approval, though it would probably not greatly affect the overall prevalence of smoking.

Advertising and promotion

Thirty million pounds was spent on tobacco company advertising in 1977, and probably rather more on sponsorship (*BMJ* 1979), whilst the total current budget for tobacco promotion was recently estimated at £80 million a year. British American Tobacco's 'State Express Challenge' alone contributed £400,000 to sport in 1979 (*BMJ* 1980), and in one typical week of that year ten hours of BBC television was devoted to events sponsored by the various tobacco companies. The upsurge in sponsorship, especially of events being televised, has been a part of the cigarette companies' response to the 1965 ban on television advertisements. Another attempt to circumvent the ban was to introduce, and advertise, cigars with a name and packaging similar to that of the prohibited cigarette brands, whilst the use of gift coupons was another aspect of the switch to alternative methods of promotion.

Because of the large number of variables involved, and the availability of counter-measures, it is difficult to assess the importance of any piecemeal government action aimed at reducing the effectiveness of advertising. The influence of advertising as a whole (and the implications of a *total* ban) are even more difficult to determine. Hamilton (1972) performed a complex regression analysis on United States data, relating cigarette consumption to advertising, income, cigarette price, and the 'health scare' over the period 1950–70. He concluded that advertising increased per capita cigarette consumption by seventy-five cigarettes per year. However, the effect of the 1964 report of the Surgeon General, clearly linking smoking with disease, was considerably greater, reducing consumption by around 250 cigarettes per year over the period 1964–70.

From 1968–70, the 'Fairness Doctrine' of the Federal Communications Commission required that cigarette advertising on radio and television be balanced by an equal number of subsidized anti-smoking commercials. Whilst the estimated effect of the tobacco companies' efforts was to increase consumption by seventy-five cigarettes per year, Hamilton calculates that the health education advertising *decreased* consumption by seven times that amount. The net effect of the 1970 ban on advertising was therefore to *increase* consumption. This illustrates the complexity of the problem.

However, the American experience, as a consequence of the 'Fairness Doctrine', was perhaps unusual. Using UK data for the period 1957–68, McGuinness and Cowling concluded that 'advertising had a positive statistically significant impact on sales, and that this impact was only partially offset by the amount of publicity given to the health effects of smoking' (McGuinness and Cowling 1975: 311). They argue that although the immediate effect of a 10 per cent increase in advertising might be an increase in sales of only one-tenth of one per cent, the long-term effect would be a much more significant increase of between two and three per cent. This is because advertising affects future sales by influencing people to *take up* smoking: 'once in the market their stream of future purchases, although ostensibly explained by the habit-forming characteristics of the commodity, can be said to have their origin in the action of a single, long-forgotten advertisement' (McGuinness and Cowling 1975: 327). The effects of advertising may therefore be far-reaching.

After reviewing the available evidence, Atkinson and Townsend (1977) suggest that a total ban on tobacco advertisements on television, together with a 75 per cent reduction in promotion in newspapers and magazines, would reduce consumption by 10 per cent. Indeed, the balance of evidence does go against the tobacco companies' standard argument that advertising, whilst it affects the share of the market obtained by different brands, has no influence on overall levels of consumption. Their second argument, that advertising must be allowed if newer and hopefully less hazardous kinds of cigarette are to be promoted, may be countered by the suggestion that it is the government and medical profession – rather than the tobacco companies – which should be responsible for making the public aware of how to reduce the risk involved in smoking.

Cigarette advertising on posters and in the press in the UK, although not banned, is controlled by a voluntary agreement between the tobacco industry and the government, 'refereed' by the

Advertising Standards Authority. Associating cigarettes with sport-
ing, sexual, and other success is excluded by the agreement and
advertisers have consequently come to rely in part on a new brand of
'visual wizardry' to sell the product (Herail and Lovatt 1979). The
originators of this trend were probably Benson and Hedges, whose
familiar gold packs appear in such unfamiliar and memorable
incarnations. This brilliant exercise in classical surrealism has
recently been imitated in a plodding way by other cigarette brands,
and has been emulated, with greater success, by advertisers of
entirely different products. The original agreement between government and the tobacco industry may have had the unlooked-for effect
of raising the aesthetic quality of advertising, but neither it, nor the
recently renegotiated voluntary agreement, is likely to have much
impact on cigarette sales.

This is in part because the emphasis has been on restricting the
quantity of advertising and the explicit claims which can be made.
However, it has been persuasively argued (Hoffman 1980) that much
more important are the implications which follow, not from the
amount or content of advertising, but from its *context*, and the fact that
it is allowed to exist at all. Thus the cigarette advertisement
appearing in a glossy magazine, preceded and followed by images of
elegant women, fast cars, and spotless kitchens, associates smoking
with glamour and success just as effectively as if such symbols had
actually appeared in the cigarette advertisement itself. However, the
most important 'implicit' message is simply that if cigarettes may be
advertised *at all* they must be a legitimate, normal, and reasonable
product. Hoffman therefore argues that advertising is critical in
maintaining the social acceptability of smoking.

Hoffman's arguments aside, many people working in the health
education field would argue that the whole concept of regulating
advertising by agreement rather than by legislation has been dis-
credited by the action of tobacco companies. Jill Turner provides a
powerful indictment of their record:

'Advertising is supposed to concentrate on the lowest tar groups, yet
in 1978 four times as much was spent on the middle range. It is
supposed not to encourage the young to take up smoking, yet in
cinemas, where 54 per cent of the audience is under 24, advertising
has increased enormously. Chesterfield has chosen three magazines for
the young to relaunch its brand name. Philip Morris has been trying
to persuade manufacturers of other goods to display cigarette packs in
their advertisements to beat the controls on direct advertising, and

every possible visual effect is used to reduce the effect of health warnings.'

(*Observer*, 6 January 1980)

A specific example of the way in which the agreement can be bypassed concerns the advertisement of Marlboro cigarettes through association with a Grand Prix car race. The posters, given a wide distribution before the event (and apparently not taken down with too great haste after it), did not have a government health warning because – although giving great prominence to the brand logo – they did not directly advertise cigarettes. The obvious association with youth, glamour, and daring was apparently unobjectionable to the ASA for the same reason. The State Express circular dropping through millions of household letterboxes was apparently also within the code of practice, since – although children would almost certainly have had direct access to many of them – the special offer they contained was restricted to adult smokers. It is examples like these that enable one to sympathize with the medical bodies' insistence on a total ban on advertising and all kinds of cigarette promotion – even if the hard evidence for the efficacy of such a ban is not overwhelming.

Health education

Entangled as they are with the influence of advertising, price, and changes in the composition of the smoking population, the effects of health education campaigns by the government and medical authorities are difficult to judge. In a review of studies of the impact of the various reports of the Royal College of Physicians and the associated education campaigns (Atkinson and Townsend 1977), the authors conclude that the initial impact is to reduce sales of cigarettes by around 5 per cent. However, sales recover over the period of a few years. Nevertheless, the overall effect of publicity surrounding the health consequences of smoking may have been to prevent the *rise* in consumption which might otherwise have taken place. The absence of a marked decline in the number of cigarettes smoked would therefore not indicate that health education programmes had been ineffective. Warner (1977) argues that 1975 levels of cigarette consumption in the US would have been 20 to 30 per cent higher than they were if it had not been for the cumulative effect of anti-smoking publicity.

In an important sense, the argument over the usefulness of further warnings on packets and more expensive health education campaigns hinges on the question of whether smokers still need to be persuaded of the risks of continued smoking and the advantages of giving up. One school of thought holds that the message has already been put across effectively and that smokers are *unable* rather than unwilling to stop. Other workers, however, argue that there are many millions of smokers (and perhaps especially those who have just started) who could and would give up if sufficiently convinced of the risks to which they were personally exposed.

That there are at least some smokers in this category was shown by Russell *et al.* (1979) who investigated the efficacy of health education advice given by general practitioners. In the course of their ordinary consultations, four hundred smokers were given one to two minutes' advice to stop smoking, and an explanatory leaflet. A year later 19 per cent were not smoking, compared with only 10 per cent of a control group who were not given any advice. The results showed that a minimal amount of effort directed personally at the smoker could double the spontaneous quit-rate. If all 20,000 family doctors in Britain were to experience the same success rate as the twenty-eight London GPs in the study, Russell *et al.* argue that there would be half a million fewer smokers in the first year alone – an achievement which could be matched by anti-smoking clinics only if their number were increased from fifty to ten thousand.

8 LEARNING AND BREAKING THE HABIT

Our understanding of how a behaviour is learned is based largely on studies of animals producing relatively simple responses in laboratory environments in which both the events eliciting a response and its consequences are carefully controlled and manipulated by the experimenter. The position of the human smoker in his natural environment is radically different. The stimuli which may be said to promote smoking are many and varied. Certain cigarettes appear to be smoked in response to particular situations – with a cup of coffee, after a meal, with friends, when a person is faced with a difficult problem, and so on. At other times, smokers seem to respond primarily to internal 'events' interpretable as the onset of a craving for nicotine. The act of smoking is itself complex: taking a cigarette, lighting it, drawing the smoke, and inhaling may all be considered separate responses. And as for the consequences of the behaviour, these also are varied and numerous, ranging from the feeling of positive pleasure accompanying the first cigarette of the day, through satisfactions derived from an increased ability to cope with anxiety and stress, to the removal of unpleasant sensations accompanying withdrawal.

Nevertheless, although extremely complex, smoking is clearly a behaviour which is learned, and which in certain circumstances may be 'unlearned'. It enters the behavioural repertoire largely through imitation, persists for a while as a casual indulgence, but then in many smokers becomes a regular and often-repeated act. At this stage it is difficult to reduce the frequency with which the behaviour occurs, let alone to abandon it entirely. In the language of animal learning, smoking has a high probability of occurrence and is strongly resistant to extinction. In these respects, behaviours analogous to smoking may be produced in the laboratory by appropriate manipulations of the animal's learning experience. Considering smoking as a learned response is therefore a potentially fruitful way of attempting to understand the acquisition and maintenance of the behaviour. Approaches based on the principles of learning theory have also been widely used in the development of techniques designed to aid the smoker in breaking the habit.

SMOKING AS A LEARNED BEHAVIOUR

The fundamental principle of learning theory is that behaviour is controlled by its consequences. The probability that an act will be repeated increases if the act results in reward. This reward may take the form of an event which in itself is pleasurable (positive reinforcement). Thus a non-satiated animal will press a bar to obtain food, water, or access to a mate. The probability that a behaviour will be repeated is also increased if the behaviour brings to an end, or prevents the occurrence of, an unpleasant stimulus (negative reinforcement). Thus an animal will press a bar to switch off an electric current or to prevent a shock being administered.

A corollary of this principle of reinforcement is that punishing consequences, or the omission of reward, decrease the probability that the related behaviour will recur. A behaviour followed a sufficient number of times by punishment or non-reward will cease to occur. This process is termed extinction.

That so many people smoke so frequently suggests that the behaviour is very effectively rewarded, whilst the fact that only a minority of smokers stop (and then with apparent difficulty) indicates that any punishments naturally associated with the act are of only minor significance in controlling the behaviour. Important determinants of the strength of a learned response are the nature and variety of the reinforcements and punishments involved, and the immediacy, frequency, and regularity with which they follow the response. What is there in the nature of the rewards which follow smoking (and in the way they are associated with the behaviour) which accounts for the strength of the habit?

Positive and negative reinforcement

Certain effects of nicotine which may have reinforcing value are listed in *Table 1*. The direct stimulation of reward pathways in the brain (discussed in Chapter 3 as a mechanism underlying the 'pleasure' of smoking) constitutes a possible source of positive reinforcement. On this interpretation, regular smokers can be seen as behaving rather like Old's rats, repeatedly pressing a bar to obtain electrical stimulation of their reward pathways. It has been suggested that activity in the reward centres is the element common to all primary reinforcers such as food, drink, and sex. On this view, smoking, and the use of certain other drugs, would constitute a short-cut to 'pleasure' which could be obtained in other (and more biologically useful) ways. Russell (1976b) has pointed out that the smoking of each cigarette, and indeed each inhalation, may mark a distinct, regular, and invariable association of the behaviour with a reinforcing 'shot' of

Table 1 Possible sources of reinforcement in smoking

	direct pharmacological effects of nicotine	nicotine – mediated changes in arousal
positive reinforcement	stimulation of 'pleasure' centres	increased alertness; enhanced performance
negative reinforcement	removal from aversive state of withdrawal	relief of anxiety and stress

pleasure. Smoking would therefore be reinforced approximately ten times during each cigarette, perhaps a total of 200 times a day, day after day for months and years. Supported by reinforcement repeated on such a scale, it would not be surprising if the behaviour were to become powerfully entrenched.

In addition to the frequency and regularity of the association, the delay between a response and its reinforcement is important in determining how effectively a behaviour will be learned. Although the optimal period varies, depending on the nature of the response and reinforcement involved, it is generally true that more immediate rewards and punishments are more effective than those which are delayed. We have noted that the interval between inhalation and the onset of nicotine's actions on the brain is less than ten seconds. There is therefore a close temporal association between the behaviour and its consequences, and we would expect that the rapid reinforcement involved would result in effective learning.

The possible stimulation of reward centres in the brain provides an instance of positive reinforcement. However, smoking may also be negatively reinforced if the behaviour brings to an end a state of noxious stimulation. Such negative reinforcement would occur if the effect of inhaling cigarette smoke was to eliminate the unpleasant consequences of nicotine deprivation. Since the removal of the aversive stimulus would rapidly follow the onset of smoking, the behaviour and its rewards (as with the positively reinforcing effects of pleasure-centre stimulation) would again be closely associated in time. Of course this form of negative reinforcement could not account for the *acquisition* of the smoking habit, since an organism would have to be exposed to nicotine on many occasions before the 'need' for the drug could be acquired. Nevertheless, negative reinforcement offers a plausible account of how smoking behaviour may be maintained, and indeed of how the smoker might find himself in the peculiarly vicious circle in which smoking, whilst reinforced by the relief it offers from nicotine withdrawal effects, itself acted to perpetuate the acquired drive for further cigarettes (Logan 1970).

The view that drug-based behaviours are maintained largely by negative reinforcement has been elaborated by Solomon (1980) in the Opponent–Process theory of acquired motivation. The theory assumes that the nervous system is organized so as to oppose or suppress emotional arousal, whether pleasurable or aversive. On this view, a stimulus which produces a positive affective state (i.e., pleasure) sets in train a compensatory process which tends to induce negative affect. This opponent process takes time to build up and time to decay. There is therefore an initial period, before effective compensation, during which pleasure is experienced, and a period of 'rebound' negative affect following the termination of the pleasurable stimulus.

The opponent-process theory also suggests that *repeated* presentation of a pleasurable stimulus *increases* the magnitude and duration of the compensatory process. This strengthening of the compensatory process leads to a progressive reduction in the positive affect produced by the original stimulus and a longer period of negative affect once it is terminated.

This effect can be illustrated using opiate administration as an example. Before the drug stimulus is first applied, the organism is in an affectively neutral state. The presence of the drug then causes a marked change in affect (the 'rush' and euphoria). This is followed by a brief period of negative affect, as the influence of the drug wears off, and a fairly rapid return to the neutral state. With repeated use, however, the opponent process becomes dominant. The pre-drug state consists of craving, the positive effect of the presence of the drug is reduced from euphoria to contentment, and the post-drug rebound is amplified from craving into 'abstinence agony'. In this way 'the positive reinforcer loses some of its power, but the negative reinforcer gains power and lasts longer' (Solomon 1980: 696). Thus drug use can be regarded as a pleasure-seeking appetitive behaviour which eventually (through the dominance of the opponent process inducing negative affect) becomes an avoidance response. In the case of smoking, the initial motivation (the desire to experience the pleasure accompanying administration of nicotine) would develop into the desire to escape from the aversive consequence of nicotine deprivation (Ternes 1977).

We have so far considered ways in which the direct pharmacological effects of nicotine may be found rewarding. The source of reward, however, may be somewhat more complicated (*Table 1*). It may derive, as Eysenck (1973) has suggested, from a nicotine-mediated change from a less-preferred to a more-preferred level of arousal. If there is an optimum level, at which an organism feels most 'comfortable', this shift in arousal may itself be positively reinforcing. On the other hand, the reinforcement may consist, for example, in the fact that the change in arousal enables effective performance to be maintained under conditions of boredom or fatigue. Processes involving negative reinforcement may also have a role. This would be the case, for example, if a cigarette enabled smokers to attenuate the aversive effects of anxiety or stress. These latter ideas amount to the suggestion that smoking may be rewarding in virtue of its usefulness, in certain contexts, as a psychological tool.

Evidence that smoking may be used in this way has already been reviewed. Nevertheless, the arousal-control approach to smoking motivation does not imply that *every* cigarette smoked is useful in such a way. Rather, it suggests that cigarettes are sometimes of great use in manipulating psychological state, and that on these occasions they are found extremely rewarding. This view of smoking is made plausible by the self-reports of smokers. For example, Mausner and Platt (1971) asked smokers to complete a diary describing the circumstances under which they smoked each cigarette, and the degree of pleasure they experienced. Apart from the many cigarettes smoked 'out of habit' (simply because others were smoking, or because cigarettes had come to be associated with certain routine activities) certain cigarettes stood out as being particularly 'needed' and especially rewarding. In part the value of these particular cigarettes was explained in terms simply of 'pleasure'. The first cigarette of the day, and cigarettes smoked after meals, were often cited in this respect.

However, there were many instances in which the rewards of smoking derived from the use of a cigarette to manipulate mood. This was especially so in situations in which smoking was thought to have reduced tension. But if the association between smoking and its rewarding effects is not invariable, how do we explain the frequent and regular smoking of cigarettes when no change in arousal is required?

Partial and secondary reinforcement

Experiments in animal learning have shown that the number of reinforcements obtained is not the only determinant of the persistence and frequency of a response. When the schedule of reinforcement is arranged so that rewards occur sometimes after a short period of responding, and at other times after a longer period, animals respond at a fast and constant rate. Moreover, when rewards cease to be provided, the behaviour takes longer to extinguish than when the association between response and reinforcement is regular and invariable (Lewis 1960). That most cigarettes are smoked without much effect on psychological state may therefore not detract from the strength of the behaviour, and may in fact make it more resistant to extinction.

The effects of partial reinforcement may explain why smoking occurs in situations in which there is no obvious need to smoke, nor pleasure to be derived from it. However, such behaviour can also be accounted for by reference to the phenomenon of secondary reinforcement. Through constant association with rewards derived from the effects of nicotine, certain other stimuli (the appearance of the cigarette, the act of smoking, and the smell and taste of tobacco) may themselves come to have reinforcing properties (Hunt and Matarazzo 1970). These secondary reinforcers are able to maintain behaviour for a long period, even when the primary source of reward is absent. For example, smokers will continue to smoke lettuce-leaf cigarettes, containing no nicotine, in the absence of the conventional tobacco product (Goldfarb, Jarvik, and Glick 1970). Of course, if smoking were to continue to be totally divorced from nicotine self-administration, we would expect that the behaviour would gradually decrease in frequency and finally cease. However, over a period of weeks, and perhaps months, the secondary reinforcers are probably sufficient to maintain the habit.

Classically conditioned responses

In addition to having secondary reinforcing properties, there is evidence that the rituals involved in drug administration may themselves come to produce the effects of the drug (Siegel 1977). This occurs through classical conditioning.

To cite a familiar example of this process, the repeated association of the sound of a bell with the presentation of food leads to a situation in which the bell alone produces salivation. In a similar way, the circumstances preceding and surrounding the use of a drug may be so reliably associated with the drug that they will produce its effects, even when the drug is absent. Thus simply bringing a dog into the room in which it has previously received insulin injections results in the same physiological changes as are produced by the insulin itself.

In the case of smoking, the sight of the cigarette and the smell of the smoke, for example, might have the power to alter arousal, reduce craving, or indeed mimic any of the effects which nicotine has on the experienced smoker. It is presumably because of such classically conditioned responses that puffing on an unlit cigarette (while smoke was provided by a lit cigarette placed in an ashtray) produced changes in the EEG similar in direction, although smaller in extent, to those which accompanied 'real' smoking (Mangan and Golding 1978): see Chapter 5 (*Figure 21*) p. 101.

These responses would of course be weakened each time the cues accompanying smoking failed to be associated with the effects of nicotine itself, and would eventually disappear. Nevertheless, reference to classical conditioning (as well as the role of secondary reinforcers) may explain the otherwise puzzling finding that smokers will for a while continue to smoke cigarettes which contain little or no nicotine.

Classically conditioned responses may also be important in determining what happens when a drug is withdrawn. Depending upon as yet unspecified details of the conditioning situation, the circumstances in which a drug is usually administered may elicit not a conditioned drug response but a conditioned *compensatory* reaction (Siegel 1977). Thus rats with a history of morphine administration may show *increased* sensitivity to painful stimuli when given a placebo in circumstances in which they were used to receiving morphine. Such learned compensatory mechanisms would tend to reduce the effect of repeated administrations of a drug and may play some part in the development of tolerance. They may also explain why withdrawal effects sometimes occur only in the circumstances in which a drug user had habitually consumed a drug. In these circumstances, the user would experience not merely the absence of the drug, but the reverse of its usual effects.

Anecdotal evidence suggests that a smoker may crave cigarettes only (or more severely) in certain well-defined contexts. Thus someone who has been unworried by the absence of cigarettes through the working day may find the temptation to smoke almost irresistible once he sits down at home to relax with a drink. It is difficult to explain such a phenomenon without reference to some form of learned association between the presence of a drug and the particular circumstances surrounding its use. Obviously it is not the absence of nicotine *per se* which is aversive, but its absence in a specific context. It is possible that such effects may be explained by some form of classically conditioned withdrawal response.

Is smoking punished?

There are a variety of routes to positive and negative reinforcement by which smoking may be rewarded. Probably all contribute to some extent to maintaining the behaviour. It is undoubtedly the variety of rewards offered by smoking, together with the frequency and immediacy with which certain reinforcements occur, which explain much of the natural history of the habit. In particular, the continuation of smoking in the face of good reasons for its abandonment may now seem less bizarre. It may in fact be logical to smoke if we are biologically programmed to behave in such a way as to maximize reward under existing contingencies of reinforcement (as classical Utilitarianism and modern Behaviourism, equally, would suggest).

Nevertheless, smoking is of course eventually 'punished' in a proportion of smokers by the occurrence of disease and premature death. But since animal experiments inform us that delayed punishment (however severe) generally has less effect on behaviour than immediate reinforcement, we should not be surprised that this prospect in itself is of only limited usefulness in persuading people to give up. Even man, with his ability to envisage and act on long-term consequences, often seems relatively uninfluenced by them. This is perhaps especially so when the consequences are not inevitable in the case of any particular individual. We are apparently well able to sustain our illusion of personal immunity in the face of odds such as the one-in-ten chance of contracting lung cancer through smoking.

For this reason, smoking cessation techniques based on learning theory have sought to associate smoking with various forms of 'artificial' punishment which can be manipulated, in the laboratory or outside, so as to be invariable, immediate, and repeatable. In parallel with the various forms of aversion therapy, attempts have been made to reduce the 'need' for smoking, and to replace the behaviour by some alternative but equally effective form of mood manipulation. A further potentially useful strategy has been to emphasize not the punishment of smoking but the rewards of non-smoking. Thus, social approval, enhanced self-esteem following the successful use of 'will-power', the absence of cough, and the increased capacity for exercise can all be regarded as reinforcers of cigarette abstinence. On the other hand, even these more proximal rewards are long delayed relative to the immediate reinforcements offered by the cigarette. Similar sorts of problem attend attempts to modify patterns of alcohol and food consumption, for example. Thus the prospect of 'punishment', to be experienced in the form of a hangover, is often insufficient to outweigh the immediate pleasure of excessive drinking, whilst the deferred rewards following loss of weight are usually inadequate to maintain rigorous dieting in the obese.

With these problems in mind we turn to a consideration of various methods which have been used in the attempt to help smokers quit.

CESSATION TECHNIQUES

It is not intended that this section should provide a comprehensive account of the many techniques which have been used to encourage smokers to stop smoking. The area is well covered by evaluative reviews: (Bernstein 1969, Hunt and Matarazzo 1973, Epstein and McCoy 1975, and Bernstein and McAlister 1976). It is nevertheless of interest to indicate the variety of approaches available (*Table 2*), and to attempt to relate their success or failure to the psychology and pharmacology of the cigarette habit.

Behaviour therapy

Smoking – like alcoholism, transvestism, and the phobias – can be considered a maladaptive learned response. As such, it ought to be amenable to the various techniques of behaviour modification which have proved useful in the treatment of certain psychiatric disorders and antisocial behaviour. Of these techniques, various forms of aversive conditioning are probably the most frequently used. In this form of therapy an unpleasant stimulus is administered at the same time as the unwanted behaviour occurs. The reaction of anxiety or discomfort produced by the noxious stimulus then becomes a conditioned response to the presence of the unwanted behaviour itself, replacing the positive reinforcement which would normally accompany and maintain it.

Table 2 Treatments for smoking

1 *behaviour therapy* aversive conditioning – electric shock   – rapid smoking operant conditioning systematic desensitization/relaxation training programmed smoking contract management/self control
2 *drugs* lobeline tranquillizers and antidepressants nicotine gum
3 *the smoking clinic/other treatments* psychotherapy/group support/information sensory deprivation hypnosis acupuncture

The use of electric shock is a traditional tool in behaviour therapy. In the laboratory, smokers receive painful shocks when they reach for a cigarette, or light it, or simply indicate they are thinking favourably about smoking. However, the problem with aversive conditioning is that the punishment is administered only in the laboratory. The smoker is well aware that in the radically different situation outside no electric shock will accompany smoking. Although the hope behind aversive conditioning is that conscious processes can be 'by-passed' (Russell 1970), there is evidence that even classically conditioned autonomic responses are affected by the subject's awareness of the 'rules' governing the administration of punishment (Bandura 1969). It is therefore likely that the anxiety response to taking a cigarette will rapidly disappear once the subject returns to the situations in which he normally smokes.

Two strategies illustrate attempts to overcome this problem.

Powell and Azrin (1968) devised a means of delivering shocks in the subject's natural smoking environment. They designed a cigarette case which administered an electric shock through electrodes attached to the upper arm whenever it was opened. As the intensity of the shock increased, the rate of smoking decreased, until, at the highest level of shock, it was approximately half that in the baseline period. Unfortunately (but not unnaturally) as the intensity of the shock increased, the length of time subjects wore the apparatus decreased, and the association between smoking and punishment was therefore gradually broken.

The association between electric shock and smoking is entirely arbitrary and the fact that learned non-smoking does not generalize to situations outside the laboratory may be partly because of this. A second strategy is therefore to use as punishment a stimulus – cigarette smoke – which will be present in the normal smoking environment (even if only in an attenuated form) and which may aid the transfer of learning from the laboratory. Various attempts to use this technique have required subjects to smoke at a much faster rate than they would choose (taking a puff every six seconds, for example) or have exposed people smoking to a stream of warm, concentrated, smoky air directed at their faces. Although success rates are very variable, Schmahl, Lichtenstein, and Harris (1972) and Lichtenstein *et al.* (1973) report that roughly 60 per cent of a combined population of seventy subjects conditioned in this way were still not smoking six months after the end of the treatment. Whilst rapid smoking and warm, smoky air seemed equally effective, there was no evidence that combining the two forms of therapy enhanced the rate of success.

There is no doubt that both forms of therapy are capable of being extremely unpleasant. In a recently published Israeli study (Merbaum, Avimier, and Goldberg 1979), it was reported that three-quarters of the subjects experiencing rapid smoking vomited at least once in the course of treatment. On six consecutive days subjects smoked in an unventilated room until they were dizzy and sick. They were then told to imagine they were with people and wanted a cigarette while the following account was given: 'Now you feel sick and have stomach cramps. As you are about to put the cigarette in your mouth you puke all over the cigarette. . . . The cigarette in your hand is very soggy and full of green vomit. . . . You throw away the cigarette and vow never to have another cigarette again. You immediately feel better.'

Although the direct consequences of such therapy are somewhat gross, the underlying learning principles are sophisticated. Thus through the use of the imagination an attempt is made to generalize the learning from the laboratory to situations in the subjects' normal smoking environment. Secondly, the effect of aversive conditioning of smoking is enhanced by the simultaneous negative reinforcement of the vow of non-smoking, since the latter provides escape from the unpleasant consequences of the former. Merbaum *et al.* report a six-month abstinence rate of 40 per cent using this technique, although other studies (e.g., Levenberg and Wagner 1976) report substantially less success.

The aversive conditioning procedures considered so far have been based largely on the punishment of the behaviour we wish to see abandoned. An alternative approach is to *reward* the absence of the behaviour. In the case of smoking, such techniques have been relatively little used. There is, however, an interesting case study which illustrates how the desired response of non-smoking might be gradually increased in frequency and duration by the procedure of operant conditioning (Barton and Barton 1978). A pigeon can be trained to peck a switch to obtain food by rewarding behaviours which approximate progressively more exactly to that required by the experimenter. In an analogous way, Barton and Barton gradually 'shaped' continuous non-smoking by reinforcing longer and longer periods spent without a cigarette. The period of non-smoking necessary to obtain the reward increased by five minutes per day until smoking was totally eliminated. In the case reported, reinforcement consisted of progressively more valuable tokens which could be redeemed for plants at a local nursery. It would be necessary to tailor such rewards to the particular enthusiasms of each smoker, and the training procedure is obviously time-consuming. The principle, however, would seem a useful complement to the more usual behaviour therapies centred on punishment.

Paradoxically, it has been suggested that non-smoking could be rewarded by the eventual provision of a cigarette. This procedure sounds bizarre, but illustrates another potentially useful strategy – that of separating the act of smoking from the cues which usually precede it and the reinforcements which habitually follow. Thus, if having a cigarette becomes contingent on the passage of a particular period of time, smoking would probably cease to occur at the times when it would be most rewarding. This non-reward of the behaviour would be expected gradually to decrease the frequency of smoking. Levinson *et al.* (1971) employed this technique of 'programmed smoking' in an experiment in which subjects smoked only when signalled to do so by a timer which was activated at random intervals. At the end of a twelve-week period, smokers reported that fewer environmental cues were relevant to their smoking. However, subjects found it difficult to reduce their consumption below ten cigarettes a day. This relatively common finding has been attributed (Bernstein and McAlister 1976) to the fact that gradual reduction in smoking increases the reinforcement value of each cigarette – irrespective of circumstances – and makes those which remain progressively harder to relinquish. The attempt to reduce smoking by breaking the link between a cigarette and its usual reward also suffers from the problem of secondary reinforcement since the cues associated with smoking will have some rewarding value, whatever the situation.

Techniques derived from learning theory have been used in attempts to eliminate smoking by punishing the behaviour, by rewarding non-smoking, and by dissociating the act of smoking from its usual sources of reward. Complementary to these approaches are forms of behaviour therapy designed to remove the need to smoke by reducing anxiety and by training smokers to use other ways of combating stress. The technique of 'systematic desensitization', developed initially for use with phobic patients, requires the subject to imagine himself in a series of situations, starting with those producing least anxiety and gradually progressing to those causing most distress. At each stage the anxiety reaction is countered by the therapist, usually through training the subject in relaxation (e.g., Wagner and Bragg 1970). The subject then moves to confront these situations in real life, hopefully taking with him the new responses he has learned. A smoker who has come to rely on a cigarette as a means of coping with stress may in this way be gradually weaned from his habitual source of support. However, the analogy between the phobic patient and a person 'taking flight' in smoking is not particularly compelling, since reducing tension is only one of the many ways in which smoking is used. It is therefore unlikely that this single approach would be effective, and desensitization has fallen out of favour as a means of 'treating' smoking (Bernstein and McAlister 1976).

The conventional wisdom is that smoking, ultimately, is conquered only through the exercise of will-power. This concept, however, is problematic. If someone has successfully quit the habit they are said to possess the quality; if they fail, they lack it. To say that someone has will-power is therefore merely *another way of saying* that they have succeeded where others fail. The concept is therefore of no use at all in explaining *how* they have succeeded. Nevertheless, the related concept of self-control does have a place in the scientific analysis of behaviour and can be interpreted in terms of learning theory.

Conventional behaviour therapy relies largely on rewards and punishments which are 'imposed' on an individual by the experimenter or therapist. The technology of self-control, on the other hand, requires that the individual sets up his *own* schedules of reinforcement (Premack 1970). The obvious advantage of this is that learning is not confined to the laboratory. The kind of rewards and punishments involved in self-control are often internal mental events such as thoughts and feelings. This poses a problem for orthodox learning theory which historically is committed to the view that only observable events may be the subject of scientific study. Despite this, more adventurous behaviourists have argued that mental events can (and indeed must) be involved in any attempt to explain and modify complex human behaviour.

The difficulty in giving up smoking, as we have noted, is that quitting (except in terms of expense) is likely to be advantageous only in the long term. However, the gap between present behaviour and future consequences *can* be bridged. One way of doing this is to use speech or imagery as a way of drawing one's attention to environmental events, such as the consequences of smoking, which are not immediately present. Thus a smoker may bring to mind the unpleasant facts about smoking at a time when he is tempted to light a cigarette and so strengthen his resolve to abstain.

Another method of bridging the temporal gap is to construct a set of artificial, but relatively immediate, rewards and punishments. The individual can do this by entering into a form of 'contract' either with himself or with others (Rachlin 1976). For example, at a time when the urge to smoke is weak, an individual enters into a commitment to give £10 to a friend if he ever smokes again. Then at some point in the future, when the urge to smoke is strong, the smoker still has a powerful reason for not smoking. In this example the 'punishment' which would follow relapse is an external environmental event. This is also the case when the 'contract' relates to the social approval of others (Tooley and Pratt 1967). However, we can equally well imagine that a contract with oneself might have the same effect, if loss of self-esteem, for example, were the forfeit.

The view that private mental events obey the same laws as public ones, and are subject to the same learning principles, was expressed by Homme (1965) who used the self-control of smoking as an example. The intending non-smoker starts by listing a number of 'behaviours' (such as thinking about an early death from lung cancer) which are incompatible with smoking. It may be assumed that such thoughts are not rewarding and do not often occur to the habitual smoker. The purpose of Homme's procedure is to increase their frequency. This is done by associating them with a behaviour which is rewarding and does occur regularly, such as drinking a cup of coffee. The smoker therefore makes a 'contract' with himself, specifying that before he makes a cup of coffee he will think about the consequences of smoking. In this way, association with the more frequently occurring behaviour is used to increase the probability of occurrence of an internal event incompatible with smoking.

Such rudimentary analyses may seem to give a somewhat inadequate account of the processes involved in self-control. But whatever the mechanisms, self-control is clearly a major factor in smoking cessation since the great majority of those who have successfully given up have used no other method.

Drugs

Drugs of one form or another have a long history of use in attempts to help people give up smoking. Three classes of substance are used. Probably the most common are drugs which are similar to nicotine in their pharmacology and which may therefore mimic its effects. The search for a nicotine substitute goes back to the 1930s, when lobeline was first used for the purpose, but no drug has proved consistently effective. Thus, although certain studies have shown a quite marked reduction in smoking rate when oral lobeline preparations were compared with placebo (e.g., Rapp, Dusza, and Blanchet 1959), other trials have produced entirely non-significant results (Bernstein 1969). Various psychotropic substances which act in ways rather different from nicotine, but whose stimulant or tranquillizing properties may be useful in helping the smoker during the difficult initial period of abstinence, have also been used. For example, Whitehead and Davies (1964) compared the effect of the mild stimulant methylphenidate with that of the minor tranquillizer diazepam, but found neither drug superior to placebo. In a recent review Bernstein (1976: 91) concluded that research with such drugs, as with lobeline, has shown their effects to be 'relatively weak, temporary, and primarily a function of placebo and other non-specific effects associated with receiving medication'.

If part of the pleasure of smoking is mediated by the release of endogenous opiates (which the work of Stein (1978) suggests may be the case), the administration of an opiate antagonist might be a useful aid in encouraging smokers to quit. There is anecdotal evidence (Mills 1980, personal communication) that clinical use of the antagonist naloxone, administered by continuous infusion, markedly decreases the patient's interest in smoking. There is also one experimental report linking subcutaneous naloxone administration with a reduced rate of cigarette consumption (Karras and Kane 1980). Although naloxone may be too short-acting to be of much practical use as an aid in smoking withdrawal, it is likely that longer-acting antagonists will become available, and their potential should be considered.

From the point of view of psychopharmacology, logically the most promising drug to use in smoking therapy is nicotine itself. Nicotine administered orally in tablet form, for reasons to do with absorption and metabolism, is ineffective. However, the recent advent of nicotine chewing gum marks a potentially important advance, especially since the work of Russell *et al.* (discussed in Chapter 4) has shown that the gum is capable of producing blood concentrations comparable with those obtained from smoking. What, then, is its therapeutic efficacy?

There is general agreement that nicotine gum reduces smoking more than a placebo preparation when used over a one- to three-week period. Thus Ohlin and Westling (1972) and Brantmark, Ohlin, and Westling (1973) report a greater decline in cigarette consumption, whilst Russell *et al.* (1976a) found a significantly greater reduction in smoke exposure (as measured by carboxyhaemoglobin levels) and Puska *et al.* a higher rate of total abstinence (Puska, Björkqvist, and Koskela 1979). However, the true test of any anti-smoking therapy lies in the longer-term success rate, and here the position is less clear. For example, Puska *et al.* report that the difference in abstention rates at six months is non-significant (35 per cent in the nicotine gum group, and 28 per cent with placebo). In contrast to these results, Malcolm *et al.* (1980) found an effect of the gum at six months, when there had been no advantage over placebo at one month. In this study, 23 per cent of subjects chewing 2 mg nicotine gum were non-smokers at a six-month follow-up, whereas only 5 per cent of the placebo group were confirmed (by COHb estimation) as having given up.

A success rate of around 20 per cent using nicotine gum, although better than placebo and control groups, is nevertheless unimpressive, and shows no improvement on the abstinence levels routinely reported from smoking clinics or studies using behaviour therapy. However, considerably stronger support for the use of nicotine gum comes from the work of Raw *et al.* (1980). One year after the start of treatment, 38 per cent of the sixty-nine people who received nicotine gum were confirmed non-smokers, compared with only 14 per cent of the forty-nine smokers who had experienced 'psychological treatment' such as rapid smoking. Of the fifteen subjects who chewed the nicotine gum for more than three months, ten successfully gave up smoking. This high rate of success is virtually identical to that reported by Wilhelmsen and Hjalmarsson (1980) for smokers who continued with the gum for more than sixteen weeks. An important determinant of success would therefore seem to be the duration for which the gum is used (Russell, Raw, and Jarvis 1980c). However, this factor does not account for the marked discrepancy between the results of Raw's group and those of Malcolm *et al.* The explanation for the greater success of Raw's Maudsley smoking-clinic patients probably lies in the type of smoker involved. The mean cigarette consumption of the group given nicotine gum by Raw *et al.* was thirty-two per day, compared with twenty-six in the case of Malcolm's patients. Related to the average consumption of smokers as a whole (nineteen per day according to Lee 1976), both groups are composed largely of heavy smokers. The sample studied by Raw, however, is considerably more atypical of the general smoking population than that involved in the other study. Brantmark *et al.* found that nicotine gum was more successful, compared with placebo, among heavy than among light smokers, supporting the view that the usefulness of the gum may be confined to the treatment of people who habitually consume large numbers of cigarettes (Brantmark, Ohlin, and Westling 1973).

The smoking clinic and other treatments

In parallel with the use of drugs and the various laboratory-based behaviour therapies, there are many hundreds of clinics which provide information, encouragement, and support for smokers who wish to quit. Many clinics offer variations on the 'Five-Day Plan' originated in the United States by the Seventh Day Adventist Church, and first described by McFarland *et al.* (1964). The five evening meetings are devoted to a mixture of information about smoking and exhortation, combined with advice on changes in diet, physical exercise, and social activities over the initial period of abstinence. Although the attempt to invoke the aid of 'a Power greater than man' (McFarland *et al.* 1964: 887) and the use of hot and cold showers may not find universal acceptance, the value of informal group discussion and of dividing participants into mutually supportive pairs (the 'buddy system') has been recognized.

The originators of the therapy claimed 70–80 per cent abstinence after five days, and around 30 per cent at three months. However, the proportion of confirmed non-smokers (arbitrarily taken as abstinence one year after the start of therapy) is almost certainly less than this (Riches 1978). A slightly different tradition of smoking clinics originated from the work of Ejrup in Sweden. These, however, are probably generally no more effective than the Five-Day Plan, and Russell (1970) reports that the success rates of smoking clinics range from 12 to 28 per cent. Perhaps discouraged by this low rate of success, smokers and clinicians alike have interested themselves in less conventional forms of therapy such as acupuncture, hypnosis, and sensory deprivation.

Choy *et al.* report (Choy, Purnell, and Jaffe 1978) that over half of a group of thirty-three smokers were abstinent two to twenty-five months after treatment by the insertion of a stainless steel stud in each ear. The variable interval of follow-up, however, makes this success rate difficult to compare with that using other methods. The usefulness of the study as an evaluation of acupuncture is also lessened by the fact that the treatment was combined with giving information and advice, and the administration of diazepam. Nevertheless, the suggestion (supported by Grobglas and Levy 1978) that acupuncture may produce an immediate strong dislike for the taste or smell of tobacco is of interest.

Although the technique has captured the popular imagination, the usefulness of hypnosis is equally unclear, despite the success reported in individual cases (e.g., Von Dedenroth 1964). Similar to hypnosis (in that both may increase suggestibility) is the technique of sensory deprivation, which has been used by Suedfeld and Ikard (1974) in the 'treatment' of smoking. In this experiment, smokers were confined individually for twenty-four hours in a dark and sound-proofed chamber and fed on a liquid diet. One year after the deprivation experience, subjects were smoking only half the number of cigarettes originally consumed. This compares with a reduced consumption of 16 per cent in a control group. The treatment therefore seemed moderately effective, if somewhat impractical.

Relapse and success

The general problem with smoking cessation techniques is not to obtain an initial change in behaviour but to *sustain* that change: 'The good news is that almost any intervention can be effective in eliminating or drastically reducing smoking behaviour. The bad news is that these changes tend to be relatively short-lived' (Bernstein and McAlister 1976: 89).

The problem of relapse was considered by Hunt, Barnett, and Branch (1971) who collated data from eighty-seven studies which had used a wide range of anti-smoking therapies. Taking all the results together, the following pattern emerges: as soon as treatment ends, there is a steep decline in the proportion of people who are still not smoking, such that after three months only 35 per cent are abstinent and at six months 25 per cent. The rate of relapse then slows, with roughly 20 per cent not smoking at the end of one year. Hunt *et al.* suggest that these 20 per cent were likely to remain abstinent, and constituted the true average rate of success of conventional approaches.

This is obviously in excess of the proportion of the smoking population that would be expected to give up smoking spontaneously. Smokers who take the trouble to attend any form of smoking therapy can be assumed to be more motivated to give up than those who do not attend. On the other hand, they also probably represent a self-selected sample who have tried before on their own and failed, perhaps a number of times. It is therefore difficult to judge whether an average rate of success of 20 per cent is something to be pleased or unhappy about.

If the overall rate of success is low (both for clinic groups and for those quitting spontaneously) there are nevertheless certain kinds of smoker who seem more likely to give up than others (*Table 3*). A number of individual reports suggest that men find it easier to stop smoking than women (e.g., Burns 1969). Reviewing over thirty studies in which figures for men and women had been separately quoted, Gritz (1978) concluded that, in the majority of cases, differences were non-significant. Nevertheless, where differences did occur, men were consistently more successful than women. In population surveys, the proportion of ex-smokers is greater among men than among women in both Britain and the USA. It is not clear why this should be so, although women and men have been found to differ in the reasons they give for smoking. Using the Tomkins's

Table 3 Factors which predict success in stopping smoking

---

sociological
  Male sex
  Higher education

personality
  Greater extraversion
  Emotional stability

smoking history
  Low overall consumption
  Fewer years a smoker
  Non-inhalation

other drug use
  Low coffee and alcohol consumption

---

typology, Ikard *et al.* report (Ikard, Green, and Hall 1969) a greater frequency of 'negative affect' smoking among women, indicating that cigarettes are used not to provide stimulation and accompany relaxation, but to combat feelings such as anger and anxiety. Interestingly, a higher level of negative affect smoking was one of the factors which distinguished a population of 'addicted' smokers attending a clinic from the 'normal' smoking population (Russell, Peto, and Patel 1974). It may therefore be that cigarettes which are used habitually to reduce negative affect are more difficult to give up than those smoked for other reasons.

Personality variables also relate to success in quitting. In the longitudinal study cited in Chapter 6, Cherry and Kiernan (1976) compared the personality of people who stopped smoking spontaneously with that of people who continued. (Nearly 500 members of the study who smoked and inhaled when they were twenty, and who had been smoking for over four years, had given up before they reached the age of twenty-five.) The proportion of subjects who had stopped was greater among the more extravert subjects. Amongst men, the ability to give up was also positively associated with a low neuroticism score. In a smaller (and older) group of 120 patients with chest disease, Burns (1969) found a similar association between successful quitting and personality.

Cherry and Kiernan also reported that low levels of cigarette consumption were predictive of greater success in giving up. This finding is supported by evidence from the major, long-term, prospective studies which are investigating risk factors for heart disease in large groups of American men and women. In the Framingham study, Gordon, Kannel, and McGee (1974) concluded that the majority of those who quit smoking over an eighteen-year period were men who had originally smoked twenty or fewer cigarettes per day. This result is confirmed and extended by the work of Friedman *et al.* (1979) who have been studying smoking in a population of over 25,000 Californians. Compared to continuing smokers, those who gave up had (on average) originally smoked fewer cigarettes, had a shorter history of smoking, and were less likely to report that they inhaled. The group of successful quitters also contained a significantly greater proportion of people with college education, and was composed of individuals who on average consumed less alcohol and coffee than those who continued to smoke. It therefore seems that (with the exception of sex) those able to give up smoking differ from those who continue in the same ways that distinguish the population of non-smokers from that of smokers.

9 LESS HAZARDOUS SMOKING?

There is every likelihood that large numbers of people will continue to smoke for years to come. Many existing smokers are unable, or unwilling, to give up and new smokers are currently joining the smoking population at nearly the same rate as old smokers die or quit. The composition of the smoking population may be changing (in age, sex, and social class) but the total is not shrinking, or at least not at such a rate that an end to the problem of smoking is in prospect. Health education, legislation, changes in social attitudes, and the availability of various aids for the would-be non-smoker will continue to have some effect on patterns of consumption and the prevalence of the habit, but it is unlikely that their immediate impact can be greatly increased, or that any new and radically more effective approaches will be devised.

The evidence available suggests that the diseases associated with smoking relate to the intake of smoke constituents in a dose-dependent way; the greater the exposure to smoke constituents, the greater the risk. Those who smoke many cigarettes are at greater risk than those who smoke few; smokers of plain cigarettes run a greater risk than smokers of lower-yielding filter brands; and smokers of many years' standing are more threatened than those with a shorter smoking history. Thus Wynder has written, 'Epidemiological studies have consistently demonstrated a dose-response relationship between tobacco smoke and the development of . . . cardiovascular diseases, tobacco-related cancer and chronic obstructive pulmonary diseases. Such evidence indicates that a long-term reduction in tobacco smoke exposure will be followed by a reduction in tobacco-related diseases' (Wynder 1980: 4).

As a complement to the emphasis on encouraging smokers to give up, and dissuading non-smokers from taking up the habit, there therefore exists another strategy – that of reducing the extent to which continuing smokers are exposed to the harmful constituents in tobacco smoke. This can be done either by reducing the total dose of smoke which smokers obtain, or by altering the composition of the smoke so that those substances most closely related to disease are selectively reduced. We will consider ways in which either or both of these aims may be accomplished, but turn initially to a brief account of the major constituents of tobacco smoke and their possible role in disease.

ADVERSE EFFECTS OF MAJOR SMOKE CONSTITUENTS

Cigarette smoke contains both gases and solids, and over thirty of the many constituents have been suspected of being harmful to health. However, the most important contributors to the hazards of smoking are judged to be carbon monoxide, in the gas phase, and tar and nicotine in the solid phase (Royal College of Physicians 1977; Surgeon General 1979).

Carbon monoxide

Apart from nitrogen, oxygen, and water vapour, which are all present in air, carbon monoxide makes up the largest proportion of the gaseous phase, contributing up to 5 per cent of the total gases in cigarette smoke. Carbon monoxide is absorbed from cigarette smoke only if it is inhaled, but once in the body it combines with haemoglobin to form carboxyhaemoglobin (COHb). The affinity of carbon monoxide for haemoglobin is 200 times greater than that of oxygen, and in addition COHb dissociates much less readily and more slowly than oxyhaemoglobin. Thus the presence of carbon monoxide tends to reduce the oxygen-carrying capacity of the blood and to impair the oxygen supply to the tissues. In smokers, the amount of carbon monoxide that enters the bloodstream depends on the carbon monoxide yield of the cigarette and the degree to which the smoke is inhaled. Most smokers show a rise of between 1 and 2 per cent COHb with each cigarette. There may be a cumulative effect so that the COHb concentration rises slowly during the day, reaching concentrations of up to 15 per cent by the evening in heavy smokers. Most of the carbon monoxide is then eliminated during the night by slow release back into the lungs.

In the short term, healthy smokers do not seem to suffer noticeably from the levels of COHb in their blood. Compensatory changes such as increases in total haemoglobin (Eisen and Hammond 1956) and increase in blood flow to vital organs (Stewart 1974) probably occur. In general only slight impairment of mental or physical performance has been demonstrated in humans with blood concentrations of COHb in the region of 5 to 10 per cent (Ayres, Gianelli, and Muller 1970; McFarland 1970; Beard and Grandstaff 1970; Mikulka *et al.* 1970; Hanks 1970).

However, in the presence of myocardial disease, where the oxygen supply to myocardial tissues is already critically reduced, a raised COHb concentration in the blood can act as an aggravating factor. Ayres *et al.* demonstrated myocardial hypoxia in patients with coronary disease when COHb concentration rose above 6 per cent (Ayres, Gianelli, and Muller 1970). They also observed increases in cardiac output and heart rate associated with small rises in COHb concentrations. These haemodynamic responses increase the oxygen demand of the already hypoxic myocardial tissue and might initiate a fatal episode of ventricular fibrillation, even at low levels of COHb. Ayres *et al.* consider that carbon monoxide might add to the cardio-vascular effects of nicotine in precipitating tobacco angina, a symptom first recorded in 1858 on the French ship *Embuscade*, where it was attributed to the high concentration of tobacco smoke below deck. For similar reasons, raised COHb levels could precipitate intermittent claudication in patients with peripheral arterial disease. Again, in respiratory diseases in which poor perfusion and ventilation limit oxygen uptake from the lungs, the presence of carbon monoxide in inspired air can aggravate respiratory failure.

Carbon monoxide has also been incriminated as one of the factors accounting for the association of maternal smoking during pregnancy with a lower than average birth weight of the infant and a higher than average rate of abortion, stillbirth, and neonatal death (Butler, Goldstein, and Ross 1972). The risks to the infants of smoking mothers appear to be approximately doubled, and this effect is independent of parity, duration of gestation, maternal size, age, or social class (Low 1959; Herriott, Billewicz, and Aylten 1962). The effects on birth weight appear to be directly related to the number of cigarettes smoked (*Lancet* 1979). As discussed by Longo (1970) the foetus is more vulnerable than the mother to raised COHb concentrations, and the concentrations found in the blood of smoking mothers could be sufficient to cause foetal hypoxia and damage to tissue enzymes, resulting in impairment of growth. Other contri-buting factors in cigarette smoke include nicotine, which causes uterine vasoconstriction, and cyanide, which depletes stores of vitamin B12 (McGarry and Andrews 1972).

Whether or not a raised COHb concentration causes long-term adverse effects in man remains controversial. Astrup (1967) and Astrup, Kjeldsen, and Wanstrup (1970) suggested that it is a cause of atherosclerotic arterial disease, but direct proof of a causative role is lacking (Surgeon General 1979). Nevertheless, there does appear to be a correlation between COHb levels in tobacco smokers and the risk of atherosclerotic diseases including ischaemic heart disease (Wald *et al.* 1973; Heliövarra *et al.* 1978). The US Surgeon General concluded that throughout his report 'Carbon monoxide, in particular has been identified . . . as a possible critical factor in coronary heart disease, atherosclerosis and sudden death . . . chronic respiratory disease (and) foetal growth retardation' (Surgeon General 1979: 411).

There is no evidence that carbon monoxide contributes to the satisfaction of smoking or that smokers show compensatory changes in smoking behaviour dependent on the carbon monoxide yields of the cigarette. Therefore, a selective reduction in the amount of this probably harmful constituent in cigarette smoke would appear to be a prudent step towards less hazardous smoking.

Tar

The main solids in cigarette smoke are tar and nicotine. Tobacco tar is usually defined as the complex of particulate matter in the smoke that is left behind on a filter after subtracting all the nicotine and moisture. Among the many substances contained in the resulting dark brown sticky mass are the polycyclic aromatic hydrocarbons, a class of compounds generally accepted as being a potential cause of cancer. Animal experiments indicate that cancer results from the interactions of cancer-initiating, cancer-promoting, and cancer-accelerating agents among these various hydrocarbons. In addition, these hydrocarbons, and probably other substances in tobacco tar, act as irritants to the lung and may be implicated in causing or aggravating bronchitis and other respiratory diseases.

Data continue to accumulate confirming the close statistical relationship between cigarette smoking in man and respiratory disease. If, as seems likely, this association depends on total tar exposure, a second step towards safer smoking would be to reduce the amount of tar available in cigarette smoke. It is not clear whether this would affect smoking behaviour.

The amount and composition of tobacco tar, and possibly its toxicity, differ according to the method of curing the tobacco leaf. At the moment UK cigarettes are manufactured almost exclusively from tobacco which has been rapidly flue-cured over a period of 24 to 36 hours in high-humidity barns heated by furnaces. This process contrasts with that in which a flow of air slowly cures the tobacco over a few months' gradual drying (Wolf 1967). The different processes produce tobaccos differing radically in pH, chemical composition, and especially sugar content. In flue-curing, the sugars are preserved, whilst in air-curing (often accompanied by induced fermentation) they are enzymatically degraded.

Lamb and Reid (1969) and Passey *et al.* (1971) reported that the smoke of flue-cured tobacco was more damaging to the respiratory system of rats than smoke from air-cured tobacco. The relevance of these studies to human smoking has been questioned (*Lancet* 1973). However, further investigation of the relative toxicity of tars obtained from differently cured tobaccos might contribute to the development of less harmful cigarettes.

Nicotine

Nicotine has widespread actions on the cardiovascular system. The typical cardiovascular response to smoking a cigarette is similar to the response to sympathetic stimulation and to exercise. There is an increase in heart rate, cardiac output, and coronary blood flow, a rise in blood pressure, peripheral vasoconstriction with a drop in skin temperature in the extremities, and an increase in muscle blood flow. At the same time there is a rise in circulating levels of adrenaline and noradrenaline (e.g., Cryer *et al.* 1976), a rise in blood sugar and fatty acids, and an increase in the adhesiveness and aggregation of blood platelets. All these changes have been well documented (Larson, Haag, and Silvette 1961; Larson and Silvette 1975); they do not occur with sham smoking and can be mimicked by intravenous injections or aerosol inhalations of nicotine. Many of the responses can be blocked by adrenergic receptor blocking drugs.

The typical response results mainly from sympathetic stimulation, but in some subjects and with different doses of nicotine, effects of parasympathetic stimulation, or of sympathetic or parasympathetic blockade, may dominate the response. For example, a fall in heart rate and blood pressure and even syncope may occur. Individual subjects tend to show their own characteristic cardiovascular response to smoking, no doubt reflecting constitutional factors (Ashton *et al.* 1979a).

There is no evidence that the cardiovascular response to nicotine leads to acute adverse effects in normal subjects. However, smoking, like exercise and sympathetic stimulation, can aggravate existing cardiovascular disease. In ischaemic heart disease, smoking may increase cardiac output, but without a concomitant increase in coronary blood flow, thus precipitating anginal pain and ischaemic changes in the electrocardiogram. Carbon monoxide probably adds to these adverse effects of nicotine (Ball and Turner 1974). Smoking can also counteract the effects of treatment with the beta adrenergic blocker propranolol in patients with angina (Fox *et al.* 1980). Other undesirable effects of nicotine in ischaemic heart disease are the increased tendency to ventricular arrhythmia (a cause of sudden death), a rise in circulating free fatty acids, and increased coagulability of the blood (Ball and Turner 1974).

In patients with peripheral arterial disease such as Raynaud's syndrome, thromboangiitis obliterans, and peripheral athero-sclerosis, the peripheral vasoconstriction induced by nicotine in addition to the raised COHb concentration, can aggravate tissue ischaemia (Ball and Turner 1974). In hypertension, nicotine produces a further rise in blood pressure and this may be a factor in the increased death rate from rupture of aortic and cerebral aneurysms in smokers (Bell and Symon 1979). In pregnancy, uterine vasoconstriction may contribute to foetal hypoxia, and smoking and nicotine chewing gum have been shown to reduce foetal breathing movements (Manning and Feyerabend 1976). Maternal smoking has also been implicated as a possible cause of congenital abnormalities in the infant (Fedrick, Alberman, and Goldstein 1971).

The involvement of smoking in the *causation* of cardiovascular disease is still controversial. However, in both men and women smoking is associated with an increased risk of ischaemic heart disease, peripheral obliterative vascular disease, strokes and hypertension, and a higher morbidity and mortality once the disease is recognized. In coronary artery disease, smoking appears to have an independent and additive effect with other associated risk factors such as obesity, physical inactivity, raised serum cholesterol, diabetes, and hypertension. Stopping smoking appears to be associated with a reduction in cardiovascular risks (e.g., Ball and Turner 1974). The relative contribution of nicotine, carbon monoxide, other smoke constituents, and constitutional factors in the aetiology of these diseases is not clear, nor is there evidence of a definite mechanism whereby nicotine, or other smoke constituents, could cause chronic cardiovascular disease.

Nevertheless, it seems clear that reducing nicotine exposure would reduce mortality and morbidity in patients who already have cardiovascular disease. This likelihood presupposes the possibility of reducing the nicotine yield of cigarettes. However, as already described, the presence of nicotine in cigarettes is for most people the reason for smoking. Reduction of nicotine yield leads to compensatory changes in smoking behaviour, and these changes (with cigarettes of their present composition) tend to increase the inhalation of tar and carbon monoxide. Similarly, cigarettes with a very low nicotine yield, beyond the possibility of compensatory smoking, are not acceptable to most smokers who quickly switch to more satisfying brands. For these reasons, a case can be made for reducing tar and carbon monoxide yields while maintaining the availability of nicotine. However, for those with cardiovascular disease, the only safe course appears to be to stop smoking; for those anxious to avoid all possible risks of its occurrence in later life, the sensible course is never to start.

Finally, mention must be made of the risks run by non-smokers exposed to others' cigarette smoke. Some risks to the unborn child of the smoking mother have already been noted. The children of cigarette smokers run a greater risk of developing respiratory disease, although whether this is directly due to exposure to cigarette smoke is not known) (Harlap and Davies 1974; Colley 1974). Recently Hirayama (1981) reported a greatly increased risk of lung cancer in the non-smoking wives of Japanese smokers. Stock (1980) has drawn attention to the fact that fourteen carcinogens in cigarette smoke occur in greater concentrations in the sidestream than in the mainstream smoke and has suggested that non-smokers enclosed in confined spaces with smokers may run a considerable risk from this form of pollution. Non-smokers, therefore, would be likely to support any move towards producing cigarettes which would be less harmful to them as well as safer for smokers.

DO WE ALREADY HAVE LESS HAZARDOUS CIGARETTES?

The role of cigarette tars in the causation of smoking-related cancers is clearer than the role of nicotine and carbon monoxide in the causation of smoking-related cardiovascular disease. The main emphasis over the past twenty years has therefore been on reducing the smoker's intake of tar. Over this period there has been a marked reduction in the standard tar delivery of cigarettes (i.e., the delivery obtained when cigarettes are machine-smoked to standard specifications of puff frequency, duration, and volume). This has resulted mainly from the almost universal switch from plain to lower-yielding filter cigarettes, although within both plain and filter categories, tar deliveries have also been reduced. Thus Lee records (Lee 1976, Table 6) that sales-weighted tar levels of UK plain and filter cigarettes dropped 29 per cent and 43 per cent respectively over the period 1965–75. The introduction of special 'low tar' brands has also made an impression. In the United States, the proportion of manufactured cigarettes with tar delivery lower than 16 mg increased from 2 per cent in 1967 to 16 per cent in 1976 (Wynder 1977). In Britain, lower tar 'mild' cigarettes now hold 20 per cent of the market (ASH 1980b). In parallel with the reduction in tar yield, the standard delivery of nicotine has also fallen, although to a slightly lesser extent (Stepney 1979b).

Since smoking-related disease takes time to develop, a considerable lag would be expected before reductions in tar delivery had any effect on epidemiological trends. Nevertheless, there is now some evidence that disease rates for certain categories of smokers are beginning to decline. Wynder (1980) cites five retrospective studies showing lower mortality amongst filter cigarette smokers. Using his own work as a basis, he concludes that people smoking filter cigarettes for ten or more years had one-third less risk of contracting cancer of the lung or larynx than smokers of plain cigarettes. Hammond (1980) discusses a prospective study, starting in 1959, which investigated mortality among over one million people. Smokers enrolled in the investigation were classified according to whether they smoked 'high' (above 26 mg), 'low' (below 18 mg) or 'medium' tar cigarettes. Subjects were then matched for age, social and economic status, and consumption. In relation to lung-cancer mortality over the period 1959–77, differences between the groups were clear. Compared with smokers of high delivery cigarettes, male low-tar smokers showed a reduction in mortality of approximately 20 per cent and female low-tar smokers a 40 per cent reduction. Although less consistent, a similar pattern was apparent for coronary heart disease; men experiencing 10 per cent reduction in mortality, and women 20 per cent.

However, this kind of evidence (even though prospective) is subject to the same criticism that has been levelled against the original epidemiological data relating smoking to disease. People who choose to smoke lower-delivery cigarettes are a self-selected group who may well be unrepresentative of the wider smoking population. It is plausible to suggest that smokers concerned enough with their health to smoke low-tar cigarettes will also be people who are better educated, wealthier, and more inclined to careful diet and exercise. They are also more likely always to have smoked cigarettes supposed to be relatively less harmful, and to have smoked fewer cigarettes and inhaled less. Certain of these factors can be controlled for when subjects in the different tar groups are matched. Others, such as attitudes towards health and extent of inhalation, would be difficult (if not impossible) to take into account. Therefore, rather than being caused by the choice of reduced-delivery cigarettes, the lower mortality among lower-tar smokers may merely reflect a host of other associated factors. Wynder *et al.* are themselves aware of this possibility (Wynder, Mabuchi, and Beattie 1970).

Fortunately, further kinds of evidence are available. One is provided by the histological work of Auerbach, Hammond, and Garfinkel (1979) which was mentioned in Chapter 1. Auerbach and his colleagues compared lung tissue from smokers who died in the 1970s with tissue taken from smokers who died in the late 1950s. In the more recent samples, fewer pre-cancerous histological abnormalities were found. These tissues were taken from people who would mostly have been long-term smokers of lower-delivery filter cigarettes, whereas the majority of people contributing the earlier samples would have had a history of smoking exclusively plain cigarettes. (In 1952 only 1 per cent of American cigarettes were filtered; in 1962, 55 per cent: Schumann 1977.) Auerbach *et al.* therefore argued that the shift to filter cigarettes was likely eventually to be reflected in a much reduced incidence of lung cancer. Although discovering a reduced frequency of histological abnormality is several steps removed from finding a decrease in cancer mortality, the argument seems plausible.

The importance of Auerbach's findings lies in the fact that the samples he was comparing were not drawn from populations of smokers who had themselves selected the type of cigarette they would smoke. They are therefore likely to be genuinely representative of the whole population of smokers, at different periods of time. However, attributing the reduced frequency of histological abnormality to a change in the type of cigarette smoked assumes that such a change is the only relevant difference between the late 1950s and the early 1970s. It could be argued that other factors (such as a reduction in atmospheric pollution, for example) might be a possible alternative cause of Auerbach's results.

It is therefore important to consider a third line of evidence, derived from comparing the carcinogenicity of tar obtained from different kinds of cigarette. A common method of establishing carcinogenicity involves repeatedly painting smoke condensate on to the exposed skin of laboratory animals. The time taken for a tumour to appear, or the proportion of animals developing tumours, is then taken as a measure of the cancer-producing potential of the substance used. The work of Wynder and Hoffman (1967) provides an example of this technique, relevant to the question of whether the health hazards of smoking may have been reduced over the past thirty years. They report that the proportion of mice developing tumours when smoke condensate was applied to their skin fell significantly over the period 1954–63. During the same period, the tumorigenicity of a constant dose of the carcinogen benzo(a)pyrene remained the same. Although the exact relationship between skin tumours in mice and cancers of the respiratory tract in humans is not clear, these results showed that the reduced cancer-producing potential of tobacco tars was a real phenomenon and not the reflection simply of increased resistance in the animals being used, or of differences in laboratory procedure. They therefore concluded that the changes were due to differences in the makeup of cigarettes, reflected in a reduction of benzo(a)pyrene and other carcinogenic constituents of tobacco smoke.

The epidemiological work discussed by Wynder and Hammond, although couched in terms of higher and lower tar delivery, essentially involves a comparison between plain and filter cigarette smokers. It might be expected that the recent emphasis on further reducing the delivery of filter brands, and on introducing specifically low-tar brands (with deliveries of 10 mg or less), would have an additional noticeable impact on mortality. The effect of these more recent changes, however, has probably yet to become apparent. Nevertheless, there are already optimists talking about a level of cigarette consumption which would be 'safe' in the sense that the associated risks would be indistinguishable from those of a non-smoker. Foremost among the advocates of this approach is Gori, of the US National Cancer Institute.

As outlined in a paper by Lynch and Gori (1980), the first stage in the argument is a review of four early studies of the relationship between smoking and disease. These studies agree in showing that the relative risk of disease decreases as the number of cigarettes smoked becomes less. Extrapolating this trend, Gori and Lynch conclude that at the level of two cigarettes per day, the risk cannot reliably be distinguished from that of a non-smoker. They then argue that two pre-1960 cigarettes are equivalent in delivery to between three and five current middle-tar cigarettes, and between ten and fifteen low-tar ones. They therefore suggest, admittedly tentatively (and subject to criticism by others working in the field of smoking and health), that smoking around a dozen current low-tar cigarettes would be a worthwhile goal for smokers unable to quit altogether, since at this level of consumption overall mortality would not be significantly increased.

Three points require emphasis. First, the figures given apply to overall mortality. Critical levels of exposure can (and have been) separately calculated for specific smoking-related diseases (Gori and Lynch 1978). When this is done, the critical level of exposure varies considerably for different diseases. Secondly, it is not suggested that smoking the equivalent of two pre-1960 cigarettes carries *no* attendant risk. Simply 'that such a risk, although real, probably cannot be observed from practical epidemiological surveys' (Lynch and Gori 1980: 42). Thirdly, it must be noted that the low-tar cigarettes Gori and Lynch are referring to (yielding 5 mg tar, 0.5 mg nicotine and 5 mg carbon monoxide) are lower in delivery than the majority of currently available (and popular) low-tar cigarettes.

However, the most important criticisms of Gori and Lynch's approach concern the assumptions they have made about smoking behaviour. First, there is the familiar point that smokers who have a low consumption of cigarettes are probably not a typical cross-section of the smoking population. Their reduced rate of ill-health is possibly attributable at least in part to the fact that they start smoking later, inhale less and have a generally more 'health-conscious' approach to life. One therefore cannot assume that the risk for a heavy smoker would eventually be reduced to that of a life-long light smoker simply by altering the number or the kind of cigarettes smoked.

The most vital objection, however, refers to the extrapolation from standardized machine-smoked deliveries to those actually obtained by the smoker. Gori and Lynch admit that their calculations 'are based on the assumption that the smoker of the low-tar and nicotine cigarettes will not change his smoking habits in terms of depth of inhalation, frequency of puffing, and butt length' (Gori and Lynch 1978: 1258). Although Gori and Lynch argue that 'findings of recent studies support this assumption' (Gori and Lynch 1978: 1258), they are surely incorrect. Evidence on the self-regulation of smoke intake was extensively reviewed in Chapter 4. The clear conclusion is that middle-tar smokers switched in the course of an experiment to lower-delivery cigarettes alter their smoking behaviour in all of the ways suggested by Gori and Lynch. While these changes in smoking are probably not sufficient to compensate entirely for the reduction in standard delivery, there is a clear tendency for the actual yield of the lower-delivery brand to be greater than that obtained by a smoking machine (e.g., Ashton, Stepney, and Thompson 1979b).

Whether smokers who voluntarily switch to lower-delivery brands show a similar adaptation of smoking behaviour is a slightly different question. The answer, however, is similar. Long-term smokers of low-tar products smoke relatively more intensively than habitual smokers of middle-tar products, taking a greater total volume of smoke from their cigarettes and smoking to a shorter butt length (Stepney 1980b). The effect of these changes in smoking behaviour is to reduce the difference in actual exposure between middle and low-tar smokers, although whether the difference in smoke intake is effectively eliminated is subject to debate.

Russell *et al.* (1980b) argue strongly that the standard nicotine delivery of a cigarette is substantially irrelevant to the question of how much nicotine a smoker will take into his body. In a study in which 330 people smoked cigarettes of their own brand Russell *et al.* found no significant differences in post-smoking blood nicotine concentration between smokers of untipped (plain), filter (i.e., middle-tar) and ventilated filter (i.e., low-tar) cigarettes. The standard nicotine yield of the brand smoked accounted for only 4 per cent of the variation in blood nicotine concentrations. They therefore conclude: 'the assumed health advantage of switching to lower-tar and lower-nicotine cigarettes may be largely offset by the tendency of smokers to compensate by increasing inhalation'. 'Whatever its cause, our results suggest that switching to cigarettes with lower tar and nicotine yields may not reduce tar and nicotine intake at all, or at most by a disappointingly small degree' (Russell *et al.* 1980b: 972, 975).

If this is correct, we are faced with the problem of explaining how the reduced risk evident in epidemiological studies has come about. In part, as already mentioned, the reduced risks run by filter-cigarette smokers may be attributable to the fact that people who choose to make the switch from plain cigarettes are already an atypically low-risk segment of the smoking population. In addition to this argument, Russell *et al.* suggest that the reduced incidence of lung cancer may be due not to lower tar exposure but to changes in the nature of the tar. Thus, the application of cigarette tar to mouse skin over the last ten to fifteen years has demonstrated a steady decrease in the carcinogenicity of the same total dose of tar. Gori (1976) suggests that this is due to changes in the design of cigarettes which have altered the way in which the tobacco is burned.

These are possible explanations for the apparent discrepancy. However, it is by no means certain that the study of Russell *et al.* truly reflects the position in which the majority of low-tar smokers find themselves. Although the sample on which the researchers based their conclusions was large, it was nevertheless highly atypical of the general population of smokers. The average daily consumption of their low-tar low-nicotine group was thirty-five cigarettes per day, compared with an average for all smokers of nineteen per day. Further, the sample consisted largely of people attending an anti-smoking clinic. Both these facts suggest the smokers studied may have been more heavily dependent on nicotine than is usual and therefore more likely to show complete compensation for lower nicotine yield. These particular smokers may also have been unusually eager to obtain a pharmacologically significant dose of nicotine in the stressful circumstances of smoking immediately before giving a venous blood sample. Moreover, even if the plasma nicotine levels in middle and low-tar smokers were very similar, their exposure to tar may nevertheless have been appreciably less. Rawbone (1980) points out that the tar-to-nicotine ratios of middle and low-tar cigarettes are different, low-tar brands providing a greater delivery of nicotine per unit of tar. Using Russell's figures for blood nicotine levels, Rawbone argues that the actual tar exposure of the low-delivery smokers would have been only three-quarters that of the middle-tar group.

A study in Cambridge (Stepney 1980b), using smaller (but more representative) groups of habitual low and middle-tar smokers, suggested that the exposure to smoke constituents was likely to be appreciably less with low-delivery brands. With low-tar cigarettes the increase in end-tidal carbon monoxide (which correlates closely with blood COHb) was only 75 per cent of that experienced by smokers of middle-tar brands, whilst the 24-hour excretion of nicotine was 76 per cent. Although it was not possible to measure directly the intake of tar in that study, it is likely that exposure to this constituent of smoke was also reduced. The delivery of tar to the smoker's mouth (as measured by the duplication of human smoking patterns on a smoking

1. The nature of the tobacco

2. Cigarette design

3. The way the cigarette is smoked

4. Inhalation

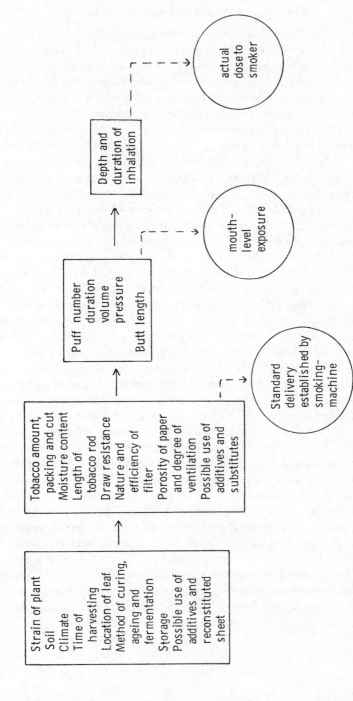

Figure 30 Factors affecting the composition of tobacco smoke and exposure to smoke constituents

machine) was significantly less in the low-tar group. Although a lower mouth-level intake does not prove that the actual dose obtained after inhalation was less (see *Figure 30*), there was no evidence from the carbon monoxide data that the proportionately greater inhalation of smoke from the low-tar cigarettes would have been sufficient to make actual tar exposure the same in the two groups.

This conclusion is substantially the same as that arrived at by Wald *et al.* (1980) who studied the inhaling habits of over a thousand middle-aged males smoking their usual brand of cigarette. Smokers of both ventilated (low-tar) and unventilated filter cigarettes inhaled more than smokers of plain (untipped) brands. This was demonstrated by relating the blood carboxyhaemoglobin levels observed in the smokers to the carbon monoxide delivery of their cigarettes. For example, smokers of low-tar (ventilated) filter cigarettes had COHb levels 39 per cent higher than smokers of plain cigarettes, despite the fact that the standard CO yields were 22 per cent lower. Nevertheless, in neither low nor middle-tar filter cigarette smokers was the increase in inhalation sufficient to result in as great an intake of tar or nicotine as that achieved by smokers of plain cigarettes. As a result, the expected benefits to health associated with smoking filter cigarettes may be reduced, but they are unlikely to be completely abolished.

Evidence from a variety of sources is therefore consistent with the view that the smoker of current reduced-delivery cigarettes is exposed to a lower risk of cancer than his counterpart of ten to thirty years ago. Epidemiological data from people smoking cigarettes of different tar delivery show a lower mortality in smokers of lower delivery cigarettes. Histological evidence from lung tissue taken from smokers of all kinds of cigarettes at different periods suggests that the risk has been reduced for smokers in general, and not merely for a self-selected, health-conscious segment of the smoking population. Laboratory studies demonstrate, on balance, that the intake of smoke constituents is less in smokers of low-tar products than in smokers of middle-tar cigarettes (although, because of compensatory changes in behaviour, the reduction in exposure is not as great as standard machine-smoked deliveries would suggest). Finally, even if current smokers *were* to obtain the same total dose of tar as their predecessors, they might still have a lower incidence of cancer because the carcinogencity of tar appears to have been reduced.

FUTURE PROSPECTS

If smoking has become somewhat less hazardous over the past thirty years, what are the prospects for a continued improvement? To some extent these depend on technological advances in the production and design of cigarettes; to some extent on the education of the smoker. However, it is also of crucial importance that agreement is reached on the strategy most likely to be successful in reducing smoking-related disease. Such agreement depends on further research to identify clearly the constituents of cigarette smoke responsible for disease, and those responsible for the rewards of smoking. By eliminating as much as possible of the former, whilst maintaining an adequate delivery of the latter, it may be possible to wean the smoker on to safer kinds of cigarette. We will discuss these issues, about which there is still much debate, but will initially briefly outline some of the techniques by which the delivery of smoke constituents may be manipulated.

The present reduced tar and nicotine deliveries have been achieved by a variety of changes in the nature of the tobacco used to manufacture cigarettes and in cigarette design (*Figure 30*). Wynder and Hoffman (1967) list examples of the way in which the yield of tar and nicotine may be manipulated. The type of tobacco used, for example, is an important variable. Cigarettes of the same weight and tobacco cut yield anything between 33.4 and 21.2 mg of dry condensate (i.e., tar plus nicotine), depending on the type of tobacco used. Even with the same type of tobacco, the conditions of cultivation are critical. Thus Burley tobacco produced tar yields varying from 20 to 40 mg per cigarette, depending on where in the world the tobacco was grown. With the same plant and same site of cultivation, the position on the stalk from which the tobacco is taken is an important determinant of yield. Hence, with cigarettes made from the same Burley strain, the standard tar delivery increased from 23 mg with tobacco from the base of the plant to 37 mg with tobacco from the top.

Turning to the design of cigarettes, the most common methods of varying delivery involve filtration and ventilation of the smoke. An effective filter will remove particulate matter (leaving the gas phase relatively unaltered), whilst increasing the porosity of the cigarette paper and perforating the tip result in the dilution of smoke drawn from the cigarette by air from outside. By an appropriate combination of filtration and ventilation it is already possible to produce virtually 'smokeless' cigarettes from which the smoker would be hard pressed to obtain 1 mg of tar, and 0.1 mg of nicotine. Such cigarettes, however, although widely advertised in the USA, are virtually unobtainable presumably because the demand for them is so slight.

There is a two-fold limitation to changes that can be made in cigarette design. The first, illustrated by the fate of 'ultra' low-delivery brands, is that while smokers have a free choice among a variety of cigarettes, any 'safer' cigarette which is unacceptable in terms of what the smoker requires will not be smoked and will therefore have no effect on the incidence of disease. The second is that any manipulation which results in a completely compensatory adaptation of smoking behaviour is worthless. Thus, halving the delivery of tar on standard machine smoking would have no effect on tar exposure if smokers smoked twice as many of the cigarettes or smoked each cigarette twice as intensively.

The problem of developing less hazardous cigarettes is further complicated by the lack of agreement on the kind of changes necessary. One school of thought holds that the delivery of tar, nicotine, and carbon monoxide ought all to be reduced, since all are implicated to some extent in smoking-related disease. Advocates of this approach are encouraged by the reduction in yields which has already taken place, and think that the cigarette manufacturer and consumer alike can be pushed further and faster down the same path. Unimpressed by the argument that smokers will compensate for the reduced availability of nicotine, they suggest that the blandness of low-delivery cigarettes may be lessened by the addition of flavourings such as are already much used in American brands.

An alternative view, vigorously advocated by Russell (1974; 1976a), holds that the delivery of tar and carbon monoxide should be minimized, whilst that of nicotine is maintained. There is logic in this approach, if it is accepted that smoking is essentially nicotine self-administration and that the minimum acceptable nicotine dose is the 1–1.5 mg per cigarette which smokers now obtain from the most widely smoked brands. Maintaining this level of nicotine in a low-tar low-carbon monoxide cigarette should both ensure acceptability and prevent the 'oversmoking' which does so much to negate the virtue of present low-tar brands.

Nevertheless, there are difficulties in Russell's approach. Whilst a reduction in all smoke constituents, through ventilation and filtration, is relatively easy to achieve, the problem of selectively reducing certain components presents a problem for tobacco technology. The difficulty might be overcome by supplementing the nicotine in tobacco, or by adding it to a non-tobacco substitute, as suggested in the 1977 report of the Royal College of Physicians. This is probably the only way in which tobacco substitutes are likely to be useful. On the assumption that people smoke for nicotine, diluting tobacco with material which produces some tar but no nicotine is unlikely to contribute to either the 'safety' or acceptability of a cigarette. It was probably this fact, as much as effective publicity against the product (Van Rossum 1978), which led to the rapid commercial failure of cigarettes containing a proportion of tobacco substitute when they were marketed in the UK in 1977.

However (somewhat ironically), the tobacco manufacturers foresee considerable problems in using a substance as toxic as nicotine in large-scale production. Even if enhanced nicotine cigarettes were a practical proposition, not all authorities would agree that their use should be encouraged. Wynder recently commented (Wynder 1980: 8–9) that although Russell's proposal was a good idea with respect to the risk of cancer, it was not known whether it was likely to be beneficial ('or even benign') with respect to cardio-vascular disease. Bock would question whether the moderate-nicotine low-tar approach was beneficial even in terms of carcino-genicity. Although expressing caution over whether results from tumour induction in animals can be directly applied to the human situation, Bock is impressed by evidence that higher nicotine concentrations increase the likelihood of eventual tumour formation when known carcinogens are applied to mouse skin. Despite the widespread assumption to the contrary, he concludes that there is now 'abundant evidence that the nicotine in cigarette smoke is a cocarcinogen' (Bock 1980: 129).

In addition to strategies aimed at reducing the delivery of some or all smoke constituents, two further suggestions have been put forward. One is that smokers should be encouraged to smoke in a less hazardous way, irrespective of the cigarette consumed. Thus health authorities have urged smokers to leave a longer butt, to take fewer puffs, and to inhale smoke less deeply. Although it is conceivable that smokers could be encouraged (or trained) to adopt a style of smoking which reduced their exposure to harmful smoke constituents, such a manoeuvre would be subject to the same limitation that besets attempts to reduce cigarette smoke delivery: both the *addiction* and the *psychological tool* models of smoking motivation suggest that nicotine intake must remain at or above the level necessary to produce the desired pharmacological effects if it is to continue to satisfy the smoker.

A second idea, which relates particularly to the situation in Britain, suggests that a change in the kind of tobacco used in cigarettes might result in a reduction in mortality, without affecting the availability of nicotine to the smoker. For example, a change to air-cured rather than flue-cured tobacco might be worthy of consideration. Wynder and Hoffman (1967) cite the finding that tar from English cigarettes produces more tumours when applied to mouse skin than tar from American brands. Although the finer cut of the tobacco and thicker cigarette paper may contribute to this difference, they are inclined to attribute it to the nature of the tobacco used. Wynder and Hoffman write: 'in general cigarettes of air-cured tobacco not only deliver less particulate matter ... but their yield of certain tumorigenic components as well as the tumorigenic activities of their smoke condensates ... are also significantly reduced' (Wynder and Hoffman 1967: 516). This finding would seem to accord with lower lung-cancer rates in France (where almost all cigarette tobacco is air-cured) and in the USA (where cigarettes are composed of a blend of air and flue-cured leaf).

However, for a number of reasons, the association between air-cured tobacco and a reduced likelihood of cancer is not straight-forward. Smoking habits in France and the USA differ from those in Britain. In France fewer smokers inhale, and the proportion of smokers was until recently considerably less than in the UK; in the USA smokers leave longer cigarette butts. Secondly, although Wynder found that air-cured tobacco tar was less carcinogenic than the tar from flue-cured cigarettes, others have found no difference, or the reverse. It is possible that a switch to air-cured tobaccos might lessen exposure to tar by reducing the extent of inhalation, perhaps because nicotine can more effectively be absorbed in the mouth from the alkaline smoke. There is no certainty, however, that the change in smoke composition resulting from the adoption of air-cured tobaccos would be of any overall benefit.

There is no shortage of suggestions as to how the smoker might be directed towards less hazardous smoking. Nevertheless, the attempt actually to reduce the risks associated with smoking is beset with difficulties. In addition to the uncertainties already described, the very concept of 'safer' smoking may discourage people from the only truly safe course of action, which is either never to start smoking or, if started, to stop. Nevertheless, the Royal College of Physicians conclude that 'this is a risk which must be taken: for if, as might be possible, the harmfulness of cigarettes were reduced by at least one half, as much illness would be prevented as by the formidable task of persuading every other smoker to stop' (Royal College of Physicians 1977: 121).

REFERENCES

ABEL, E. L. (1974) *Drugs and Behaviour*. New York: John Wiley and Sons.

ABERG, E. (1980) Agricultural Aspects of Growing Tobacco and Alternative Crops. In L. M. Ramström (ed.) *The Smoking Epidemic: Proceedings of the Fourth World Conference on Smoking and Health*. Stockholm: Almqvist & Wiksell International.

ADAMS, P.I. (1978) The Influence of Cigarette Smoke Yields on Smoking Habits. In R.E. Thornton (ed.) *Smoking Behaviour: Physiological and Psychological Influences*. Edinburgh: Churchill Livingstone.

ALPERN, H.I. and JACKSON, S.J. (1978) Stimulants and Depressants: Drug Effects on Memory. In M.A. Lipton, A. DiMascio, and K.F. Killam (eds) *Psychopharmacology: A Generation of Progress*. New York: Raven Press.

ANDERSSON, K. (1975) Effects of Cigarette Smoking on Learning and Retention. *Psychopharmacologia* **41**: 1–5.

ANDERSSON, K. and HOCKEY, G.R.J. (1977) Effects of Cigarette Smoking on Incidental Memory. *Psychopharmacology* **52**: 223–26.

ANDO, K. and YANAGITA, T. (1981) Cigarette Smoking in Rhesus Monkeys. *Psychopharmacology* **72**: 117–27.

ARMITAGE, A.K. (1973) Some Recent Observations Relating to the Absorption of Nicotine from Tobacco Smoke. In W.L. Dunn, Jr. (ed.) *Smoking Behaviour, Motives and Incentives*. Washington: Winston.

ARMITAGE, A.K. and TURNER, D.M. (1970) Absorption of Nicotine in Cigarette and Cigar Smoke Through the Oral Mucosa. *Nature* **226**: 1231–232.

ARMITAGE, A.K., HALL, G.H., and SELLERS, C.M. (1969) Effects of Nicotine on Electrocortical Activity and Acetylcholine Release from the Cat Cerebral Cortex. *British Journal of Pharmacology* **35**: 152–60.

ARMITAGE, A.K., DOLLERY, C.T., GEORGE, C.F., HOUSEMAN, T.H., LEWIS, P.J., and TURNER, D.M. (1975) Absorption and Metabolism of Nicotine from Cigarettes. *British Medical Journal* **4**: 313–16.

ARMITAGE, A.K., DOLLERY, C.T., HOUSEMAN, T.H., KOHNER, E., LEWIS, P.J., and TURNER, D.M. (1978) Absorption of Nicotine from Small Cigars. *Clinical Pharmacology and Therapeutics* **23**(2): 143–51.

ASH INFORMATION BULLETIN (1980a) Issue 62, London: 6 November.

ASH INFORMATION BULLETIN (1980b) Issue 63, London, 20 November.

ASHTON, H., and WATSON, D.W. (1970) Puffing Frequency and Nicotine Intake in Cigarette Smokers. *British Medical Journal* **3**: 679–81.

ASHTON, H., STEPNEY, R., and THOMPSON, J.W. (1978b) Smoking Behaviour and Nicotine Intake in Smokers Presented with a 'Two-Thirds' Cigarette. In R.E. Thornton (ed.) *Smoking Behaviour: Physiological and Psychological Influences.* Edinburgh: Churchill Livingstone.

ASHTON, C.H., STEPNEY, R., and THOMPSON, J.W. (1978c) Clinical Psychopharmacology Unit, Department of Pharmacological Sciences, University of Newcastle-upon-Tyne (unpublished data).

ASHTON, H., STEPNEY, R., and THOMPSON, J.W. (1979b) Self-Titration in Cigarette Smokers. *British Medical Journal* **2**: 357–60.

ASHTON, H., STEPNEY, R., and THOMPSON, J.W. (1981) Should Intake of Carbon Monoxide be Used as a Guide to Intake of Other Smoke Constituents? *British Medical Journal* **282**: 10–13.

ASHTON, H., MILLMAN, J.E., TELFORD, R., and THOMPSON, J.W. (1974) The Effects of Caffeine, Nitrazepam and Cigarette Smoking on the Contingent Negative Variation in Man. *Electroencephalography and Clinical Neurophysiology* **37**: 59–71.

ASHTON, H., SAVAGE, R.D., TELFORD, R., THOMPSON, J.W., and WATSON, D.W. (1972) The Effects of Cigarette Smoking on the Response to Stress in a Driving Simulator. *British Journal of Pharmacology* **45**: 546–56.

ASHTON, H., MILLMAN, J.E., RAWLINS, M. D., TELFORD, R., and THOMPSON, J.W. (1978a) The Use of Event-Related Slow Potentials of the Brain in the Analysis of Effects of Cigarette Smoking and Nicotine in Humans. In K. Battig (ed.) *Behavioural Effects of Nicotine.* Basel: S. Karger.

ASHTON, H., MARSH, V.R., MILLMAN, J.E., RAWLINS, M.D., STEPNEY, R., TELFORD, R., and THOMPSON, J.W. (1979a) Pattern of Behavioural, Autonomic and Electro-physiological Response to Cigarette Smoking and Nicotine in Man. In A. Remond and C. Izard (eds) *Electrophysiological Effects of Nicotine.* Amsterdam: Elsevier/N. Holland Biomedical Press.

ASHTON, H., MARSH, V.R., MILLMAN, J.E., RAWLINS, M.D., TELFORD, R., and THOMPSON, J.W. (1980) Biphasic Dose-Related Responses of the CNV (Contingent Negative Variation) to I.V. Nicotine in Man. *British Journal of Clinical Pharmacology* **10**: 579–89.

ASTRUP, P. (1967) Carbon Monoxide and Peripheral Arterial Disease. *The Scandinavian Journal of Clinical and Laboratory Investigation* (suppl.) **93**: 193–97.

ASTRUP, P., KJELDSEN, K., and WANSTRUP, J. (1970) Effects of Carbon Monoxide on the Arterial Walls. *Annals of the New York Academy of Sciences* **174**: 294–300.

ATKINSON, A.B. and TOWNSEND, J.L. (1977) Economic Aspects of Reduced Smoking. *Lancet* **2**: 492–94.

AUERBACH, O., HAMMOND, E.C., and GARFINKEL, L. (1979) Changes in Bronchial Epithelium in Relation to Cigarette Smoking, 1955–60 vs. 1970–77. *New England Journal of Medicine* **300**(8): 381–86.

AYRES, S.M., GIANELLI, S., and MULLER, H. (1970) Myocardial and Systemic Responses to Carboxyhaemoglobin. *Annals of the New York Academy of Sciences* **174**: 268–93.

BALL, K.P. (1980) How to Stop Smoking. In L.M. Ramström (ed.) *The Smoking Epidemic: Proceedings of the Fourth World Conference on Smoking and Health.* Stockholm: Almqvist & Wiksell International.

BALL, K. and TURNER, R. (1974) Smoking and the Heart. *Lancet* **2**: 822–26.

BANDURA, A. (1969) *Principles of Behavior Modification*. London: Holt, Rinehart & Winston.

BARRIE, J.M. (1890) *My Lady Nicotine*. London: Hodder & Stoughton.

BARTON, E.S. and BARTON, J.L. (1978) A Case Report on the Use of DRO in the Treatment of Smoking. *Addictive Behaviors* **3**: 1–4.

BEARD, R.R. and GRANDSTAFF, N. (1970) Carbon Monoxide Exposure and Cerebral Function. *Annals of the New York Academy of Sciences* **174**: 385–95.

BECKETT, A.H., GORROD, J.W., and JENNER, P. (1971) The Effect of Smoking on Nicotine Metabolism in Vivo in Man. *Journal of Pharmacy and Pharmacology* (suppl.) **23**: 62S–67S.

BEJEROT, C. and BEJEROT, N. (1978) Exposure Factors in Drug Use, Abuse and Addiction. In J. Fisherman (ed.) *Bases of Addiction*. Berlin: Dahlem Konferenzen.

BELL, B.A. and SYMON, L. (1979) Smoking and Subarachnoid Haemorrhage. *British Medical Journal* **1**: 577–78.

BERGLER, E. (1946) Psychopathology of Compulsive Smoking. *Psychiatric Quarterly* **20**: 297–321.

BERGLER, E. (1953) Smoking and its Infantile Precursors. *International Journal of Sexology* **6**(4): 214–20.

BERNSTEIN, D.A. (1969) Modification of Smoking Behavior: An Evaluative Review. *Psychological Bulletin* **71**(6): 418–40.

BERNSTEIN, D.A. and McALISTER, A. (1976) The Modification of Smoking Behavior: Progress and Problems. *Addictive Behaviors* **1**: 89–102.

BERNTSON, G.G., BEATTIE, M.S., and WALKER, J.M. (1976) Effects of Nicotinic and Muscarinic Compounds on Biting Attack in the Cat. *Pharmacology, Biochemistry and Behaviour* **5**: 235–39.

BEWLEY, B.R. and BLAND, J.M. (1977) Academic Performance and Social Factors Related to Cigarette Smoking by Schoolchildren. *British Journal of Preventive and Social Medicine* **31**: 18–24.

BEWLEY, B.R., BLAND, J.M., and HARRIS, R. (1974) Factors Associated with the Starting of Cigarette Smoking by Primary School Children. *British Journal of Preventive and Social Medicine* **28**: 37–44.

BEWLEY, B.R., JOHNSON, M.R.D., BLAND, J.M., and MURRAY, M. (1980) Trends in Children's Smoking. *Community Medicine* **2**: 186–89.

BJARTVEIT, K. (1981) Scandinavian Strategies. Paper presented at the ASH Tenth Anniversary Conference, Royal College of Physicians, London, 5 February 1981.

BOCK, F.G. (1980) Co-carcinogenic Properties of Nicotine. In G.B. Gori and F.G. Bock (eds) *Banbury Report 3: A Safe Cigarette?* New York: Cold Spring Harbor Laboratory.

BORGATTA, E.F. and EVANS, R.R. (1968) Social and Psychological Concomitants of Smoking Behaviour and its Change Among University Freshmen. In E.F. Borgatta and R.R. Evans (eds) *Smoking, Health and Behavior*. Chicago: Aldine.

BRANTMARK, B., OHLIN, P., and WESTLING, H. (1973) Nicotine-Containing Chewing Gum as an Anti-Smoking Aid. *Psychopharmacologia* **31**: 191–200.

BRECHER, E.M. (1972) *Licit and Illicit Drugs*. New York: Consumers Union.

BRILL, A.A. (1922) Tobacco and the Individual. *International Journal of Psychoanalysis* **3**: 430–40.

British Medical Journal (1968) Effects of Nicotine **1**: 73.

British Medical Journal (1979) Priority for Action. **1**: 1377–379.

British Medical Journal (1980) The Avoidable Holocaust. **280**: 959–60.

BROCK, T.C. (1965) Commitment to Exposure as a Determinant of Information Receptivity. *Journal of Personality and Social Psychology* **2**: 10–19.

BROCK, T.C., and BALLOUN, J.L. (1967) Behavioural Receptivity to Dissonant Information. *Journal of Personality and Social Psychology* **6**: 413–28.

BROOKS, J.E. (1953) *The Mighty Leaf: Tobacco Through the Centuries.* London: Alvin Redman.

BURCH, P.R.J. (1974) Smoking and Lung Cancer. *Lancet* 19 October: 950.

BURN, J.H. (1961) The Action of Nicotine and the Pleasure of Smoking. *Advancement of Science* **17**: 494–98.

BURNS, B.H. (1969) Chronic Chest Disease, Personality and Success in Stopping Cigarette Smoking. *British Journal of Preventive and Social Medicine* **23**: 23–27.

BUTLER, N.R., GOLDSTEIN, H., and ROSS, E.M. (1972) Cigarette Smoking in Pregnancy, its Influence on Birth Weight and Perinatal Mortality. *British Medical Journal* **1**: 127–30.

CAIN, W.S. (1980) Sensory Attributes of Cigarette Smoking. In G.B. Gori and F.G. Bock (eds) *Banbury Report 3: A Safe Cigarette?* New York: Cold Spring Harbor Laboratory.

CAPELL, P.J. (1978) Trends in Cigarette Smoking in the UK. *Health Trends* **10**: 49–54.

CHEIN, I. (1969) Psychological Functions of Drug Use. In H. Steinberg (ed.) *Scientific Basis of Drug Dependence.* London: J. & A. Churchill.

CHERRY, N. and KIERNAN, K. (1976) Personality Scores and Smoking Behaviour. *British Journal of Preventive and Social Medicine* **30**: 123–31.

CHOY, D.S.J., PURNELL, F., and JAFFE, R. (1978) Auricular Acupuncture for Cessation of Smoking. In J.L. Schwartz (ed.) *Progress in Smoking Cessation.* New York: American Cancer Society/WHO.

CLAIRMONTE, F.F. (1980) Corporate Hegemonism in World Tobacco. In L.M. Ramström (ed.) *The Smoking Epidemic: Proceedings of the Fourth World Conference on Smoking and Health.* Stockholm: Almqvist & Wiksell International.

CLARIDGE, G. (1970) *Drugs and Human Behaviour.* London: Allen Lane.

CLARK, M.S.G. (1969) Self-Administered Nicotine Solutions Preferred to Placebo by the Rat. *British Journal of Pharmacology* **35**: 367.

COAN, R.W. (1973) Personality Variables Associated with Cigarette Smoking. *Journal of Personality and Social Psychology* **26**(1): 86–104.

COLLEY, J.R.T. (1974) Respiratory Symptoms in Children and Parental Smoking and Phlegm Production. *British Medical Journal* **2**: 201–04.

COMER, A.K. and CREIGHTON, D.E. (1978) The Effect of Experimental Conditions on Smoking Behaviour. In R.E. Thornton (ed.) *Smoking Behaviour: Physiological and Psychological Influences.* Edinburgh: Churchill Livingstone.

COPPEN, A. and METCALFE, M. (1963) Cancer and Extraversion. *British Medical Journal* **2**: 18–19.

CORCORAN, D.W.J. (1965) Personality and the Inverted-U Relation. *British Journal of Psychology* **56**: 267–73.

CORINA, M. (1975) *Trust in Tobacco: The Anglo-American Struggle for Power*. London: Michael Joseph.

CORTI, COUNT E.C. (1931) *A History of Smoking*. London: Harrap.

CREIGHTON, D.E. (1973) Tobacco Smoke Retention. Paper presented at Conference on Aerosol Physics, British American Tobacco Co. Ltd., Southampton.

CREIGHTON, D.E. and LEWIS, P.H. (1978a) The Effect of Smoking Pattern on Smoke Deliveries. In R.E. Thornton (ed.) *Smoking Behaviour: Physiological and Psychological Influences*. Edinburgh: Churchill Livingstone.

CREIGHTON, D.E. and LEWIS, P.H. (1978b) The Effect of Different Cigarettes on Human Smoking Patterns. In R.E. Thornton (ed.) *Smoking Behaviour: Physiological and Psychological Influences*. Edinburgh: Churchill Livingstone.

CREIGHTON, D.E., NOBLE, M.J., and WHEWELL, R.T. (1979) A Portable Smoking Pattern Recorder. *Biotelemetry and Patient Monitoring* 6: 186–91.

CRYER, P.E., HAYMOND, M.W., SANTIAGO, J.V., and SHAH, S.D. (1976) Norepinephrine and Epinephrine Release and Adrenergic Mediation of Smoking-Associated Hemodynamic and Metabolic Events. *New England Journal of Medicine* 295: 573–77.

DENEAU, G.A. and INOKI, R. (1967) Nicotine Self-Administration in Monkeys. *Annals of the New York Academy of Science* 142: 277–79.

DOLE, V.P. (1978) A Clinician's View of Addiction. In J. Fishman (ed.) *Bases of Addiction*. Berlin: Dahlem Konferenzen.

DOLL, R. and HILL, A.B. (1952) A Study of the Aetiology of Carcinoma of the Lung. *British Medical Journal* 2: 1271–286.

DOMINO, E.F. (1973) Neuropsychopharmacology of Nicotine and Tobacco Smoking. In W.L. Dunn (ed.) *Smoking Behavior: Motives and Incentives*. Washington: Winston.

DOMINO, E.F. (1979) Behavioral, Electrophysiological, Endocrine and Skeletal Muscle Actions of Nicotine and Tobacco Smoking. In A. Remond and C. Izard (eds) *Electrophysiological Effects of Nicotine*. Amsterdam: Elsevier/N. Holland Biomedical Press.

DOUGLAS, R.J. (1975) The Development of Hippocampal Function: Implications for Theory and for Therapy. In R.L. Isaacson and K.H. Pribram (eds) *The Hippocampus*. New York: Plenum Press.

DRACHMAN, D.A. (1978) Central Cholinergic System and Memory. In M.A. Lipton, A. DiMascio, and K.F. Killam (eds) *Psychopharmacology: A Generation of Progress*. New York: Raven Press.

DUNN, W.L. (1978) Smoking as a Possible Inhibitor of Arousal. In K. Bättig (ed.) *Behavioral Effects of Nicotine*. Basel: S. Karger.

EINON, G.S. (1974) *Introduction to the Nervous System*. Milton Keynes: Open University Press.

EISEN, M.E. and HAMMOND, E.C. (1956) The Effect of Smoking on Packed Cell Volume, Red Cell Counts, Hemoglobin and Platelet Counts. *Journal of the Canadian Medical Association* 75: 520–27.

EISER, J.R., SUTTON, S.R. and WOBER, M. (1977) Smokers, Non-Smokers and the Attribution of Addiction. *British Journal of Social and Clinical Psychology* 16: 329–36.

EISER, J.R., SUTTON, S.R. and WOBER, M. (1979) Smoking, Seat Belts, and Beliefs about Health. *Addictive Behaviors* 4: 331–38.

EMERY, F.E., HILGENDORF, E.L. and IRVING, B.L. (1968) *The Psychological Dynamics of Smoking*. London: Tobacco Research Council Research Paper 10.

EPSTEIN, L.H. and McCoy, J.F. (1975) Issues in Smoking Control. *Addictive Behaviors* 1: 65–72.

EYSENCK, H.J. (1965) *Smoking, Health and Personality*. London: Weidenfeld & Nicolson.

EYSENCK, H.J. (1973) Personality and the Maintenance of the Smoking Habit. In W.L. Dunn (ed.) *Smoking Behavior: Motives and Incentives*. Washington: Winston.

EYSENCK, H.J. and EAVES, L.J. (1980) *The Causes and Effects of Smoking*. London: Maurice Temple Smith.

EYSENCK, H.J. and O'CONNOR, K. (1979) Smoking, Arousal and Personality. In A. Remond and C. Izard (eds) *Electrophysiological Effects of Nicotine*. Amsterdam: Elsevier/N. Holland Biomedical Press.

EYSENCK, H.J., TARRANT, M., WOOLF, M., and ENGLAND, L. (1960) Smoking and Personality. *British Medical Journal* 1: 1456–460.

FEDRICK, J., ALBERMAN, E.D. and GOLDSTEIN, H. (1971) Possible Teratogenic Effect of Cigarette Smoking. *Nature* 231: 559–60.

FESTINGER, L. (1957) *A Theory of Cognitive Dissonance*. Evanston, Illinois: Row, Peterson.

FEYERABEND, C. and RUSSELL, M.A.H. (1978) Effect of Urinary pH and Nicotine Excretion Rate on Plasma Nicotine During Cigarette Smoking and Chewing Nicotine Gum. *British Journal of Clinical Pharmacology* 5: 293–97.

FINNEGAN, J.K., LARSON, P.J., and HAAG, H.B. (1945) The Role of Nicotine in the Cigarette Habit. *Science* 102: 94–96.

FISHER, R.A. (1958) Lung Cancer and Cigarettes. *Nature* 182: 108.

FLOOD, J.F., BENNETT, E.L., ORME, A.E., ROSENZWIEG, M.R., and JARVIK, M.E. (1978) Memory: Modification of Anisomycin-Induced Amnesia by Stimulants and Depressants. *Science* 199: 324–26.

FORBES, W.F., ROBINSON, J.C., HANLEY, J.A., and COLBURN, H.N. (1976) Studies on the Nicotine Exposure of Individual Smokers. *International Journal of the Addictions* 11: 933–50.

Fox, K., JONATHAN, A., WILLIAMS, H., and SELWYN, A. (1980) Interaction between Cigarettes and Propranolol in Treatment of Angina Pectoris. *British Medical Journal* 281: 191–93.

FRANKENHAEUSER, M., MYRSTEN, A-L., POST, B., and JOHANSSON, G. (1971) Behavioural and Physiological Effects of Cigarette Smoking in a Monotonous Situation. *Psychopharmacologia* 22: 1–7.

FRANKENHAEUSER, M., POST, B., HAGDAHL, R., and WRANGSJOE, B. (1964) Effects of a Depressant Drug as Modified by Experimentally-Induced Expectation. *Perceptual and Motor Skills* 18: 513–22.

FREEDMAN, S., and FLETCHER, C.M. (1976) Changes of Smoking Habits and Cough in Men Smoking Cigarettes with 30% NSM Tobacco Substitute. *British Medical Journal* 1: 1427–430.

FREUD, S. (1905) Three Essays on the Theory of Sexuality. In *On Sexuality*, Pelican Freud Library (vol. 7). London: Harmondsworth (1977).

FRIBERG, L., KAIJ, L., DENCKER, S.J., and JONSSON, E. (1959) Smoking Habits of Monozygotic and Dizygotic Twins. *British Medical Journal* **1**: 1090–092.

FRIEDMAN, G.D., SIEGELAUB, A.B., DALES, L.G., and SELTZER, C.C. (1979) Characteristics Predictive of Coronary Heart Disease in Ex-Smokers before they Stopped Smoking: Comparison with Persistent Smokers and Non-Smokers. *Journal of Chronic Diseases* **32**: 175–90.

FRITH, C.D. (1971a) The Effect of Varying the Nicotine Content of Cigarettes on Human Smoking Behaviour. *Psychopharmacologia* **19**: 188–92.

FRITH, C.D. (1971b) Smoking Behaviour and its Relation to the Smoker's Immediate Experience. *British Journal of Social and Clinical Psychology* **10**: 73–78.

General Household Survey, Office of Population Censuses and Surveys (1980). London: HMSO.

GLAD, W. and ADESSO, V.J. (1976) The Relative Importance of Socially Induced Tension and Behavioral Contagion for Smoking Behavior. *Journal of Abnormal Psychology* **85**: 119–21.

GOLDFARB, T.L., JARVIK, M.E., and GLICK, S.D. (1970) Cigarette Nicotine Content as a Determinant of Human Smoking Behavior. *Psychopharmacologia* **17**: 89–93.

GOLDFARB, T., GRITZ, E.R., JARVIK, M.E., and STOLERMAN, I.P. (1976) Reactions to Cigarettes as a Function of Nicotine and 'Tar'. *Clinical Pharmacology and Therapeutics* **19**: 767–72.

GOODMAN, L.S. and GILMAN, A. (1970) (eds) *The Pharmacological Basis of Therapeutics* (4th edition). London: Macmillan.

GORDON, T., KANNEL, W.B., and McGEE, G. (1974) Death and Coronary Attacks in Men After Giving up Cigarette Smoking. *Lancet* **2**: 1345–348.

GORI, G.B. (1976) Low-Risk Cigarettes: A Prescription. *Science* **194**: 1243–246.

GORI, G.B. and LYNCH, C.J. (1978) Toward Less Hazardous Cigarettes. *Journal of the American Medical Association* **240**(12): 1255–259.

GRAY, J.A. (1970) The Psychophysiological Basis of Introversion–Extraversion. *Behavioural Research and Therapy* **8**: 249–66.

GREEN, G.H. (1923) Some Notes on Smoking. *International Journal of Psychoanalysis* **4**: 323–25.

GRIFFITHS, R.R., BIGELOW, G.E., and LIEBSON, L. (1976) Facilitation of Human Tobacco Self-Administration by Ethanol: A Behavioural Analysis. *Journal of the Experimental Analysis of Behaviour* **25**: 279–92.

GRITZ., E.R. (1978) Women and Smoking. In J.L. Schwartz (ed.) *Progress in Smoking Cessation*. New York: American Cancer Society/WHO.

GROBGLAS, A. and LEVY, J. (1978) Ear Acupuncture in the Fight Against the Smoking Habit. In *1978 Directory of Ongoing Research in Smoking and Health*. Rockville, Maryland: United States Department of Health, Education and Welfare.

GUILLERM, R. and RADZISZEWSKI, E. (1978) Analysis of Smoking Pattern Including Intake of Carbon Monoxide and Influence of Changes in Cigarette Design. In R.E. Thornton (ed.) *Smoking Behaviour: Physiological and Psychological Influences*. Edinburgh: Churchill Livingstone.

GUILLERM, R., MASUREL, G., BROUSOLLE, B., HYACINTHE, R., SIMON, A., and HEE, J. (1974) Effets Cliniques et Fonctionnels Respiratoires de la Substitution d'une Cigarette à Fumée Peu Irritante à la Cigarette

Habituelle dans un Groupe de Grands Fumeurs. *Les Bronches* **24**: 209–31.

HAINES, A.P., IMESON, J.D., and MEADE, T.W. (1980) Psychoneurotic Profiles of Smokers and Non-Smokers. *British Medical Journal* **1**: 1422.

HAINES, C.F., MAHAJAN, D.K., MILJKOVIC, D., MILJKOVIC, M., and VESSELL, E.S. (1974) Radioimmunoassay of Plasma Nicotine in Habituated and Naive Smokers. *Clinical Pharmacology and Therapeutics* **16**: 1083–089.

HALL, G.H. (1970) Effects of Nicotine and Tobacco Smoke on the Electrical Activity of the Cerebral Cortex and Olfactory Bulb. *British Journal of Pharmacology* **38**: 271–86.

HALL, G.H. and MORRISON, C.F. (1973) New Evidence for a Relationship Between Tobacco Smoking, Nicotine Dependence and Stress. *Nature* **243**: 199–201.

HALL, G.H. and TURNER, D.M. (1972) Effects of Nicotine on the Release of 3H-Noradrenaline from the Hypothalamus. *Biochemical Pharmacology* **21**: 1829–838.

HAMILTON, J.L. (1972) The Demand for Cigarettes: Advertising, the Health Scare and the Cigarette Advertising Ban. *Review of Economics and Statistics* **54**: 401–11.

HAMILTON, W.F. (1978) Why Smoke a Pipe? *British Medical Journal* **1**: 583.

HAMMOND, E.C. (1980) The Long-Term Benefits of Reducing Tar and Nicotine in Cigarettes. In G.B. Gori and F.G. Bock (eds) *Banbury Report 3: A Safe Cigarette?* New York: Cold Spring Harbor Laboratory.

HANKS, T.G. (1970) Human Performance of a Psychomotor Test as a Function of Exposure to Carbon Monoxide. *Annals of the New York Academy of Sciences* **174**: 421–24.

HARLAP, S. and DAVIES, A.M. (1974) Infant Admissions to Hospital and Maternal Smoking. *Lancet* **1**: 529.

HEIMSTRA, N.W. (1973) The Effects of Smoking on Mood Change. In W.L. Dunn (ed.) *Smoking Behaviour: Motives and Incentives.* Washington: Winston.

HEIMSTRA, N.W., BANCROFT, N.R., and DeKOCK, A.R. (1967) Effects of Smoking upon Sustained Performance in a Simulated Driving Task. *Annals of the New York Academy of Science* **142**: 295–307.

HELIÖVARRA, M., KARVONEN, M.J., VILHUMEN, R., and PUNSAR, S. (1978) Smoking, Carbon Monoxide, and Atherosclerotic Diseases. *British Medical Journal* **1**: 268–70.

HERAIL, R.J. and LOVATT, E.A. (1979) Why Anti-Smoking Advertising Loses Out. *World Medicine* **14**: 15–17.

HERMAN, C.P. (1974) External and Internal Cues as Determinants of the Smoking Behavior of Light and Heavy Smokers. *Journal of Personality and Social Psychology* **30**: 664–72.

HERR, M. (1978) *Dispatches.* London: Picador.

HERRIOTT, A., BILLEWICZ, W.Z., and AYLTEN, F.E. (1962) Cigarette Smoking in Pregnancy. *Lancet* **1**: 771–73.

HIRAYAMA, T. (1981) Non-Smoking Wives of Heavy Smokers have a Higher Risk of Lung Cancer: a Study from Japan. *British Medical Journal* **282**: 183–85.

HOFFMAN, W.E. (1980) The Impact of Tobacco Advertising and Promotion on Cigarette Consumption. In L.M. Ramström (ed.) *The Smoking Epidemic: Proceedings of the Fourth World Conference on Smoking and Health.* Stockholm:

Almqvist & Wiksell International.

HOMME, L.E. (1965) Perspectives in Psychology: XXIV. Control of Coverants, the Operants of the Mind. *Psychological Record* **15**: 501–11.

HORN, D. (1978) Who is Quitting and Why? In J.L. Schwartz (ed.) *Progress in Smoking Cessation*. New York: American Cancer Society/WHO.

HOWE, M. and SUMMERFIELD, A.B. (1979) Orality and Smoking. *British Journal of Medical Psychology* **52**: 85–90.

HULL, C.L. (1924) The Influence of Tobacco Smoking on Mental and Motor Efficiency. *Psychological Monographs* **33**(3): 1–160.

HUNT, W.A. and MATARAZZO, J.D. (1973) Three Years Later: Recent Developments in the Modification of Smoking Behavior. *Journal of Abnormal Psychology* **81**: 107–114.

HUNT, W.A., BARNETT, L.W. and BRANCH, L.G. (1971) Relapse Rates in Addiction Programs. *Journal of Clinical Psychology* **27**: 455–56.

HUNT, W.A. and MATARAZZO, J.D. (1970) Habit Mechanisms in Smoking. In W.A. Hunt (ed.) *Learning Mechanisms in Smoking*. Chicago: Aldine.

HUTCHINSON, R.R. and Emley, G.S. (1973) Effects of Nicotine on Avoidance, Conditioned Suppression and Aggression Response Measures in Animals and Man. In W.L. Dunn (ed.) *Smoking Behavior: Motives and Incentives*. Washington: Winston.

HUXLEY, A. (1970) *The Devils of Loudun*. London: Chatto and Windus.

IKARD, F.F., GREEN, D.E., and HORN, D. (1969) A Scale to Differentiate Between Types of Smoking as Related to the Management of Affect. *International Journal of the Addictions* **4**(4): 649–59.

INGLIS, B. (1975) *The Forbidden Game: A Social History of Drugs*. London: Hodder & Stoughton.

ISAAC, P.F. and RAND, M.J. (1969) Blood Levels of Nicotine and Physiological Effects After Inhalation of Tobacco Smoke. *European Journal of Pharmacology* **8**: 269–83.

ISAAC, P.F. and RAND, M.J. (1972) Cigarette Smoking and Plasma Levels of Nicotine. *Nature* **236**: 308–10.

ISAACSON, R.L. and PRIBRAM, K.H. (1975) *The Hippocampus* (vols. 1 and 2). New York: Plenum Press.

JACOBS, M.A., KNAPP, P.H., ANDERSON, L.S., KARUSH, N., MEISSNER, R., and RICHMAN, S.J. (1965) Relationship of Oral Frustration Factors with Heavy Cigarette Smoking in Males. *Journal of Nervous and Mental Disease* **141** (2): 161–71.

JACOBSON, N.L., JACOBSON, A.A., and PHILLIP, J. (1979) Non-Combustible Cigarette: Alternative Method of Nicotine Delivery. *Chest* **76**: 355–56.

JAFFE, J.H. (1978) Applying What We Know from Other Addictions. In J.L. Schwartz (ed.) *Progress in Smoking Cessation*. New York: American Cancer Society/WHO.

JAMES I (1604) *A Counterblaste to Tobacco*. London.

JARVIK, M.E. (1967) Tobacco Smoking in Monkeys. *Annals of the New York Academy of Science* **142**: 280–94.

JARVIK, M.E. (1970) The Role of Nicotine in the Smoking Habit. In W.A. Hunt (ed.) *Learning Mechanisms in Smoking*. Chicago: Aldine.

JARVIK, M.E. (1973) Further Observations on Nicotine as the Reinforcing Agent in Smoking. In W.L. Dunn (ed.) *Smoking Behavior: Motives and*

Incentives. Washington: Winston.

JARVIK, M.E., GLICK, S.D., and NAKAMURA, R.K. (1970) Inhibition of Cigarette Smoking by Orally Administered Nicotine. *Clinical Pharmacology and Therapeutics* **11**: 574–76.

JESSOR, R. (1978) Psychosocial Factors in the Patterning of Drinking Behavior. In J. Fishman (ed.) *The Bases of Addiction*. Berlin: Dahlem Konferenzen.

JOHNSTON, L.M. (1942) Tobacco Smoking and Nicotine. *Lancet* **2**: 742.

JOHNSTON, L. (1957) *The Disease of Tobacco Smoking and its Cure*. London: Christopher Johnson.

JONES, E. (1953) *Sigmund Freud: Life and Work* (vols. 1–3). London: Hogarth Press.

KARRAS, A. and KANE, J.M. (1980) Naloxone Reduces Cigarette Consumption. *Life Sciences* **27**: 1541–545.

KISSEN, D.M. and EYSENCK, H.J. (1962) Personality in Male Lung Cancer Patients. *Journal of Psychosomatic Research* **6**: 123–27.

KNAPP, P.H., BLISS, G.M., and WELLS, H. (1963) Addictive Aspects in Heavy Cigarette Smoking. *American Journal of Psychiatry* **119**: 966–71.

KNOTT, V.J. and VENABLES, P.H. (1977) EEG Alpha Correlates of Non-Smokers, Smokers, Smoking and Smoking Deprivation. *Psychophysiology* **14**: 150–56.

KOHN, P.M. and ANNIS, H.M. (1977) Drug Use and Four Kinds of Novelty Seeking. *British Journal of Addiction* **72**: 135–41.

KOSKOWSKI, W. (1955) *The Habit of Tobacco Smoking*. London: Staples Press.

KOZLOWSKI, L.T., HERMAN, C.P., and FRECKER, R.C. (1980) What Researchers Make of What Cigarette Smokers Say: Filtering Smokers' Hot Air. *Lancet* **1**: 699–70.

KRASNEGOR, N.A. (1980) Withdrawal, Relapse and Abstinence. In L.M. Ramström (ed.) *The Smoking Epidemic: Proceedings of the Fourth World Conference on Smoking and Health*. Stockholm: Almqvist & Wiksell International.

KUMAR, R., COOKE, E.C., LADER, M.H., and RUSSELL, M.A.H. (1977) Is Nicotine Important in Tobacco Smoking? *Clinical Pharmacology and Therapeutics* **21**: 520–29.

LACEY, J.J. (1967) Somatic Response Patterning and Stress–Some Revisions of Activation Theory. In M.H. Appley and R. Trumbull (eds) *Psychological Stress*. New York: Appleton Century Crofts.

LAMB, P. and REID, L. (1969) Goblet Cell Increase in Rat Bronchial Epithelium after Exposure to Cigarette and Cigar Tobacco Smoke. *British Medical Journal* **1**: 33–35.

LAMBIASE, M. and SERRA, C. (1957) Fume e sistema nervoso. I. Modificazioni dell' attivita elettrica corticale da fumo. *Acta Neurologica* (Napoli) **12**: 475–93.

Lancet (1973) Sugar in Tobacco: Theory and Fact. **1**: 187–89.

Lancet (1979) Smoking and Intrauterine Growth. **1**: 536.

LARSON, P.S. and SILVETTE, H. (1975) *Tobacco: Experimental and Clinical Studies, Supplement III*. Baltimore: Williams & Wilkins.

LARSON, P.S., HAAG, H.B., and SILVETTE (1961) *Tobacco: Experimental and Clinical Studies*. Baltimore: Williams & Wilkins.

LEE, P.N. (1976) *Statistics of Smoking in the UK* (7th edition). London: Tobacco Research Council.

LEHRER, T. (1978) Cessation of Smoking in Clinics: The Problem of Relapse and the 'Quasi-Sick' Role. In J.L. Schwartz (ed.) *Progress in Smoking Cessation*. New York: American Cancer Society/WHO.

LE SHAN, L. (1959) Psychological States as Factors in the Development of Malignant Disease. *Journal of the National Cancer Institute* **22**: 1–18.

LEVENBERG, S.B. and WAGNER, M.K. (1976) Smoking Cessation: Long-Term Irrelevance of Mode of Treatment. *Journal of Behaviour Therapy and Experimental Psychiatry* **7**: 93–95.

LEVINSON, B.L., SHAPIRO, D., SCHWARTZ, G.E., and TURSKY, B. (1971) Smoking Elimination by Gradual Reduction. *Behavior Therapy* **2**: 477–87.

LEWIS, D.J. (1960) Partial Reinforcement: A Selective Review of the Literature since 1950. *Psychological Bulletin* **57**: 1–28.

LICHTENSTEIN, E., HARRIS, D.E., BIRCHLER, G.R., WAHL, J.M., and SCHMAHL, D.P. (1973) Comparison of Rapid Smoking, Warm, Smoky Air and Attention Placebo in the Modification of Smoking Behaviors. *Journal of Consulting and Clinical Psychology* **40**: 92–8.

LINDESMITH, A.R. (1965) Problems in the Social Psychology of Addiction. In D.M. Wilner and G.G. Kassebaum (eds) *Narcotics*. New York: McGraw Hill.

LOGAN, F.A. (1970) The Smoking Habit. In W.A. Hunt (ed.) *Learning Mechanisms in Smoking*. Chicago: Aldine.

LONGO, L. (1970) Carbon Monoxide in the Pregnant Mother and Fetus and its Exchange across the Placenta. *Annals of the New York Academy of Sciences* **174**: 313–41.

LORENZ, K.Z. (1961) *King Solomon's Ring*. London: Methuen.

LOW, C.R. (1959) Effects of Mothers' Smoking Habits on Birth Weight of their Children. *British Medical Journal* **2**: 673–75.

LUCCHESI, B.R., SCHUSTER, C.R., and EMLEY, G.S. (1967) The Role of Nicotine as a Determinant of Cigarette Smoking Frequency in Man with Observations of Certain Cardiovascular Effects Associated with the Tobacco Alkaloid. *Clinical Pharmacology and Therapeutics* **8**: 789–96.

LYNCH, C.J. and GORI, G.B. (1980) Non-Detectable Risk Levels in Cigarette Smoking. In G.B. Gori and F.G. Bock (eds) *Banbury Report 3: A Safe Cigarette?* New York: Cold Spring Harbor Laboratory.

MCARTHUR, C., WALDRON, E., and DICKINSON, J. (1958) The Psychology of Smoking. *Journal of Abnormal and Social Psychology* **56**: 267–75.

MCELHENY, V.K. (1980) Preface. In G.B. Gori and F.G. Bock (eds) *Banbury Report 3: A Safe Cigarette?* New York: Cold Spring Harbor Laboratory.

MCEWAN, I. (1976) *First Love: Last Rites*. London: Picador.

MCFARLAND, J.W., GIMBEL, H.W., DONALD, W.A.J., and FOLKENBERG, E.J. (1964) The Five-Day Program to Help Individuals Stop Smoking. *Connecticut Medicine* **28**: 885–90.

MCFARLAND, R. (1970) The Effects of Exposure to Small Quantities of Carbon Monoxide on Vision. *Annals of the New York Academy of Sciences* **174**: 301–12.

MCGARRY, J.M. and ANDREWS, J. (1972) Smoking in Pregnancy and Vitamin B_{12} Metabolism. *British Medical Journal* **70**: 639–41.

McGuinness, T. and Cowling, K. (1975) Advertising and the Aggregate Demand for Cigarettes. *European Economic Review* **6**: 311–28.

McKennell, A.C. (1973) *A Comparison of Two Smoking Typologies*. London: Tobacco Research Council.

McPeake, J.D. and DiMascio, A. (1965) Drug–Personality Interaction in the Learning of a Nonsense Syllable Task. *Journal of Psychiatric Research* **3**: 105–11.

McRae, R.R., Costa, P.T., and Bossé, R. (1978) Anxiety, Extraversion and Smoking. *British Journal of Social and Clinical Psychology* **17**: 269–73.

Madden, J.S. (1979) *Alcohol and Drug Dependence*. Bristol: Wright.

Mahler, H. (1980) Meeting a World Challenge. In L. M. Ramström (ed.) *The Smoking Epidemic: Proceedings of the Fourth World Conference on Smoking and Health*. Stockholm: Almqvist & Wiksell International.

Malcolm, R.E., Sillett, R.W., Turner, J.A.McM., and Ball, K.P. (1980) The Use of Nicotine Chewing Gum as an Aid to Stopping Smoking. *Psychopharmacology* **70**: 295–96.

Mangan, G.L. and Golding, J. (1978) An 'Enhancement' Model of Smoking Maintenance? In R.E. Thornton (ed.) *Smoking Behaviour: Physiological and Psychological Influences*. Edinburgh: Churchill Livingstone.

Manning, F.A. and Feyerabend, C. (1976) Cigarette Smoking and Foetal Breathing Movements. *British Journal of Obstetrics and Gynaecology* **83**: 262–64.

Margule, D.L., Moisset, B., Lewis, M.J., Shibuya, H., and Pert, C. (1978) Endorphin is Associated with Overeating in Genetically Obese Mice and Rats. *Science* **202**: 988–91.

Marongiu, P. (1980) Recent Trends and Longer Term Outlook in the World Tobacco Economy. In L.M. Ramström (ed.) *The Smoking Epidemic: Proceedings of the Fourth World Conference on Smoking and Health*. Stockholm: Almqvist & Wiksell International.

Matarazzo, J.D. and Saslow, G. (1960) Psychological and Related Characteristics of Smokers and Non-Smokers. *Psychological Bulletin* **57**: 493–513.

Mausner, B. and Platt, E.S. (1971) *Smoking: A Behavioral Analysis*. New York: Pergamon.

Maxwell International Estimates (1979) How the Brands Ranked. *World Tobacco* (July): 67–74.

Mazière, M., Comar, D., Marazano, C., and Berger, G. (1976) Nicotine-[11]C: Synthesis and Distribution Kinetics in Animals. *European Journal of Nuclear Medicine* **1**: 255–58.

Meares, R., Grimwade, J., Bickley, M., and Wood, C. (1971) Smoking and Neuroticism. *Lancet* **2**: 770–71.

Merbaum, M., Avimier, R., and Goldberg, J. (1979) The Relationship Between Aversion, Group Training and Vomiting in the Reduction of Smoking Behavior. *Addictive Behaviors* **4**: 279–85.

Mikulka, P., O'Donnell, R., Hernig, P., and Theodore, J. (1970) The Effect of Carbon Monoxide on Human Performance. *Annals of the New York Academy of Sciences* **174**: 409–20.

Miller, L.L. (1979) Cannabis and the Brain with Special Reference to the Limbic System. In G.G. Nahas and W.D.M. Paton (eds) *Marijuana: Bio-*

logical Effects. Oxford: Pergamon Press.

MORRIS, D. (1977) *Manwatching.* London: Jonathan Cape.

MORRISON, C.F. and ARMITAGE, A.K. (1967) Effects of Nicotine upon the Free Operant Behaviour of Rats and Spontaneous Motor Activity of Mice. *Annals of the New York Academy of Science* **142**: 268–76.

MOSHY, R.A. (1967) Reconstituted Tobacco Sheet. In Wynder, E.L. and Hoffman, D. *Tobacco and Tobacco Smoke.* New York: Academic Press.

MURPHREE, H.B., PFEIFFER, C.C., and PRICE, L.M. (1967) Electroencephalographic Changes in Man Following Smoking. *Annals of the New York Academy of Science* **142**: 245–60.

MYRSTEN, A-L. and ANDERSSON, K. (1975) Interaction between Effects of Alcohol Intake and Cigarette Smoking. *Blutalkohol* **12**: 253–65.

MYRSTEN, A-L., ANDERSSON, K., FRANKENHAEUSER, M., and ELGEROT, A. (1975) Immediate Effects of Cigarette Smoking as Related to Different Smoking Habits. *Perceptual and Motor Skills* **40**: 515–23.

NELSEN, J.M. (1978) Psychological Consequences of Chronic Nicotinisation: A Focus on Arousal. In K. Bättig (ed.) *Behavioural Effects of Nicotine.* Basel: S. Karger.

New Scientist (1980) Child Smokers Show Deviant Personality. 28 February: 655.

Observer Magazine (1978) 31 December.

OHLIN, P. and WESTLING, H. (1972) Nicotine-Containing Chewing Gum as a Substitute for Smoking. In R.G. Richardson (ed.) *Proceedings of the Second World Conference on Smoking and Health.* London: Pitman Medical.

OLDS, J. (1962) Hypothalamic Substrates of Reward. *Physiological Reviews* **42**: 554–604.

PASSEY, R.D., BLACKMORE, M., WARBRICK-SMITH, D., and JONES, R. (1971) Smoking Risks of Different Tobaccos. *British Medical Journal* **4**: 198–201.

PATON, W.D.M., PERTWEE, R.G., and TYLDEN, E. (1973) Clinical Aspects of Cannabis Action. In R. Mechoulam (ed.) *Marijuana.* New York: Academic Press.

PEARL, R. (1938) Tobacco Smoking and Longevity. *Science* **87** (2253): 216–17.

PERVIN, L.A. and YATKO, R.J. (1965) Cigarette Smoking and Alternative Methods of Reducing Dissonance. *Journal of Personality and Social Psychology* **2**: 30–6.

POWELL, G.E., STEWART, R.A., and GRYLLS, D.G. (1979) The Personality of Young Smokers. *British Journal of Addictions* **74**: 311–15.

POWELL, J. and AZRIN, N. (1968) The Effects of Shock as a Punisher for Cigarette Smoking. *Journal of Applied Behavior Analysis* **1**: 63–71.

PREMACK, D. (1970) Mechanisms of Self-Control. In W.A. Hunt (ed.) *Learning Mechanisms in Smoking.* Chicago: Aldine.

PRENDERGAST, T.J. and PREBLE, M.R. (1973) Drug Use and Its Relation to Alcohol and Cigarette Consumption in the Military Community of West Germany. *International Journal of the Addictions* **8** (5): 741–54.

PROTHRO, E.T. (1953) Identification of American, British and Lebanese Cigarettes. *Journal of Applied Psychology* **37** (1): 54–6.

PUSKA, P., BJÖRKQVIST, S., and KOSKELA, K. (1979) Nicotine-Containing Chewing Gum in Smoking Cessation: A Double Blind Trial with Half Year Follow-Up. *Addictive Behaviors* **4**: 141–46.

RACHLIN, H. (1976) *Introduction to Modern Behaviorism*. San Francisco: W.H. Freeman.

RAMOND, C.K., RACHAL, L.H., and MARKS, M.R. (1950) Brand Discrimination Among Cigarette Smokers. *Journal of Applied Psychology* **34**: 282–84.

RAPP, G.W., DUSZA, B.T., and BLANCHET, L. (1959) Absorption and Utility of Lobeline as a Smoking Deterrent. *American Journal of Medical Sciences* **237**: 287–92.

RAW, M., JARVIS, M.J., FEYERABEND, C., and RUSSELL, M.A.H. (1980) Comparison of Nicotine Chewing-Gum and Psychological Treatments for Dependent Smokers. *British Medical Journal* **281**: 481–82.

RAWBONE, R.G. (1980) Low-Tar Smoking Versus Middle-Tar Smoking. *British Medical Journal* **281**: 309.

RAWBONE, R.G., MURPHY, K., TATE, M.E., and KANE, S.J. (1978) The Analysis of Smoking Parameters, Inhalation and Absorption of Tobacco Smoke in Studies of Human Smoking Behaviour. In R.E. Thornton (ed.) *Smoking Behaviour: Physiological and Psychological Influences*. Edinburgh: Churchill Livingstone.

RICHES, R. (1978) Evaluation of Five Smoking Cessation Programs known as the 'Five Day Plan'. In *1978 Directory of Ongoing Research in Smoking and Health*. Rockville, Maryland: United States Department of Health, Education and Welfare.

ROBINS, L., HELZER, J., and DAVIS, D. (1975) Narcotic Use in South-east Asia and Afterward. *Archives of General Psychiatry* **32**: 955–61.

ROE, F.J.C. and LEE, P.N. (1978) Inhaling Habits of Pipe Smokers. *British Medical Journal* **1**: 648.

ROSENMAN, R.H. (1979) Personality, Type A Behaviour Pattern and Coronary Heart Disease. In R.W. Elsdon-Dew *et al.* (eds) *The Cardiovascular, Metabolic and Psychological Interface*. London: Royal Society of Medicine/ Academic Press.

ROUTTENBERG, A. (1968) The Two-Arousal Hypothesis: Reticular Formation and Limbic System. *Psychological Review* **75** (1): 51–80.

ROYAL COLLEGE OF PHYSICIANS (1977) *Smoking or Health*. London: Pitman Medical.

ROYAL COLLEGE OF PSYCHIATRISTS (1979) *Alcohol and Alcoholism*. London: Tavistock Publications.

RUSSELL, M.A.H. (1970) Effect of Electric Aversion on Cigarette Smoking. *British Medical Journal* **1**: 82–86.

RUSSELL, M.A.H. (1971) Cigarette Smoking: Natural History of a Dependence Disorder. *British Journal of Medical Psychology* **44**: 1–16.

RUSSELL, M.A.H. (1974) Realistic Goals for Smoking and Health. *Lancet* **1**: 254–58.

RUSSELL, M.A.H. (1976a) Low-Tar Medium-Nicotine Cigarettes: A New Approach to Safer Smoking. *British Medical Journal* **1**: 1430–433.

RUSSELL, M.A.H. (1976b) Tobacco Smoking and Nicotine Dependence. In R.J. Gibbins *et al.* (eds) *Research Advances in Alcohol and Drug Problems* (vol. 3). New York: Wiley and Sons.

RUSSELL, M.A.H. (1977) Tube with the 7-Second Fuse. *The Guardian*, 31 March.

RUSSELL, M.A.H. (1978a) Smoking Addiction. In J.L. Schwartz (ed.) *Progress in Smoking Cessation*. New York: American Cancer Society/WHO.

RUSSELL, M.A.H. (1978b) Cigarette Smoking: A Dependence on High-Nicotine Boli. *Drug Metabolism Reviews* **8** (1): 29–57.

RUSSELL, M.A.H. and FEYERABEND, C. (1980) Smoking as a Dependence Disorder. In L.M. Ramström (ed.) *The Smoking Epidemic: Proceedings of the Fourth World Conference on Smoking and Health*. Stockholm: Almqvist & Wiksell International.

RUSSELL, M.A.H., FEYERABEND, C., and COLE, P.V. (1976b) Plasma Nicotine Levels After Cigarette Smoking and Chewing Nicotine Gum. *British Medical Journal* **1**: 1043–046.

RUSSELL, M.A.H., JARVIS, M.J., and FEYERABEND, C. (1980a) A New Age for Snuff? *Lancet* **1**: 474–75.

RUSSELL, M.A.H., PETO, J., and PATEL, U.A. (1974) The Classification of Smoking by a Factorial Structure of Motives. *Journal of the Royal Statistical Society* **137**: 313–46.

RUSSELL, M.A.H., RAW, M., and JARVIS, M.J. (1980c) Clinical Use of Nicotine Chewing-Gum. *British Medical Journal* **280**: 1599–1602.

RUSSELL, M.A.H., JARVIS, M., IYER, R., and FEYERABEND, C. (1980b) Relation of Nicotine Yield of Cigarettes to Blood Nicotine Concentrations in Smokers. *British Medical Journal* **280**: 972–76.

RUSSELL, M.A.H., WILSON, C., FEYERABEND, C., and COLE, P.V. (1976a) Effect of Nicotine Chewing Gum on Smoking Behaviour and as an Aid to Cigarette Withdrawal. *British Medical Journal* **2**: 391–93.

RUSSELL, M.A.H., WILSON, C., TAYLOR, C., and BAKER, C.D. (1979) Effect of General Practitioners' Advice Against Smoking. *British Medical Journal* **2**: 231–35.

RUSSELL, M.A.H., WILSON, C., TAYLOR, C., and BAKER, C.D. (1980d) Smoking Habits of Men and Women. *British Medical Journal* **281**: 17–20.

RUSSELL, M.A.H., SUTTON, S.R., FEYERABEND, C., COLE, P.V., and SALOOJEE, Y. (1977) Nicotine Chewing Gum as a Substitute for Smoking. *British Medical Journal* **1**: 1060–063.

RUSSELL, M.A.H., WILSON, C., PATEL, U.A., COLE, P.V., and FEYERABEND, C. (1973) Comparison of the Effect on Tobacco Consumption and Carbon Monoxide Absorption of Changing to High and Low-Nicotine Cigarettes. *British Medical Journal* **4**: 512–16.

SCHACHTER, S. (1977) Nicotine Regulation in Heavy and Light Smokers. *Journal of Experimental Psychology: General* **106**: 5–12.

SCHACHTER, S. (1978) Pharmacological and Psychological Determinants of Smoking. In R.E. Thornton (ed.) *Smoking Behaviour: Physiological and Psychological Influences*. Edinburgh: Churchill Livingstone.

SCHACHTER, S., KOZLOWSKI, L. T., and SILVERSTEIN, B. (1977a) Effects of Urinary pH on Cigarette Smoking. *Journal of Experimental Psychology: General* **106** (1): 13–19.

SCHACHTER, S., SILVERSTEIN, B., KOZLOWSKI, L.T., HERMAN, C.P., and LIEBLING, B. (1977b) Effects of Stress on Cigarette Smoking and Urinary pH. *Journal of Experimental Psychology: General* **106** (1): 24–30.

SCHMAHL, D.P., LICHTENSTEIN, E., and HARRIS, D.E. (1972) Successful Treatment of Habitual Smokers with Warm, Smoky Air and Rapid

Smoking. *Journal of Consulting and Clinical Psychology* **38**: 105–11.

SCHMITERLOW, C.G., HANSSON, E., ANDERSSON, G., APPELGREN, L.E., and HOFFMAN, P.C. (1967) Distribution of Nicotine in the Central Nervous System. *Annals of the New York Academy of Sciences* **142**: 2–14.

SCHNEIDER, N.G., POPEK, P., JARVIK, M.E., and GRITZ, E.R. (1977) The Use of Nicotine Gum During Cessation of Smoking. *American Journal of Psychiatry* **134**: 439–40.

SCHUBERT, D.S.P. (1965) Arousal Seeking as a Central Factor in Tobacco Smoking Among College Students. *International Journal of Social Psychiatry* **11:** 221–25.

SCHUMAN, L.M. (1977) Patterns of Smoking Behaviour. In M.E. Jarvik *et al.* (eds) *Research on Smoking Behavior (NIDA Monograph No. 17).* Rockville, Maryland: National Institute on Drug Abuse.

SEHM, M. (1979) University of Helsinki, Department of Statistics, personal communication.

SHIFFMAN, S.M. (1979) The Tobacco Withdrawal Syndrome. In N.A. Krasnegor (ed.) *Cigarette Smoking as a Dependence Process,* NIDA Research Monograph 23. Rockville: Maryland.

SIEGEL, S. (1977) Learning and Psychopharmacology. In M.E. Jarvik (ed.) *Psychopharmacology in the Practice of Medicine.* New York: Appleton-Century Crofts.

SILVERSTEIN, B., KOZLOWSKI, L.T., and SCHACHTER, S. (1977) Social Life, Cigarette Smoking and Urinary pH. *Journal of Experimental Psychology: General* **106** (1): 20–23.

SMITH, G.M. (1970) Personality and Smoking: A Review of the Literature. In W.G. Hunt (ed.) *Learning Mechanisms in Smoking.* Chicago: Aldine.

SOLOMON, R.L. (1980) An Opponent-Process Theory of Acquired Motivation. *American Psychologist* **35** (8): 691–712.

SPELMAN, M.S. and LEY, P. (1966) Knowledge of Lung Cancer and Smoking Habits. *British Journal of Social and Clinical Psychology* **5**: 207–10.

STEIN, L. (1978) Reward Transmitters: Catecholamines and Opioid Peptides. In M.A. Lipton, A. DiMascio, and K.F. Killam (eds) *Psychopharmacology: A Generation of Progress.* New York: Raven Press.

STEIN, L. and WISE, C.D. (1969) Release of Norepinephrine from Hypothalamus and Amygdala by Rewarding Median Forebrain Bundle Stimulation and Amphetamine. *Journal of Comparative Physiological Psychology* **67**: 189–198.

STEPNEY, R. (1979a) *The Role of Nicotine in Smoking Motivation.* M.Sc. thesis, University of Newcastle-upon-Tyne.

STEPNEY, R. (1979b) Tar:Nicotine Ratio of Cigarettes (1973–79). *Lancet* **2**: 422–23.

STEPNEY, R. (1979c) Men of Habit. *World Medicine* **14**: 39–41.

STEPNEY, R. (1980a) Cigarette Consumption and Nicotine Delivery. *British Journal of Addiction* **75** (1): 81–88.

STEPNEY, R. (1980b) Intake of Carbon Monoxide, Tar and Nicotine in Habitual Middle and Low-Tar Smokers. Paper presented to the *Meeting on Carbon Monoxide and Smoke Intake.* Southampton, March 1980.

STEPNEY, R. (1980c) Smoking Behaviour: A Psychology of the Cigarette Habit. *British Journal of Diseases of the Chest* **74**: 325–44.

STEPNEY, R. (1981) Would a Medium-Nicotine Low-Tar Cigarette Be Less Hazardous to Health? *British Medical Journal* (in press).

STEWART, R.D. (1974) The Effects of Low Concentrations of Carbon Monoxide in Man. In R. Rylander (ed.) *Environmental Tobacco Smoke: Effects on the Non-Smoker*. University of Geneva Press.

STOCK, S.L. (1980) Risks the Passive Smoker Runs. *Lancet* 2: 1082.

SUEDFELD, P. and IKARD, F.F. (1974) Use of Sensory Deprivation in Facilitating the Reduction of Cigarette Smoking. *Journal of Consulting and Clinical Psychology* 42 (6): 888–95.

SURGEON GENERAL (1979) *Smoking and Health*. Washington: United States Department of Health, Education and Welfare.

TAHA, A. and BALL, K. (1980) Smoking and Africa: The Coming Epidemic. *British Medical Journal* 280 (6219): 991–93.

TARRIÈRE, C. and HARTEMANN, F. (1964) Investigation into the Effects of Tobacco Smoke on a Visual Vigilance Task. In *Proceedings of Second International Congress of Ergonomics, Dortmund* (suppl. to *Ergonomics*): 525–30.

TERNES, J.W. (1977) An Opponent-Process Theory of Habitual Behavior, with Special Reference to Smoking. In M.E. Jarvik *et al.* (eds) *Research on Smoking Behavior (NIDA Monograph No. 17)*. Rockville, Maryland: National Institute on Drug Abuse.

THOMAS, C.B. (1973) The Relationship of Smoking and Habits of Nervous Tension. In W.L. Dunn (ed.) *Smoking Behavior: Motives and Incentives*. Washington: Winston.

Tobacco (1979) Brand Shares of the UK Cigarette Market 1978. August 1979: 20–21.

TODD, G.F. (1975) *Changes in Smoking Patterns in the UK*. London: Tobacco Research Council.

TOMKINS, S.S. (1966) Psychological Model for Smoking Behaviour. *American Journal of Public Health* 56: 17–20.

TOOLEY, J.T. and PRATT, S. (1967) An Experimental Procedure for the Extinction of Smoking Behavior. *Psychological Record* 17: 209–18.

TURNBULL, M.J. and KELVIN, A.S. (1971) Cigarette Dependence. *British Medical Journal* 3: 115–17.

TURNER, J.A.McM., SILLETT, R.W., and BALL, K.P. (1974) Some Effects of Changing to Low-Tar and Low-Nicotine Cigarettes. *Lancet* 2: 737–39.

TURNER, J.A.McM., SILLETT, R.W., and McNICOL, M.W. (1977) Effect of Cigar Smoking on Carboxyhaemoglobin and Plasma Nicotine Concentrations in Primary Pipe and Cigar Smokers and Ex-Cigarette Smokers. *British Medical Journal* 2: 1387–389.

TURNER, J.A.McM., SILLETT, R.W., and McNICOL, M.W. (1981) The Inhaling Habits of Pipe Smokers. *British Journal of Diseases of the Chest* 75: 71–76.

TURNER, J.A., SILLETT, R.W., TAYLOR, D.M., and McNICOL, M.W. (1977) The Effects of Supplementary Nicotine in Regular Cigarette Smokers. *Postgraduate Medical Journal* 53: 683–86.

ULETT, J., and ITIL, T. (1969) Quantitative Electroencephalogram in Smoking and Smoking Deprivation. *Science* 164: 969–70.

VAN PROOSDIJ, C. (1960) *Smoking: Its Influence on the Individual and its Role in Social Medicine*. Amsterdam: Elsevier.

VAN ROSSUM, R. (1978) The Great Substitute Disaster. *The Grocer* 16 September 1978.

VON DEDENROTH, T.E.A. (1964) The Use of Hypnosis with 'Tobacco-maniacs'. *American Journal of Clinical Hypnosis* **6** (4): 326–31.

WAGNER, M.K. and BRAGG, R.A. (1970) Comparing Behavior Modification Approaches to Habit Decrement-Smoking. *Journal of Consulting and Clinical Psychology* **34** (2): 258–63.

WALD, N.J., IDLE, M., BOREHAM, J., and BAILEY, A. (1980) Inhaling Habits Among Smokers of Different Types of Cigarette. *Thorax* **35** (12): 925–28.

WALD, N., HOWARD, S., SMITH, P.G., and KJELDSEN, K. (1973) Association between Atherosclerotic Diseases and Carboxyhaemoglobin Levels in Tobacco Smokers. *British Medical Journal* **1**: 761–65.

WARBURTON, D.M. and WESNES, K. (1978) Individual Differences in Smoking and Attentional Performance. In R.E. Thornton (ed.) *Smoking Behaviour: Physiological and Psychological Influences*. Edinburgh: Churchill Livingstone.

WARNER, K.E. (1977) The Effects of the Anti-Smoking Campaign on Cigarette Consumption. *American Journal of Public Health* **67** (7): 645–50.

WESNES, K. and WARBURTON, D.M. (1978) The Effects of Cigarette Smoking and Nicotine Tablets upon Human Attention. In R.E. Thornton (ed.) *Smoking Behaviour: Physiological and Psychological Influences*. Edinburgh: Churchill Livingstone.

Which? (1980) Smoking. August 1980: 473–77.

WHITEHEAD, R.W. and DAVIES, J.M. (1964) A Study of Methylphenidate and Diazepam as Possible Smoking Deterrents. *Current Therapeutic Research* **6** (5): 363–67.

WICKSTRÖM, B. (1980) Cigarette Marketing in the Third World. In L.M. Ramström (ed.) *The Smoking Epidemic: Proceedings of the Fourth World Conference on Smoking and Health*. Stockholm: Almqvist & Wiksell International.

WILHELMSEN, L. and HJALMARSSON, A. (1980) Smoking Cessation Experience in Sweden. *Canadian Family Physician* **26**: 737–43.

WILLIAMS, A.F. (1973) Personality and other Characteristics Associated with Cigarette Smoking among Young Teenagers. *Journal of Health and Social Behaviour* **14**: 374–80.

WITTGENSTEIN, L. (1972) *Philosophical Investigations*. Oxford: Blackwell.

WOLF, F.A. (1967) Tobacco Production and Processing. In Wynder, E.L. and Hoffman, D. *Tobacco and Tobacco Smoke*. New York: Academic Press.

World Health Organisation (1979) *Controlling the Smoking Epidemic: Report of the WHO Expert Committee on Smoking Control*. Geneva: WHO.

WYNDER, E.L. (1977) Interrelationship of Smoking to Other Variables and Preventive Approaches. In M.E. Jarvik *et al.* (eds) *Research on Smoking Behavior*. United States Department of Health, Education and Welfare, Research Monograph 17.

WYNDER, E.L. (1980) Some Concepts of the Less Harmful Cigarette. In G.B. Gori and F.G. Bock (eds) *Banbury Report 3: A Safe Cigarette?* New York: Cold Spring Harbor Laboratory.

WYNDER, E.L. and HOFFMAN, D. (1967) *Tobacco and Tobacco Smoke*. New York: Academic Press.

WYNDER, E.L., MABUCHI, K., and BEATTIE, E.J. (1970) The Epidemiology of Lung Cancer: Recent Trends. *Journal of the American Medical Association* **213** (13): 2221–228.

WYNDER, E.L., BROSS, I.J., CORNFIELD, J., and O'DONNELL, W.E. (1956) Lung Cancer in Women. *New England Journal of Medicine* **255** (24): 1111–121.

YOUNG, G. (1980) The Politics of Smoking. In L.M. Ramström (ed.) *The Smoking Epidemic: Proceedings of the Fourth World Conference on Smoking and Health.* Stockholm: Almqvist & Wiksell International.

ZAGONA, S.V. and ZURCHER, L.A. (1965) An Analysis of some Psychosocial Variables Associated with Smoking Behavior in a College Sample. *Psychological Reports* **17**: 967–78.

ZUCKER, R.A. and VAN HORN, H. (1972) Sibling Social Structure and Oral Behaviour. *Quarterly Journal of Studies on Alcohol* **33**: 193–97.

SUBJECT INDEX

NAME INDEX